T0339903

# The Good Forest

CARL & SALLY GABLE FUND

*for Southern Colonial American History*

EARLY
AMERICAN
PLACES

# The Good Forest

## The Salzburgers, Success, and the Plan for Georgia

### KAREN AUMAN

*The University of Georgia Press*
ATHENS

Published in part with generous support from the
Carl and Sally Gable Fund for Southern Colonial American History

Set in 10.5/13.5 Adobe Caslon Pro Regular
by Kaelin Chappell Broaddus

Most University of Georgia Press titles are
available from popular e-book vendors.

Printed digitally

Library of Congress Cataloging-in-Publication Data

Names: Auman, Karen, author.
Title: The good forest : the Salzburgers, success, and the plan for Georgia / Karen Auman.
Other titles: Early American places.
Description: Athens : University of Georgia Press, [2024] |
Series: Early American places | Includes bibliographical references and index.
Identifiers: LCCN 2023039681 | ISBN 9780820366104 (hardback) | ISBN 9780820366098
(paperback) | ISBN 9780820366111 (EPUB) | ISBN 9780820366128 (PDF)
Subjects: LCSH: Salzburgers—Georgia—Ebenezer (Effingham County) | Salzburgers—
Georgia—Ebenezer (Effingham County)—Politics and government. | German Americans—
Georgia—Ebenezer (Effingham County)—History—18th century. | Yuchi Indians—
Georgia—Ebenezer (Effingham County) | Creek Indians—Georgia—Ebenezer (Effingham
County) | Slavery—Georgia—Ebenezer (Effingham County)—History—18th century.
| Ebenezer (Effingham County, Ga.)—Race relations—History—18th century.
Classification: LCC F295.S1 A96 2024 | DDC 975.8/72200431073—dc23/eng/20231213
LC record available at https://lccn.loc.gov/2023039681

*For my mother Elaine and late father Bill,
and for my whole family.*

# CONTENTS

# FOREWORD

At the peak of his career as the preeminent historian of the American frontier, Frederick Jackson Turner turned to the regional specifics of those dynamics that he believed "explained American development." Georgia occupied a particular place in his thinking: "What Maine was to the New England states, Georgia was to the southern seaboard, with the difference that it was deeply touched by influences characteristically Western. Because of the traits of her leaders and the rude aggressive policies of her people, Georgia belonged as much to the West as to the South. From colonial times the Georgia settlers had been engaged in an almost incessant struggle against the savages on her border, and had the instincts of a frontier society."[1]

A long view of the state's history lends substantial support to his claim. Yet that distant aspect neglects to recognize that the colony, if not the state, came into being around high principles unusual for the time, however much it also served as a defensive buffer to Spanish Florida. The fact that the founding Trustees sought to settle England's increasingly landless and desperate poor on "free" lands that would allow them to pursue the independence associated with yeoman farmers is well known, both in principle and in its rapid dissolution. So, too, the short-lived ban on enslavement. Less appreciated, and perhaps more instructive as a case of high intentions gone unremarked, is that of the Ebenezer colony.

Karen Auman's *The Good Forest: The Salzburgers, Success, and the Plan for Georgia* tells a different story of the state, at least across its early decades. The forty-five German Lutherans who arrived on the coast in 1734 were a different sort of desperate than the 114 English whom Oglethorpe had disembarked near what would become Savannah in the winter of 1733. Persecuted for their Protestant faith in Catholic Salzburg, the Georgia Trustees' promise of fifty-acre freeholds by which to pursue competency seemed biblical in promise. Much more than their English neighbors, the Salzburger colonists embraced to the colony's founding principles and proved themselves worthy.

The swiftness with which the Trustees' humanitarian vision gave way to the "South Carolina" model of intensive slave-based monocropping (rice, then cotton) and competitive emulation of that colony's cynical Indian policies, forged in the deer hide and Indian slave trade, Auman argues, discredits both the presence and the principles that defined the Salzburger settlements. In fact, Auman suggests that the successes of the Salzburger colonists in establishing farms, towns, mills, and even an orphanage, as well as what is now the oldest (European) remaining house of worship in the state puts the lie to our widespread assumption that climate and environment made anything but a slave-based plantation society impossible.

Auman's graceful prose and compelling argumentation suggest a very different, if unrealized, narrative of early Georgia. Pious, self-sufficient, industrious, and less arrogant in their Indian policy than their English neighbors, under the leadership of pastor Johann Martin Boltzius, Ebenezer colony's founding exiles offer a different origin story than the failure narrative associated with their English neighbors. That they hewed to their Lutheran principles even in the face of slavery's capacity to produce wealth, just across the Savannah River, attests to their general character. Even the title Auman employs, *The Good Forest*, surprises the reader with the Salzburgers' capacity to see what Puritans were then calling "the wilderness" as a place perhaps perilous but also capable of challenge, communion, and spiritual growth.

The Salzburgers also seem to have respected Indigenous culture and boundaries more than their English neighbors. The Yuchi, living north of the original colony on the west bank of the Savannah River, served as guides when the "good forest" became refuge for wandering livestock. Living in close proximity to Yuchis and Muskogees, the colonists sometimes practiced the kind of intimate interpersonal frontier diplomacy with which more famous figures like Oglethorpe, Tomochichi, and Mary Musgrove are associated. Yet Salzburgers would grow wary of their Indigenous neighbors as tensions between the colony and the backcountry intensified, especially as Savannah granted Yuchi lands for expanding colonial footprints, and in time turned away from missionary work toward Christian conversion.

After the failure of the Trustee's original vision and success of the "Malcontents" in forcing the legalization of slavery into the colony's economy, the Salzburger colony wrestled with its conscience—and lost. Allowing the enslavement of fellow human beings seems beyond Christian conscience to-day, but Pastor Boltzius accommodated the practice with the provision that enslavers must be limited to no more than four enslaved people, must bap-tize them, and must treat them as Christian brethren.

That the Salzburger experiment with colonization, however much shaped by Christian principles, would founder in time on the shoals of American slavery, will surprise no one. But Karen Auman's insightful and sensitive book deepens our understanding of the promise lost in those early decades and our appreciation for the richness of early Georgia history. I am delighted to add the Gable Endowment name to this fine book.

James F. Brooks
Gable Chair in Early American History
University of Georgia

# The Good Forest

The first Salzburgers stepped off their boats and onto the Georgia shore on March 12, 1734.[1] They had first spotted land five days earlier, a sight so wonderful after eight weeks of difficult sailing that the group of German Lutherans broke into the hymn "Lord God We Praise Thee!"[2] The winds, tides, and a sandbar kept the people on the ship for a few days after seeing land, but when they could finally begin to disembark they were greeted by a shout of joy and the firing of several cannon from nearly all the people of Savannah.[3] As they reached the ground along the shores of the Savannah River, the Salzburgers found the American landscape beautiful and began the difficult venture of establishing a new town in the Georgia forest.

Their trip across the Atlantic from England had taken two months, but really their journey began much earlier, in the alpine valleys south of the city of Salzburg. There, living as Protestants, they were expelled by their prince archbishop ruler by a November 1731 decree that required all who were not Roman Catholic to leave their homeland. With uncertain futures, the Salzburger refugees had walked to towns in Saxony and Bavaria, seeking aid and hoping for a permanent place to stay. Those Salzburgers who settled in the American South migrated because they were swayed by the Georgia Trustees' promise of free transport, land, and provisions to the refugees. While most exiled Salzburgers remained in German lands, a few risked all to settle in America in a new society on the southern fringe of the British mainland colonies. After the initial group, another six transports of Georgia Salzburgers and other Germans migrated to America and together established a series of settlements along the Savannah River.

The new British American colony was chartered in 1732 as a charity run by the Trustees for the Establishment of the Colony of Georgia in America, commonly known as the Georgia Trustees. These men strove to create a new kind of colony, and a new kind of society, in the American Lowcountry. Their plan was for a colony of fifty-acre family farms, without slavery, that would provide a new beginning for Britain's worthy poor and the persecuted Protestants of Europe. The Salzburgers' shared experience of being forcibly removed from their homes for the sake of the Protestant religion convinced the Trustees that these refugees were the sort of people they had in mind when they pictured helping the worthy poor. The religious overtones of sending an exiled people to the American wilderness to be saved fit neatly with the Salzburgers' background. The Georgian forest would save them, physically and spiritually.

Although many Georgia Salzburgers died within the first few years of arriving, by the early 1740s the German settlements were on firm footing and growing. By the end of Trustee rule in 1752 the Salzburgers, settling along the Savannah River, had built three towns, three churches, a gristmill, sawmills (for the lumber market), and an orphanage. They had cleared the forest to create farms that "went on for miles" around their main town Ebenezer, successfully feeding themselves by the late 1730s; they were also the largest producers of silk in Georgia.[4] Salzburger settlements radiated north and south from Ebenezer, forming a German zone along the river beginning about twenty miles upstream from the town of Savannah. Though never wealthy, the Salzburgers—and the other Germans who settled with them—were the Trustees' success story.

During the Trustee period, the Salzburgers' town of Ebenezer was the second largest in the colony after Savannah and probably the largest in 1752 at the end of the Trustee period, though it is very difficult to estimate population in early Georgia. Although we have good ship manifests for the colonists sent by the Trustees, including the Salzburgers and other Germans, we do not have thorough records of births, deaths, marriages, and departures in early Georgia. There are reports and estimates of numbers given by some Trustees as well as by those who were unhappy with Trustee rule. Each, obviously, had motives for over- or understating the population size as they argued about the success of the colony. Estimates of the Georgia population in 1750 are between 2,900 and 5,000; the Salzburgers composed three congregations, which supports estimates of between 1,200 and 1,500 residents and makes this self-sustaining community of Lutherans about one-third to one-half of the total Georgia population in the early 1750s.[5]

The early history of Georgia is often characterized as one of failure, with the Trustees painted as too idealistic, trying to establish a sort of small farm utopia through the strong arm of paternalism. The Salzburgers' experience should cause us to reconsider efforts to paint Georgia with a broad brush of failure and force us to entertain a more nuanced understanding of the colonial period.

Saying that the Salzburger story matters is not to say that the Georgia Trustees' project was an unquestioned and glorious success. There were serious failures in Georgia by the Trustees, and by all accounts large numbers of English-speaking settlers voted with their feet and left the colony. A group of disaffected colonists, known as the Malcontents, challenged the Trustees to change their rules in a bid to make Georgia more like neighboring South Carolina. That group eventually won the battle in Parliament and in British public opinion, causing the funding for the Trustees' experiment to dry up. In America, the Georgia Salzburgers were perhaps the only settlers who worked to fully implement the Trustees' plans, and they were the Trustees' bright hope and evidence that the Trustees' ideas could work. The Salzburgers needed the support of the Trustees to advance their settlement, and the Trustees promoted the success of the Salzburgers in marketing their plan for Georgia. Despite Salzburger success, the Malcontents' message dominated, and support for the Trustees' plans dwindled. The Georgia Trustees met for the last time in June 1752, when they defaced their official seal; Georgia entered a new era as a royal colony.[6]

Because the Malcontents won the dispute, the long-standing standard narrative for colonial Georgia emerged in which the Trustee years (1732–1752) were a failure, with success achieved only after the territory became a royal colony that operated with plantation slavery. The theme of Trustee failure has been used as the framing device for understanding events in colonial Georgia on a wide range of topics, sometimes explicitly invoked and other times implied.[7] Many of the best-known histories of Georgia adopt the failure model for understanding important matters such as the introduction of slavery, colonial economics, and the role of British imperial rivalries, each accepting the assumption that it was ridiculous from the start to think of founding a colony in the Lowcountry region that did not include slavery.[8] In doing so, these histories accept the Malcontents' main arguments that only a slave-based plantation society could prosper in the American Southeast.

While the adoption of slavery in 1750 and the rapid "Carolinization" of Georgia after 1752 into a plantation economy is an important part of the colony's story, the historiographic model carries with it an implication that only a slave society was feasible in the Lowcountry. It is true that Georgia struggled economically under Trustee rule and then blossomed after slavery was allowed. This is largely because after 1752 settlers eager to form large plantations poured in from South Carolina and brought enslaved Africans to create the large Lowcountry zone, economically and socially similar to other plantation societies in the Chesapeake and Caribbean. Yet to fully accept the idea that because a slave-based society thrived in post-Trustee Georgia meant it was necessarily the only way to succeed is to accept a sort of environmental determinism. The notion hearkens to the racist idea that only people of African descent could work in the hot, humid Georgia climate, an idea current at the time (and seen in the Malcontents' arguments) and that sadly has persisted throughout much of U.S. history. The Salzburgers actively pushed back against that idea, noting that they, Europeans, worked their own fields and fed themselves.

Further, the framing that Georgia failed under the Trustees and was a success only after the introduction of slavery belies an unspoken assumption that economic systems were the primary motors of change within the colony. While economics are an important part of understanding the social systems of any British colony, the Salzburgers and the Trustees were also concerned with the moral character of the settlement.

More recent work on early Georgia by Noeleen McIlvenna refreshingly moves away from the success-failure ties to slavery, arguing that class struggles were the important change agents. In this analysis, the "worthy poor" would not submit to wealthier colonists and also Trustee domination. They simply would not conform to Trustees' plans for them to labor on small farms.[9] This rejection of a servile stance by the poor led the wealthy to more actively demand the right to use the labor of enslaved Africans.[10] Yet, unlike the English-speaking settlers convincingly analyzed by McIlvenna, the Salzburgers did *mostly* conform to the Trustee plans. Because the Salzburgers were helped by philanthropists in Germany and England who were allied with the Trustees, the Germans actively worked to follow the colony's rules, such as to encourage continued charitable support from the philanthropic elites.

The Salzburgers left many records from Colonial Georgia, so they appear frequently in historical works but often in quotes about conditions and less often as figures of analysis. Part of the reason for this is that the Salzburgers preferred to deal with the Trustees and other Protestant philanthropic sponsors rather than be involved in local debates directly. Ebenezer's geographic position and the presence of the Salzburgers figure in histories of Georgia's Indian relations.[11] Additionally, Salzburger pastor Johann Martin Boltzius had direct interactions with important religious figures who passed through colonial Georgia. His influence as part of the history of evangelists George Whitefield and John Wesley, the founder of Methodism, has been studied.[12] While these works help to integrate the Germans with the broader colony, they do not explain the Salzburger community.

Relatively few academic works focus on the Salzburgers and their settlements. Perhaps the best known was written by George Fenwick Jones, a professor of German. He dedicated much of his academic work to transcribing and translating the diaries written by the Salzburger pastors, a great service to all scholars of early Georgia. He used his extensive knowledge of their experience to write *The Salzburger Saga* (1984), a narrative history.[13] The book tells their story but does not carry a strong argument or attempt to integrate the Salzburgers into the historiography of Trustee Georgia. His is an informative recounting of the story.

James Van Horn Melton brings updated research and insight into the Salzburgers' experience in his 2015 book *Religion, Community, and Slavery on the Colonial Southern Frontier*.[14] Using archives in Salzburg, Melton researched the lives of several of the first exiles, discovering that the first group consisted mostly of mining families from the Gastein region of Salzburg. His book supplements our dependence upon the pastors' official diaries with the experiences of some of the actual Salzburgers. The first half of the book analyzes their European experiences, while the second half centers the debate over slavery in Georgia and its effects on and within the Salzburgers' settlements.

The historiography of slavery in Georgia is long and often calls upon the Salzburger diaries because of their support for the Trustees' ban. Betty Wood's *Slavery in Colonial Georgia, 1730–1775* is considered a classic on the topic.[15] While Wood presents the Salzburgers and their opinions, she stays focused on the broader colonial issue of slavery. Other works about slavery in Georgia and the Lowcountry, as well as about plantation economies in the British American South, inform this book.[16]

Although the slavery debates are critical to understanding Georgia, *The Good Forest* argues that the moral, social, religious, and cultural elements of establishing the Germanic settlements on the Savannah River remove the "success-failure" paradigm associated with the slavery ban as a way of understanding Trustee Georgia. The experiences of the Salzburger community need to be integrated into our understanding of early Georgia. Yes, many early settlers wanted to own slaves and therefore left, leaving behind a depleted colony. However, with few exceptions, the Germans stayed and built a self-sustaining community. In many ways for the Salzburger settlements the introduction of slavery led to more difficulty for the group as cultural rifts developed between the poor and the few wealthy who accumulated land and slaves. The story of the Salzburgers reveals the possibilities and limits of colonization and helps us rethink the Trustees' experiment.

This book is situated in the pre-Revolutionary years in Georgia, focused primarily on Georgia's Trustee years (1732–1752). The first section, comprising chapters 1 through 3, describes the plan for Georgia and the Salzburgers' role in it, with a discussion on how they came to be the "Salzburger exiles" who were sponsored by British and German philanthropies. Because the Salzburgers became the Trustees' ideal settlers, it is important to understand what the plan for Georgia entailed. The chapter on the Trustees argues that they were not naïve or ill prepared but were responding to the challenges they faced in British society in the years leading up to the founding of the colony. Chapter 3 argues that without support from a transnational and transatlantic network of Protestant philanthropists the Salzburger settlement in Georgia would have never even happened. The German Lutheran philanthropists formed an informal network of Pietist believers who supported the Georgia Salzburgers, and their strong ecumenical partnership with the British Anglican philanthropy the Society for Promoting Christian Knowledge (SPCK) made possible the Salzburger community's success in Georgia.

The subsequent chapters focus on the settlement project in Georgia and how the Salzburgers built their community and economy. The Georgia Germans took an alternative approach to establishing settlements on colonial frontiers than the other colonizers sent by the Trustees to America. The Salzburgers had the advantage of settling as a group, initially organizing their work cooperatively and later creating economic projects that benefited all of them, such as a mill complex. The Georgia Germans' community was also different from those of more studied German groups such as the Moravians, the Dunkers, and other "peace churches" who typically settled in the Mid-Atlantic. For example, the Moravians, a well-studied group of German Pietists who arrived in Georgia in 1735, at the same time as the second transport of Salzburgers, created a strongly hierarchical, controlled society. By 1741 most of the Moravians had left Georgia for Pennsylvania's Lehigh Valley, where they held land communally, built group homes segregated by gender, and managed economic programs with a top-down administration. To preserve their tight-knit society, the Moravians remained mostly separate from

Anglo settlers. Other small groups of Germans, such as the Dunkers and Amish, also kept separate from Anglo settlers but did not pursue the types of communal economic programs as the Moravians.[17]

Understanding the Georgia Salzburgers' settlements adds to our knowledge of German colonizing in British North America. The settlers at Ebenezer chose to build their community in a very different manner from other Georgia colonists and from Germans in British America, in part because of the singular and capable leadership of their first pastor, Johann Martin Boltzius (1703–1765), and because they took on the task of incorporating Germans throughout the Lowcountry. Ebenezer began as a group of exiled Salzburgers, but it soon after accumulated "persecuted Protestants" out of a variety of German-speaking kingdoms and principalities.[18] The colonizing project quickly became focused on establishing a functioning community that included Protestant Germans from throughout central Europe. Chapter 4 addresses the ways the Salzburgers came to know, live, and survive in the Georgia environment, a world very different from their alpine and central European homelands. Their understanding of the Lowcountry environment was heavily freighted with religious ideas of God's people being preserved and refined in a wilderness.

The following three chapters turn to how the Salzburgers imagined themselves as subjects in the British Empire, built a sense of community in Georgia, and developed economic projects. As part of the 111,000 German immigrants who arrived in America in the first half of the eighteenth century, the Salzburgers formed a portion of "the first large wave of free political aliens" in the British colonies.[19] Contrary to our standard understanding of Germans in America remaining apart from Anglo politics, the Salzburgers were engaged and active members of the British Empire who worked to influence British policy and the administration of Georgia. The result in Ebenezer was a group who upheld a strong loyalty to the British monarch, King George II, as well as a shared sense of civic responsibility to the empire and community that included sometimes criticizing English settlers for not being good subjects.

Key themes run throughout the book. The first is the explication of how the Salzburgers colonized. They built a tight-knit community and a self-sustaining society that was a draw for German-speaking migrants. The group created settlements unlike those in the Carolinas and the rest of the colonial South, at a time when the Georgia Malcontents claimed that was impossible. The Salzburger experience in Georgia thus adds to our understanding of how European settlement worked in eighteenth-century America, particularly in contact zones such as Ebenezer, which bordered Yuchi and Muskogee lands and was the farthest south, least developed colony in mainland British North America.

Any study of the Salzburgers must include a discussion of the role of the Pietist religious network in the colonization, a second theme. Ebenezer was an important node in a web of Pietist faith, an outpost firmly planted in American soil by God's design to bless the lives of Atlantic Germans.[20] For example, in 1742, when Halle Pietists arranged to send to Pennsylvania their first Lutheran minister, Heinrich Melchior Mühlenberg, they had him first stop at Ebenezer to learn about life and religion in America. The network also aided chain migration to America, as settlers communicated within their groups about the colonial opportunity.

This Lutheran network expands our understanding of the way webs of exchange operated in the British Atlantic and builds upon recent work that examines trade, travel, and knowledge-building networks.[21] The Pietists were important beyond merely adding to the material or religious comfort of the Salzburgers, as these Germans were necessary partners with the British for the colonial project to succeed. German Lutherans provided key funding when British resources were insufficient and were a prime source for recruiting Protestant settlers. The Trustees so relied on this German network that in the 1740s two Augsburg men were made Trustees: Samuel Urlsperger, a man who already had strong ties to London, and Christian von Münch, an Augsburg banker and merchant.

The Pietist connection to America has received special interest in recent decades, as the records of the Francke Foundations in Halle have become more widely available after the reunification of Germany. In the eighteenth century Francke's Pietist Lutheranism had profound impacts on several other religious groups, including the Moravians (whose leaders Count Zinzendorf and Bishop Spangenberger trained at Halle), the Quakers in England, and John Wesley's Methodists. Skilled historians have traced these influences in America, with a strong focus on Pennsylvania and the Mid-Atlantic.[22] This book builds on our understanding of the role of the German networks in America by incorporating the South.

Closely related to the importance of religious networks was the outsized role of British and German Protestant philanthropy in supporting the Salzburgers. One of the Georgia Malcontents' complaints was that the people at Ebenezer received more aid and support than the other settlers, and this was likely true. The Salzburgers benefited from a robust Protestant philanthropic network with the SPCK in London and the Pietist Lutheran network centered around the Francke Foundations in Halle, Saxony—known today as Halle (Saale) to differentiate it from Halle in western Germany. Working in concert with the Trustees, these charities paid for ministers and schoolteachers; sent food, clothing, shoes, and other material goods; and funded large construction projects such as mills, a silk filature, and the Lutheran church in Ebenezer. This extra aid reminds us that colonizing was a very expensive proposition and nearly always required more resources than the founding projectors originally anticipated. It also demonstrates the ways the British used religious philanthropy to build their empire.

As a by-product of their philanthropy, Germans who did not intend to migrate to America invested heavily in this British colony and empire. As Ebenezer became more securely established, some of the German backers began to invest in the Georgia plan for economic gain. For example, Christian von Münch, an Augsburg banker and charitable supporter of the Salzburgers, also dabbled in the American silk trade and sent staff to investigate business opportunities for him. The commitment by Germans to the British cause can be partly explained because the king of England, George II, was himself a German-born Lutheran as well as the Elector of Hannover in the Holy Roman Empire. His personal links to German Protestantism may have encouraged other support.

The story of the Georgia Salzburgers begins in late 1731, with an expulsion order targeted at those who would not renounce their Protestant faith. The timing of their exile in the early 1730s coincided with the founding of Georgia. The existing links between German and English philanthropists brought the two together, and soon the Georgia Trustees incorporated support for religious exiles—nearly always referred to as "Poor Persecuted Protestants"—in their marketing and colonizing plans. The first transport of Salzburgers brought just forty-five men, women, and children to Georgia in March 1734, but it was soon followed by many more who established a home along the banks of the Savannah River.

## Terminology

The Salzburgers settled on land that was the home of the Yamacraw and Yuchi tribes. When it is evident in the records, the tribal name is used in this book. However, it is not always clear from the sources to which group of people the Salzburgers are referring. Indeed, it is possible the Germans themselves did not always know. In those and other cases, a more general collective noun must be used. As Karen O. Kupperman points out, the Museum of the American Indian suggests "Native American," "Indian," "American Indian," and "Native" as acceptable terms.[23] I follow her lead and use these collective nouns interchangeably when specific tribes cannot be identified.

The Yamacraw and Yuchi tribes affiliated with the larger Muskogee Confederation, and where appropriate I use that name. The main body of the Muskogee was broadly divided into two major groups: the Upper Towns on the Coosa and Tallapoosa rivers (mainly in modern Alabama) and the Lower Towns on the Chattahoochee and Flint rivers (in modern Georgia). The contemporary sources, and until fairly recently modern academics, referred to these groups as the Upper Creeks and Lower Creeks.

## A Note on Sources

We are fortunate to have many sources from and about the Salzburgers, although a majority are from their religious leaders, making it sometimes difficult to know what the settlers themselves believed. Johann Martin Boltzius, assigned as chief pastor to the Salzburgers from the beginning and the de facto civil authority until the late 1740s, authored thousands of pages beginning with his journey out of Europe with the first transport of exiles. The records also include writings by his catechists and assistants, comprising Israel Christian Gronau until his death in 1745 and his replacement, Hermann Lemke. Later the Salzburgers were served by the Halle-trained pastors Christian Rabenhorst and Christian Triebner. The pastors kept an official diary, a copy of which was periodically sent to Europe, edited by Halle-aligned Lutheran minister Samuel Urlsperger in Augsburg and published in German. Extracts were also translated and printed in England, often used as a marketing tool by the Trustees to raise funds and garner support for their charitable endeavor. Urlsperger's edited editions survive, as do many of Boltzius's original diaries. Boltzius knew the diaries would receive a broad audience in Europe and Britain and was mindful of the need for philanthropic aid. Although at times he was remarkably frank in his writing, it seems very likely he would have self-censored these diaries. Urlsperger, functioning as editor, also censored parts of the diaries. Through the lifelong effort of Dr. George Fenwick Jones and some of his students, these diaries have been transcribed and translated into English in an eighteen-volume set titled *Detailed Reports on the Salzburger Emigrants Who Settled in America* (abbreviated "DR vol:page" in the notes). In this set Jones was able to refer to the original diaries, held at the Francke Foundations archive in Halle an der Saale, and he restored passages that had been edited out by Urlsperger. We are also fortunate to have approximately two hundred letters by Boltzius and other Salzburgers, in both English and German, to individuals and organizations in Britain and Germany. Some of the English-language letters are preserved in the records of the SPCK, the Georgia Trustees, and the British Board of Trade and Plantations. Russell C. Kleckley, in collaboration with Jürgen Gröschl at the Francke Foundations, published a two-volume work that transcribed and translated 158 of Boltzius's letters that are held in the Francke Foundations' archives. When using material contained in either the published letters or the *Detailed Reports*, I use the printed English translation and cite the page numbers. I provide my own translations of additional German-language letters, documents, and materials.

I have mostly retained original spelling, capitalization, and punctuation when quoting a source, but I have converted "ye" to "the" and removed archaic contractions for clarity. During the Trustee period, Britain used the old-style Julian calendar, with the year starting on March 25, while Germans used the Gregorian calendar with a January 1 start date. In practice, the British often clarified the date when corresponding with Germans by marking both years, such as February 2, 1734/1735. In all cases I have modernized the dates, so that the year begins on January 1. In the example above the date would be written February 2, 1735. I have not, however, included the twelve-day adjustment needed to fully convert to the Gregorian calendar.

# CHAPTER 1

# Exile

The pounding on the door came late at night while all inside were sleeping. Soldiers and bailiffs stormed into the home, pulled the father out of his bed, put him in irons, and dragged him to prison. Next, the enforcers searched for and confiscated suspicious and banned Protestant books. The bailiff then moved to the next house, gathering a group of Protestant "Heretick Dogs" on a wagon to be sent to jail.[1] The prisoners were thrown into the dungeon of the Hohensalzburg Fortress (the castle on the top of the hill used by the rulers of Salzburg), where they were held for weeks. There, they were examined for evidence of illegal activity, such as participating in meetings that espoused the Protestant faith. Other Salzburg Protestant prisoners reported being held in a corn loft for seven weeks, without protection from the freezing elements. One Protestant was arrested and held for thirty weeks before he paid a fine and was finally released.[2]

These Salzburg Protestants resided on the hard lines of the Catholic Counter-Reformation, when Catholic princes fought back against the tide of Protestantism. Although Martin Luther had encouraged obedience to secular authority, Protestantism's challenge to the Roman Catholic Church was also seen as a challenge to the secular leadership. This was especially true in Salzburg, where the secular and the religious were combined into the authority of the single leader appointed by the pope, the prince archbishop.

Prince Archbishop Leopold Anton Eleutherius von Firmian ascended to the throne in 1727, and his reign was characterized by vigorous efforts to weed out Protestantism in his realm. Tensions between Firmian and his many Protestant subjects, most of whom lived primarily in the rural alpine valleys along the Salzach River and its tributaries, built to a crescendo in the early 1730s. Inquisitions, arrests, confiscations, and threats failed to compel the Protestants to conform to Roman Catholicism. Finally, on November 11, 1731, Firmian issued an expulsion order: all Protestants had to leave the territory.[3]

Most of the expelled Protestants came from the Pongau, a region south of the city of Salzburg settled by families on small plots wedged into the narrow valley floors. Area residents descended from families who had adhered to Lutheran and Calvinist doctrines for generations, some since at least the 1500s. The mountains south of the city of Salzburg formed a mining district—many of the first exiles were miners—and it seems most likely that it was miners who brought word of the new type of Christianity to the archbishopric in the 1500s. Miners frequently had a migratory work pattern, traveling to other German states to work temporarily in mines. Historian James Van Horn Melton has documented a miner named Martin Lodinger, who in 1532 sought Martin Luther's advice regarding the anti-Protestant persecution in Salzburg. To remain true to his beliefs, Lodinger chose self-exile, leaving the Pongau. Two of his epistles to fellow Protestants were published and continued to circulate in the 1730s, inspiring devotion to the faith in the face of persecution for generations.[4]

The miners' ongoing migratory work patterns meant that Pongau families had access to Protestant literature when they worked in Protestant German states. Often, they returned to Salzburg territory with devotional literature and hymnals. These books were an important means of sustaining and promoting Protestantism in the Catholic archbishopric devoid of Lutheran or Calvinist clergy. The writings became a particular focus of Firmian's inquisition, as they were viewed as spreading false religion and subverting his authority. Also, they were a tangible way to quickly determine if a family was Protestant.

Among the Salzburgers' favorite books was Josef Schaitberger's *Sendbrief*, first printed in 1691, with more editions (that included additional material) in the early 1700s.[5] Schaitberger was a native of Hallein, in the archbishopric of Salzburg. In 1686, following his arrest and imprisonment, Schaitberger was expelled from Salzburg, eventually settling in Nuremberg, where he was influenced by a Pietist form of Lutheranism. The *Sendbrief* is a collection of his letters (*sendbriefe*) to all Protestants back home; as he was a Salzburger, his writings carried weight and appeal. He emphasized Pietist belief in an inner spirituality and focused on conversion of the soul. Schaitberger's writings stressed the need to uphold and maintain Lutheran doctrine and practices, as he also denigrated Roman Catholicism. The book was so treasured by the Protestant Salzburgers that a copy could be used as currency to pay a debt.[6]

One of the markers of Pietist Protestantism was gathering in what they called conventicles in fellow believers' homes. There, Lutherans would read from the Bible, read devotional literature, sing hymns, and pray together. Schaitberger approved of this practice and discussed it in his *Sendbrief*, and the Salzburgers of the 1730s similarly practiced these religious meetings in their homes.

The rebellious literature and the ongoing meetings devoted to Protestantism became the focus of Prince Archbishop von Firmian's efforts to bring his principality into conformance with Roman Catholicism. Firmian's decree made clear that he viewed Protestants as being in open rebellion against him "under Pretence of Persecution in Matters of Religion."[7] Prior to the expulsion edict he had ordered all Lutherans and Calvinists in his territories to stop meeting in their homes to discuss the Protestant religion, to cease public preaching, and to end all "commotions." Firmian claimed that if they complied with law and abandoned public support for Lutheranism, the archbishop's commissioners who traveled to the mountain regions would allow each Protestant to "exercise his Religion in secret at his own House."[8] However, by the early 1730s Firmian believed the Protestants continued to "assemble themselves in a tumultuous manner . . . publickly" and to "threaten to exterminate Catholicks with Fire and Sword," and crucially, they refused to recognize the temporal and spiritual leadership of the archbishop. He wrote that, as a result, he was forced to expel these "rebellious and disloyal Subjects."[9]

Archbishop von Firmian's 1731 Edict of Expulsion gave Protestants very little time to leave. Those who owned land had three months to sell their property and leave; unpropertied tradesmen, servants, and laborers had only eight days. According to the 1648 Treaty of Westphalia that had ended the Thirty Years' War in central Europe, Firmian had the right to expel people not of his faith, but the terms required allowing three years for removal so that subjects could make arrangements. The Holy Roman emperor Charles VI and the pope both urged Firmian to obey the terms of the treaty, but their pleas had little effect and the expulsion proceeded apace.[10] In total over twenty thousand Protestants were forced to leave Salzburg, representing as much as one-sixth of the principality's population.[11]

The exiles flooded into southern German towns in Swabia and Bavaria, seeking refuge in any Protestant city that would accept them. Per the rules of the Treaty of Westphalia, the forced migrants were given a passport from the archbishopric that made clear the travelers were not criminals and were leaving Salzburg because they "professeth the Protestant Religion."[12] This passport was intended to provide unencumbered travel as the Salzburgers left their hometown, although in practice they often met resistance in Catholic-led kingdoms and principalities.

As large groups of refugees flooded into southern German towns, the call quickly went out for aid, and the plight of the Salzburger "persecuted Protestants" became a cause célèbre throughout Europe. More than three hundred pamphlets, letters, and news stories were printed and reprinted about the exiles.[13] These pamphlets and broadsides were also translated into Dutch, French, and English and were widely read throughout Protestant Europe and used to raise funds and material support. Circulated with the pamphlets were drawings, paintings, and commemorative medals depicting long trains of exiles, usually portrayed with very few belongings and often holding the Bible.[14] The Protestant marketing effort always included testimony that the Salzburgers were an upstanding and persecuted people, noting that they had been questioned by Lutheran ministers and found to be sincere and devout in their faith. It was reported that the Salzburgers frequently sang Martin Luther's hymn "God Is Our Refuge in Distress," which the English-speaking world now knows as "A Mighty Fortress Is Our God."[15] By this time the hymn was a kind of Protestant anthem, confirming the firm belief that God would shelter, protect, and fight for them against the evils of Roman Catholic power.[16] That the Salzburgers knew and loved the song is evidence of how connected they were to the broader Protestant world, despite their remote location in a Catholic principality.

As word rapidly spread throughout Europe in late 1731 and early 1732 that the Salzburgers had been "driven out of their native Country for the Sake of their Religion, and forced to leave their All behind them," Samuel Urlsperger knew he must organize immediately to help these people.[17] As the senior Lutheran minister in Augsburg, Bavaria, he learned in December that eight hundred refugees were soon expected to arrive at his city.[18] These Salzburgers arrived at the gates of Augsburg in the dead of winter, most with very little money and few possessions. Urlsperger mobilized to help his fellow Lutherans.

The refugees had traveled from their homes in the alpine valleys south of Salzburg searching for a Protestant town in which to stay, but Augsburg was a complicated choice and Urlsperger's desire to help met many obstacles. Symbolic of the religious division that had existed in central Europe for two centuries, the Free Imperial City of Augsburg had a system of government in which the Catholic and Protestant magistrates took turns ruling; the fate of the Salzburgers depended upon which group of magistrates was in charge on the day. The Catholic leaders would not let the exiles stay in the city, and the Salzburgers were forced to camp outside the town wall, at great expense to Augsburg's Protestants who were caring for them.[19] At last the Catholic hierarchy relented, and the exiles were allowed to stay inside the town in Protestant-run inns or in private homes.

Despite Urlsperger's success in navigating the religious politics of his town, it was clear that the opposition of the Catholics and the material burden of support meant that a large group of refugees could not stay in Augsburg long. Something had to be done to help them find a more permanent settlement. Worse still, reports came that thousands more Salzburgers were en route, looking for refuge; their arrival would further stretch the resources of Augsburg's Protestant community. The need was beyond the ability of Urlsperger and the local Lutheran communities to accommodate.

To rally support for the Salzburgers Urlsperger called upon a network of philanthropic Protestants that included the London-based Society for Promoting Christian Knowledge (SPCK) and Pietist Lutherans whose spiritual home was the Francke Foundations in Halle in Prussia (formerly part of Saxony). As a young man Samuel Urlsperger had studied with Francke in Halle an der Saale (so called to distinguish it from other communities named Halle), before leaving in 1709 to serve as the assistant pastor to Anton Wilhelm Böhme, who was the German Lutheran royal chaplain at the Savoy Church in London. While in London Urlsperger became a member of the Anglican SPCK, a philanthropy that took an ecumenical view and incorporated the Lutheran pastors into their group. By 1713 Urlsperger returned to Germany, where he remained a corresponding member of the Society and maintained his connections to the world of Protestant English philanthropy.

In Augsburg, Urlsperger first contacted the Francke Foundations in Halle for aid. In early 1732 he also wrote to Friedrich Michael Ziegenhagen, King George II's Lutheran chaplain in London who was part of the Pietist Lutheran network having studied in Halle and another German member of the SPCK.[20] Ziegenhagen contacted Henry Newman, the Society's long-serving American-born secretary, to discuss the matter at the group's next meeting.[21] Urlsperger's appeal to the SPCK received a favorable response, and the society in England sent financial aid quickly.[22] The British donations were part of a response from throughout Europe, as aid began flowing to Bavaria and Swabia to help feed and clothe the Salzburgers.

In early 1732 Prussian king Frederick William I offered protection and permanent settlement in East Prussia. Eventually, most of the twenty thou-

sand Salzburger refugees chose to move there, in territory that is today near
the modern-day borders of Poland, Lithuania, and the Russian Kaliningrad
Oblast. The Prussian offer was, arguably, the safest opportunity for the Salzburgers. They would live in a place protected by a Protestant king and were
promised land that they could farm. The over-eight-hundred-mile overland
journey, though arduous, was imaginable to the exiles.

In early 1733 word of another settlement offer came to the Salzburgers.
A few regular members of the SPCK in England, including John Perceval
(sometimes spelled Percival), the future Earl of Egmont, James Oglethorpe,
Thomas Coram, and James Vernon, were at the same time working to establish the colony of Georgia in America, intended as a refuge for the worthy poor. By spring 1732 the philanthropic Trustees considered sending some
"poor persecuted Protestants" to their new colony, and in July they agreed
to a special collection to enact their plan.[23] The SPCK proposed that they
help defray some of the expense of settling Salzburgers in Georgia by paying for their journey from Augsburg to England. Finally, in October 1732 the
common council of the Georgia Trustees—the charity that held the charter
for the colony—resolved to work through the SPCK and "their correspondent in Germany," Samuel Urlsperger, to see "whether any Salzburger families would be willing to become British Subjects and to settle" in America.[24]
One challenge was that by the time the Georgia Trustees were ready to in-
vite Salzburgers, the main body of the exiles were already finding permanent homes in Europe. Still, groups of a few hundred at a time trickled out
of Salzburg and into southern German lands in 1733. The exiles who eventually went to Georgia left their homes in mid- to late 1732 and early 1733 and
were not part of the first-wave Protestants forced to leave, probably because
many of them came from the Gastein Valley sixty to seventy miles south
of the Salzburg city center, where it took longer for the authorities to reach
them. This was the group that first heard of the Trustees' offer to send three
hundred of them to Georgia.

The Georgia offer was generous. The Trustees promised the Salzburgers
that all travel expenses would be paid by their charity. Upon arrival in Georgia the Salzburgers would receive an allowance of food for one year, plus the
tools and seed needed to start a farm. Males would receive three lots of land: a
town lot for a home, a plot on the edge of town suitable for a kitchen garden,
and a "Lot for Tillage" reasonably near the town.[25] In practice this meant an
approximately one-half-acre town lot, a five-acre plot near town, and a forty-
five-acre "plantation" on which to grow crops for market. Those who migrated
to Georgia would become denizens of Britain, subjects of the British mon-

arch, and would have "all the Rights and priviledges of Englishmen," including "the free exercise of their religion."[26] In return the Trustees demanded that they "shall obey such Orders and Regulation . . . as the Trustees shall think necessary."[27] In addition, the SPCK agreed to pay the wages of a German Lutheran minister and a catechist to accompany the group and settle in America.[28]

Although this appeared to be a very substantial offer, it took much of 1733 to recruit Salzburgers for migration to America and to negotiate the details of settlement. Urlsperger reported that he had difficulty finding enough willing Salzburgers. Many were "very much afraid of the sea," recognizing that a journey across the Atlantic was potentially dangerous.[29] They were concerned about migrating to America knowing, or suspecting, that starting a new colony would be difficult, lacking the infrastructure on offer in Prussia and other European locales. Through Urlsperger's communications with the SPCK and the Trustees, the refugees asked that, in addition to the guaranteed freedom of religion, their children and posterity would also have the benefit of pastors and catechists. Further, they wanted guarantees that they would be settled near each other and not be made servants but have their own lands. They were also concerned that the people in Georgia would "have Patience with their Manners and Language and not jeer at them."[30] Early in the main Salzburger migration a group had taken up an offer to settle in Zeeland (in the Netherlands) and quickly became dissatisfied with the situation. They reported that they were mocked for their manners and were unhappy with the quality of land and opportunities. In 1733 the Zeeland Salzburgers left and became migrants once again, and many of them ended up moving to Prussia. Those Salzburgers who were being recruited for British America had heard about the Zeeland group and knew it would be difficult to return to Europe. They wanted assurances. The Trustees assured the potential colonists that each of their concerns would be met: they would have paid clergy, would be settled together in a community, and would not be made servants. There was little they could do about guaranteeing the demeanor of the colonists toward the Salzburgers, but in the end the two groups were settled in Georgia several days' journey away from each other, limiting the chances for cruel interactions.

A key sticking point was the title for the land on offer. The plan for Georgia required that the land be held in tail-male, meaning it could not be inherited by Salzburger daughters. For the Trustees, this was an important defense against one person assembling a large landholding by marrying female heirs, and the policy was somewhat consistent with British common law and practice. Under strict primogeniture, the eldest son inherited every-thing. However, in Salzburg and neighboring regions, it was common for daughters to inherit land if there were no male heirs.[31] The Georgia Trustees would not budge on this issue, which may explain why Urlsperger could find only forty-one Salzburgers willing to migrate as part of the first group.[32]

After finding an initial group of Salzburgers willing to migrate to Amer-ica, Urlsperger reported that the Roman Catholic magistrates in Augs-burg were making it difficult for him and the exiles. Urlsperger had noti-fied the town that they planned to use Augsburg as a gathering place for up to three hundred Salzburgers who would migrate to British America. There, he hoped, the town's Protestants could organize and supply the migrants for their long journey. As during the first wave of migrants, the Catholic mag-istrates in the city refused entry to the exiles.[33] Urlsperger also tried to re-cruit from the Salzburger group returning from Zeeland but had no success with them. He had a group of forty-one migrants ready to leave in the fall of 1733 and worried that the group might be too small. The Trustees, confident in their plans, believed the success of the initial group would be an incen-tive for others to follow.[34] They commissioned Philip Georg Friedrich von Reck to escort the first Salzburgers from Bavaria to Georgia. Reck was the nephew of King George II's envoy to the Holy Roman Empire's Perpetual Diet in Regensburg, and his presence on the journey signaled royal approval for the venture. Eventually the first group of forty-one migrants, called the first transport of Salzburgers, left the Augsburg area on October 31, 1733. Fi-nally, on March 12, 1734, they arrived in Georgia.[35]

Part of the Trustees' offer to the refugees was that a German Lutheran minister would live with them in Georgia. To fulfill this commitment, they turned to Urlsperger and Francke for recommendations. Johann Martin Boltzius, who at the time was a thirty-year-old teacher at the Latin school of the Francke Foundations in Halle, agreed to join the migration. Boltzius was born in Forst in Lower Lusatia; his uncle was a pastor, and it was he who arranged for Johann Martin to receive an education at Berlin and then at the University of Halle.[36] Boltzius was accompanied to America by Israel Christian Gronau, a tutor at the Halle school. Gronau, the son of a pastor, had volunteered to serve the Salzburgers who migrated to Prussia but in-stead agreed to serve as catechist to the exiles in Georgia. Boltzius and Gro-nau were both devout Pietists but had not yet been ordained in the Lutheran ministry. They rushed to Wernigerode, where they were ordained on No-vember 11, 1733, and then to Rotterdam, where they met the first transport of Salzburgers.[37] Together the group sailed first to Dover, arriving in England in mid-December. Already six weeks had passed since the Salzburgers had left southern Germany. Bad weather kept them in their ships off Dover's shore until January, when, finally, they departed for America.

The Salzburgers named their new settlement Ebenezer while they were still aboard the *Purysburg* traveling across the Atlantic—before they had seen the American coastline, before they had slogged miles inland from the Savannah River through swamps and mud, and before half of them had become sick. They chose this new name as a group, as part of the discussions that took place aboard the ship about the unknown paths their lives were taking in their migration.[38] The voyage had been fraught, with winds so strong that at one point the ship's main mast broke, and many of the travelers had become seasick. They endured together and comforted themselves with scripture. The name Ebenezer came from the Old Testament and carried with it two meanings, the first from the words the prophet Samuel spoke as he raised a symbolic stone: "Thus far the Lord has helped us."[39] The second understanding came from a literal translation of the Hebrew, meaning a "stone of help" from God. Both nuances seemed fitting for the group, in line with the hymn they had sung in Augsburg, "God Is Our Refuge in Distress." They believed God had supported and led them through difficult trials to bring them to a new, and blessed, land. The Salzburgers believed that they would be tested, tried, and refined by God in this American wilderness and that the Georgia forest would ultimately save them, as the desert had saved the Israelites.

Ebenezer's location in Georgia was initially assigned to the Salzburger migrants by Trustee James Oglethorpe. Oglethorpe was the only Trustee who traveled to America, and in the early years of the colony he served as its de facto civil leader. A week after the first group arrived in the colony on March 12, 1734, Oglethorpe arranged to take Reck, Gronau, and a few others to the location he had predetermined would be the new Salzburger home.[40] Eight single men followed on March 20 to begin building homes for the settlers. A South Carolina benefactor, possibly plantation owners Jonathan and Hugh Bryan, loaned fourteen enslaved workers to build roads and shelters.[41] Boltzius and Reck's account of the early days describes the Salzburger migrants' toil to carve a space in the forest for their settlement but rarely mentions the work of the enslaved.

By April there were enough crude shelters that the rest of the Salzburgers began moving north toward their new town, stopping in Abercorn because they could not reach Ebenezer via the Savannah River. They had to construct an overland road through swampland from Abercorn to the Ebenezer site and carry all of their provisions and baggage by foot. In these first weeks Salzburger Tobias Lackner died.[42]

These early trials and disappointments presaged an often difficult life in Georgia. The early years were characterized by scarcity of food, tenuous shelter, and plentiful disease and death. Even so the Salzburgers eventually built a community that expanded beyond Ebenezer to incorporate more Germans in Georgia. The Salzburgers would not have established self-sustaining farms and community without the intervention, and ongoing support, of Protestant philanthropists. The three groups who worked across religious boundaries—the British charitable corporation the Trustees for Establishing the Colony of Georgia, the Anglican-led SPCK, and the German Pietist Lutheran community centered on the Francke Foundations at Halle—had united in common cause to settle Protestant refugees in America. Now that the Salzburgers had arrived at their new home, the long-term, sustained provision of aid would be put to the test.

# CHAPTER 2

---

# The Georgia Trustees

That any Salzburger exiles ended up in Georgia came about through the confluence of three philanthropic groups choosing to work together: Protestants in Germany and Britain and the Georgia Trustees. The exiles' migrations out of Salzburg in 1732 and continuing into 1733 was just the right timing for some people to believe settling in America was a good option, which seems obvious only in hindsight. If they had left their alpine homes a few years earlier, the colony of Georgia would not have existed and the Salzburgers would have likely settled in Prussia with the majority of the exiles. If the Salzburgers had been forced out a few years later, in the late 1730s, the Trustees would likely have felt they did not have the funding needed for their migration. By that time the Trustees were beginning to deal with grumbling colonists and public relations battles over the goals and structure of their project. Leaving their homes when they did, the Georgia Salzburgers sought a new home, were persuaded by the Trustees' project for a new colony, and took a massive risk that it would succeed.

To fully appreciate the relationship between the Trustees and the Salzburgers and how these Germans came to be idealized as the right sort of settlers, it is important to understand the Georgia Trustees and their colonization plans' inspiration, methods, and goals. The group formed as a charity to help the poor (while benefiting the empire) and adjusted their policies in response to the realities of funding and support for establishing a new colony. The Georgia Salzburgers were often portrayed as the ideal settlers, in part because they seemed to implement the Trustees' original plans for the colony. Agreeing that the Georgia forest could physically rescue them, the Salz-burgers quickly came to see the new colony also as a place where they were also spiritually saved. In practice, the Salzburgers were reliant upon Trustee goodwill to send money, supplies, and more Germans, which caused the mi-grants to stay closely aligned with the original aims of the colony. After the first few years, when some Georgia settlers challenged the colonizing plan for Georgia, the Salzburgers were held out as *the* proof that the colony could succeed under Trustee leadership because they appeared to agree with the founders' plans.

## Georgia's Beginnings

In 1731 James Oglethorpe explained in a letter his motivation behind creating the colony of Georgia. "By this means [we] hope to take so many wretches from the utmost misery and settle them in a comfortable way of living, and of providing well for their children."[1] With this philanthropic goal in mind, and beginning in 1729, Oglethorpe and John Lord Viscount Perceval (created the First Earl of Egmont in 1733), along with some additional members of Parliament, leading clergymen, and London merchants, planned for a corpo-rate body that would serve the poor of Britain and benefit the empire. In 1732 the men formed the Trustees for the Establishment of the Colony of Geor-gia in America with a colonization plan that was unique in Britain's history of empire. The group was a private charity, counting on some government fi-nancing, designed to address the plight of the "worthy poor" in London by colonizing land in the American mainland Southeast. The Trustees formed nearly fifty years after the establishment of Carolina, and they chose to de-viate from a well-established pattern for American colonies, imagining that colonialism could simultaneously serve the empire and fulfill charitable aspi-rations. They proposed helping Britain's poor by having the Trustees' charity pay the cost of transport to America and upon arrival deed each settler fifty acres of land, all necessary tools, and one year of food and supplies. By setting up families as free farmers in America, they hoped to elevate the poor, to turn them into morally upright, productive, and valued members of society, and to make them contributors to the empire's general weal.

The original Trustees' colonial idea emerged from work done on a 1729 parliamentary committee created to investigate the state of government prisons. Oglethorpe and Egmont had served on this Gaols Committee and were alarmed by conditions in debtor prisons, particularly those endured by people the MPs believed were simply honorable poor who had fallen into

debt.[2] As a result, eight of the MPs on the prison committee banded together to form the Georgia Trustees.[3] That they believed a colony was a viable solution to London poverty is testament to the faith in empire held by
leading Britons in the early eighteenth century as well as the flexibility that
still existed in colonization plans for new ventures.

Oglethorpe, Egmont, and the other philanthropists planned to use public
donations to finance the transport of impoverished migrants to immediately become free, independent people in the new colonies. Their fundraising
began by redirecting the charitable legacy funds established by the estate
of Anglican clergyman Dr. Thomas Bray, the founder of the Society for
Promoting Christian Knowledge (SPCK). After Bray spent a short time
in Maryland in 1700, much of his charitable works focused on the British American colonies, including founding the Society for the Propagation
of the Gospel in Foreign Parts (SPG), which sent Anglican missionaries
to America.[4] When Bray died in 1730 Oglethorpe and Perceval were already part of the Associates of Dr. Bray, a group formed to carry out the
philanthropic work. The Bray Associates formed the seed group of men
who founded Georgia and included future Trustees Thomas Coram (who
founded the London Foundling Hospital in 1739), Rev. Stephen Hales, and
James Vernon, an active supporter of the Salzburgers throughout the Trustee
period. Before they had their colonial charter, the Bray Associates used their
meetings to begin working on the Georgia project, writing marketing pamphlets to promote the idea and even interviewing possible settlers.[5]

Not only would the Georgia colony be different in setting up a structure that intended to relieve the poor, but the Georgia Trustees also chose a
unique administrative model. No other American colony had been founded
as a charitable corporation, and the Trustees pledged not to benefit finan-
cially from the venture to demonstrate integrity and to lend confidence to
potential donors. The charter that the Trustees received from King George
II in June 1732 included elements found in earlier colonization plans; however it also included a long section that declared that none of the Trustees
should "take, or receive, directly or indirectly, any salary, fee, perquisite, benefit or profit whatsoever."[6] This innovation was crafted by the early Trustees
in response to financial corruption scandals that had rocked London in the
1720s to assure potential donors.[7]

Perhaps the most unusual feature of the Georgia plan was this promise
of disinterest, as colonies were always about earning a profit for the inves-
tors. The Trustees took an oath that they would not profit, and their designs
made clear that none of them would be granted land in the colony. This vow

was an important part of the selling of the plan to King George II and his Privy Council. The king stalled on signing the charter for a few months, forcing Egmont and others to work through Prime Minister Robert Walpole to obtain approval. Frustrated with the delays, Egmont met with Walpole in February 1732 to press for the signature, emphasizing that they were "restrained at our own desire by oath from making any advantage directly or indirectly" from the colony, and therefore the government should be asking them to start the colony, rather than forcing the Trustees to repeatedly beg for approval.[8] The promise of disinterest was apparently influential with the Privy Council and in getting the king's approval, because Lord Wilmington, the president of the Privy Council, singled out the pledge for praise. Shortly after the charter was signed, Wilmington told a group of Trustees that he "wished it might prove a pattern for all future new settlements in America, if such a number of gentlemen might be found who would give their service for nothing."[9] On April 23, 1732, Egmont received word that the king had finally signed the new charter.

In addition to the unusual emphasis on public disinterest, the plan for Georgia included rules that marked it as unique in imperial Britain. The Trustees banned slavery and deeded land only in tail-male, meaning daughters and wives could not inherit. These two rules became the source of much discontent for the colonists in America but were at the heart of the colonizing plan conceived by Oglethorpe, Egmont, and the clergy who made up the original Trustees. Their thinking about land and labor was influenced by the political philosophy known as Agrarian Law, favored by a group in Parliament known as the Country Party. The early Trustees were not always aligned politically—Egmont was nominally a Whig and Oglethorpe a Tory-leaning independent—yet many of them seemed to agree with the ideas of the unofficial Country Party element in Parliament.[10] Members of this loosely organized group were unhappy with the new way of running government under Robert Walpole, who served as George II's Lord of the Treasury and is now generally considered to have been the first prime minister. Whig and Tory members of the Country Party opposed the consolidation of power in the court and advocated keeping power and prerogatives in the hands of the landed gentry. They favored the needs of rural Britons over the growing power and influence of urban London. The original plans of the Trustees fit squarely with Country Party thinking in that they planned to create a society that favored land ownership over consolidated commercial interests, in which upstanding subjects would be rural, not urban, dwellers, in part because they believed the country environment strengthened traditional morals.

The pamphlets, sermons, and meeting minutes of the Trustees reveal the influence of seventeenth-century thinker James Harrington, whose ideas were popular with the Country Party. Harrington's most influential work, *The Commonwealth of Oceana*, outlined the ideal society and form of government, which he described as ruled by Agrarian Law. Published in 1656, during Oliver Cromwell's Protectorate, Harrington's *Oceana* placed the source of power in land ownership, to the exclusion of other forms of property. Although he wrote of a natural aristocracy, he advocated the distribution of land so that there would not be a small landed aristocracy. To that end, under his theory of Agrarian Law, a man with an estate valued at more than two thousand pounds should divide it between his sons, essentially upending English primogeniture. Further, under Harrington's ideas, anyone who held land valued at more than two thousand pounds would not be allowed to acquire any more property as "that would raise his income above that sum."[11] In other words, this utopian society would feature a broad base of landholders, each with some political rights. In his study of political philosophy, Harrington argued that Rome fell in large part because the emperors had, "thro a negligence committed in their Agrarian Laws, let in the sink of Luxury, and forfeited the inestimable treasure of liberty."[12] The Romans had failed to properly distribute land among the people and had thereby created a small aristocracy, steeped in luxury and subject to attack from without, and they all ultimately suffered the loss of liberty.

Harrington had proposed a republic, with voting by landholders and a bicameral legislature. The Trustees were not so radical as to envision that type of colony, and in fact they did not implement an elected assembly until 1750, after years of settlers' complaints and well after all the other British colonies had local representation. However, they did try to implement the core ideas of Agrarian Law. The phrase itself was used only sparingly in the Trustees' published materials, but it did appear. For example, in one of the Trustees' published annual sermons on Georgia, Philip Bearcroft praised the "happy influence of this Agrarian Law," where a man could "sit with wife and children under own Vines and Fruit Trees" and enjoy "a virtuous Frugality."[13] The original Trustees believed that a society that properly implemented the Agrarian Law would be a virtuous society.

We can see Harrington's ideas at work most prominently in the foundational policies of the Trustees surrounding land and slavery. First, for them the key to improving the life and character of the poor was to give them land. But the Trustees limited Georgia land grants to fifty acres per head of household (always a male), similar to the ideas of Agrarian Law and very different from the law in neighboring South Carolina. Wives and daughters could not inherit because the Trustees believed that an unscrupulous man could accumulate vast stretches of land through multiple marriages. They sought to create an ideal society where power was decentralized in the hands of many rural property holders. A Trustee pamphlet argued that "experience has shown the Inconvenience of Privat Persons possessing too large Quantities of Land in our colonies," which led to uncultivated land.[14] In Georgia, the Trustees wrote, a family would have their own land, which naturally would have the "best Motive for industry."[15] The implication was that plantation owners who profited from enslaved laborers were inherently lazy, while landowning farming families would be industrious and upright citizens.

Another innovation in colonizing came with the second key policy for Georgia—the ban on slavery. This was not due to any great feeling of sympathy for the enslaved individuals, as some Trustees invested in slave-based economies elsewhere. Georgia founder James Oglethorpe and Trustee John LaRoche both held administrative positions with the Royal African Company, which was engaged in the transatlantic slave trade.[16] In addition, as mentioned earlier, in the early days of the colony Oglethorpe accepted the labor of enslaved men when it was loaned to them by South Carolinians to help the Germans fell trees and build roads and structures.[17]

The Trustees marketed several reasons for their ban. Not permitting settlers to hold enslaved people was presented as necessary for colonial defense. The British feared that the Spanish in neighboring Florida would incite the enslaved people to rebel and revolt. Indeed, Spain did work to undermine the British Lowcountry by promising freedom to any enslaved person who escaped to Florida.[18] The need for the ban as a defense carried the day with the British Parliament. When the 1735 law that codified Trustee policy was passed, it was named the "Act for rendering the Colony of Georgia More Defencible by Prohibiting the Importation and Use of Black Slaves."[19]

Importantly, another key reason the original Trustees wanted the ban in Georgia was that they believed slavery was antithetical to creating a society of families living on small farms. The Trustees were familiar with South Carolina and the West Indies, where slavery accompanied a system of large plantations in which one man, or one family, controlled thousands of acres of land. That plantation owner and enslaver did not perform the physical labor but rather lived in luxury on the work of others, contrary to the Trustees' plan for small farming families. In a 1741 pamphlet the Georgia Trustees laid out their reasoning for the ban. They cited concerns for defense, the cost of purchasing enslaved individuals, and concern that the enslaver "would be less disposed to labour himself."[20] Further, the Trustees believed that wealthy colonists who enslaved Africans might "be more induced to absent themselves, and live in other Places, leaving the care of their planta- tions . . . to Overseers."[21] For the Trustees, creating a society that uplifted the poor and needy of Britain and Europe required a ban on slavery. The Trustee pamphlets never mention the violence and disease suffered by the enslaved under South Carolina's plantation system, further evidence that they were not early forerunners of humanitarian abolition but were primar- ily concerned about the moral character of Euro-Americans in Georgia.

The two policies—limited land holdings and the ban on slavery—were at the heart of the Trustees' social engineering plans. They believed that the success of the colony depended upon creating a moral environment where the poor could thrive, and that environment could not be built without these rules in place. This is why the Trustees so adamantly adhered to the plan, even as these ideas were at the heart of many of the Georgia settlers' discontent.[22]

Until Spring 1732 all Georgia Trustees were either members of Parliament or clergymen. However, they were soon joined by a cadre of merchants inter- ested in both the philanthropic and the commercial prospects in the Amer- ican South. There had been earlier proposals for a colony south of the Sa- vannah River, with pamphlets circulated in London outlining the reasons for settling the region. The 1717 pamphlet by Sir Robert Montgomery titled *A Discourse Concerning the Design'd Establishment of a New Colony to the South of Carolina, in the Most Delightful Country of the Universe* argued for a new Lowcountry colony.[23] Montgomery's plan highlighted the benefit of having a colony to act as a buffer and defense of South Carolina against the Indians and Spanish in Florida. This and other proposals emphasized the commer- cial opportunities that would accrue to Britain if they held a new colony at Mediterranean latitudes. The territory that became Georgia could provide "Coffee, Tea, Figs, Raisins, Currants, Almonds, Olives, Silk, Wine, [and] Cochineal," which were all products that Britain was "forc'd to buy at mighty Rates from Countries lying in the very Latitude of our Plantations."[24]

When word of the Trustees' colonial plan began to spread, the mem- ory of these earlier proposals sparked the interests of the London merchant community. At the same time the philanthropic Trustees needed funding beyond simple charitable donations for the poor, as experience had shown that establishing a new colony was expensive and would need the support of many people. For this reason, the Trustees began to expand their body to include important London merchants. By June 1732, when they finally received their charter with the king's seal attached, the Trustees' corporation included several men experienced in Atlantic trade. These new men were sorely needed, as the Trustees had only £175 at that time, and they estimated they would need £10,000.[25] The pledge to not gain personally from the venture applied to the merchant Trustees, but they seemed to have restricted that to mean not owning or speculating on land. Although the merchants joined the Georgia Trustees with an eye on developing trade in competition with France and Spain, in the early days of the colony these men were most useful for their connections to the London business and political community in the drive to raise funds.

Trustee Frances Eyles came from a well-connected, wealthy trading family whose father had been the Lord Mayor of London. He was joined by Trustee William Chapman, the son of a wealthy London alderman and the owner of the largest cloth export firm in the city. Chapman participated in the triangle trade, carrying cloth to Africa in his own ships, which then picked up enslaved people to sell in America on the return run. Perhaps the most influential merchant to support the Trustees was Sir Gilbert Heathcote, a leader of London's financial and commercial community who expressed interest in advancing the Georgia project in late 1731 and early 1732. Heathcote helped the Trustees negotiate and receive their charter as he lent his name to the plan and, with Egmont, personally presented a draft of the proposal to the secretary of state, the Duke of Newcastle.[26] Considered one of the wealthiest commoners of the early 1700s and well known in London as the former Lord Mayor and as a leader in the wine trade and the trade in the East and West Indies, Heathcote had been the agent for Jamaica and held the victualing contract for British troops there.[27] Sir Gilbert Heathcote died in 1733 and did not officially join the Trustees, but his nephew, Sir George Heathcote, did. George was also an alderman of London.

### Advertising and Funding
### the Georgia Project

Due to the influence of these experienced merchants and financiers, the Trustees began describing their plan in terms of three interrelated goals: to help the poor by creating an ideal society in the Georgia forests, to provide important trade goods to Britain, and to serve as a defense for the southern colonies. The Trustees wrote that the three goals were compatible as they argued that the poor would become important producers of raw materials needed for British trade. And having a colony of many small land holdings meant people living relatively close together, instead of spreading out on large plantations, a pattern that worked well for defense, as each head of household was required to serve in the militia. This enticing new framing of the colonial project garnered the support of several audiences and made the colony appealing to the British public and to members of Parliament. As "persecuted protestants" the Salzburgers fit the criteria of worthy poor, and as migrants they aligned their community with the other two ideals.

One way the Trustees raised funds and spread the word about their new colony was by publishing a series of pamphlets, most of which listed the corporate body as the author but were probably written by their secretary, Benjamin Martyn, in consultation with Oglethorpe, Egmont, and others. Upon receiving their charter with the king's seal in June 1732, they quickly published three works. The first was *Some Account of the Designs of the Trustees for Establishing the Colony of Georgia in America*, a short, five-page pamphlet that laid out the possibilities for the colony in the three key areas of charity, defense, and commerce. Oglethorpe released his own seventy-seven-page treatise, *A New and Accurate Account of the Provinces of South-Carolina and Georgia*, which argued that the new colony could not fail.[28] To build his case, Oglethorpe recounted the history of colonies under the Roman Republic, mentioned the beneficial climate of the Lowcountry, and provided descriptions of the flora and fauna of the region and of the mercantile possibilities that existed for Georgia. Some believed that migration to the colony would drain British resources, an idea that Oglethorpe tackled with calculations to show that a poor family who moved to Georgia instead of remaining in England would be a net economic benefit to Britain. He wrote that in England a hundred each of poor men, women, and children could, at best, earn a thousand pounds in a year and would still require another thousand pounds of charitable donations to survive. In Georgia, he calculated, the same three hundred people would earn six thousand pounds and, better still, would consume four thousand pounds of British goods.[29] This type of thinking—that American colonial residents were still a useful part of a greater Britain—is representative of the shift of understanding about the interrelatedness of colony and metropole, arguing that Britain would be stronger relative to its rivals France and Spain by having a strong empire.

In 1732 the Trustees also republished a set of earlier tracts about the benefits of colonization in general. Titled *Select Tracts Relating to Colonies*, the pamphlet included an essay by Sir Francis Bacon and some of William

Penn's promotional writing.[30] This publication was aimed at reassuring British citizens that colonies were historically successful and useful to European nations and, by inference, that donors would be doing good not just for the poor but for Britain as a whole.

In addition to publishing tracts, the Trustees placed notices in magazines that circulated in London coffeehouses, in cities throughout Britain, and in America. The June 30, 1732, issue of *Gentlemen's Magazine* announced the new colony's charter and listed the names of the Trustees.[31] A month later, they placed an item explaining the seal, which featured "two Figures of Rivers," signifying the Savannah and Altamaha, and a representation of the "Genius of the Colony . . . with the Cap of Liberty upon her head" and a cornucopia nearby.[32] All of this was carefully designed to convey the bright prospects for Georgia. Included was a description of their motto, "Non sibi sed aliis," meaning "Not for self, but for others." This was another way to emphasize the charitable nature of the enterprise and to reinforce the pledge of personal disinterest.

As the group began to receive donations, the Trustees publicized those, too, as when they announced that the parish of St. Botolph Aldgate had "contributed very handsomely" to the colony.[33] This was a way of simultaneously thanking the donors and applying social pressure for more funds. As soon as they had positive reports from Georgia, the Trustees placed notices in magazines, in part to show the success and also to demonstrate that the funds were being put to good use.

The primary means of gathering charitable donations was not through the printed word but through developing a network of people commissioned to solicit and collect donations. In June 1732 the Trustees wrote the aldermen of London, Liverpool, and smaller boroughs, but initially they did not make direct personal calls to each individual alderman.[34] In response, they received supportive requests for commissions to collect for the charity from the cities of Liverpool, Bodmin, and Hereford, but noticeably absent were any commissions from London.[35] Having Eyles, Chapman, and Heathcote as Trustees now became invaluable as they used their influence within the upper circles of the London merchant community to make personal appeals. Due to their efforts the group received requests to have a commission from "members of the governing boards of the Levant Company, the Russia Company, the East India Company . . . [and] the South Sea Company" and from the "three leading Sephardic Jewish financiers in Lombard Street."[36] These commercial donors could provide much greater funds than parish charitable collections. Sir Gilbert Heathcote presented the Georgia plan to the directors of the Bank of England, emphasizing that the colony would be a "means of increasing our Trade and Navigation, and raising of Raw Silk, for which 500,000£ a Year is paid to Piedmont [in Italy]."[37] All but two of the directors made personal subscriptions totaling £315.[38]

Even with all this effort, the colony never raised enough money from private donations, and from the beginning the Trustees looked to the government for help. In May 1732, before they even had their signed royal charter, the Trustees petitioned Parliament for a £10,000 grant. Parliament refused that year but did vote the funds in May 1733.[39] In March 1735 Parliament voted another £26,000, and government support was firmly entrenched in the financial structure of the Georgia "charitable" colony. Historian Richard Dunn calculated that from 1732 to 1752 the Trustees spent £155,000, with £136,000 (88 percent) coming from Parliament; another £100,000 was spent by Parliament on the colony's defense, much of that during the War of Jenkins' Ear (1739–1742), when Georgia was on the front lines of Britain's war against Spain.[40]

While the Georgia plan was distinctive, being established as a charity and ruled by a group of Trustees, the funding structure made the project doubly unique as the only British American colony funded almost entirely by parliamentary grants. Expanding the goals beyond helping the worthy poor, and the total dependence upon government funding, meant that the Trustees had to regularly convince the public of the worthiness of their plans. They did this through pamphlets and published sermons. The Salzburgers' settlement featured prominently in the marketing because they came the closest to following the philanthropic design of the original Trustees in creating a community of small farms.

## Administering the Colony

The Georgia plan, with rules about land ownership, slavery, and inheritance, has been described as a "straight-jacket system."[41] The Earl of Egmont, perhaps because of his leading role in the group and his unbending attitude toward slavery in the colony, often comes in for criticism. History has judged him a "romantic" who was filled with "utopian zeal" for American projects, as evidenced by his long-term support of Anglo-Irish Dean George Berkeley's failed plans for a school for enslaved Africans in the Americas.[42] In other histories the Trustees are portrayed as naïve, obstinate, and too steeped in utopian ideals to understand the pragmatic needs of a colony. The state of Georgia's official collection of colonial records includes a comment that "the

plan of government first instituted by the Trustees was utopian and impracticable."[43] They *were* very obstinate in their core principles of distributed
land ownership and the ban on slavery because the Trustees viewed them as
required to meet their goals. Their intransigence on these issues met strong
resistance from many colonists and led to the Trustees ultimately surrender-
ing their charter to the Crown in 1752, but they were not naïve or inexpe-
rienced. They exerted great effort to gather the best information and were
often willing to respond to colonists' requests to provide every needful thing.

As a body, the Trustees approached establishing Georgia by gathering
the best available knowledge about the region and by studying previous colonial projects. It is clear from the writings that the Trustees were familiar
with earlier colonizing attempts, as was natural for those set to invest a great
deal of energy and resources on establishing a new colony.

Georgia, as the youngest British colony on mainland North America, had
several precedents, but the Trustees looked most closely at South Carolina
and Virginia. Comparing Georgia to early Virginia, the Trustees noted that
the first colonists at Jamestown entered a world where the "Coast and Climate" were unknown and where the Indians were "at Enmity with the first
Planters," eliding the complex and often violent relationship between Jamestown and the local Powhatan Confederacy.[44] Georgia had neither of these
problems, the Trustees reasoned, since the coast and climate were similar to
those in South Carolina, and they believed that the Native Americans in the
region had retreated inland after suffering losses in the Yamasee War of 1715.
While it was true that the Yamasee had retreated, of course the lands targeted by the Trustees were still owned and used by Native Americans. For
all of their study and information gathering, the Trustees seemed somewhat
unaware of the powerful Muskogee Confederation towns in Georgia or the
fact that the coastal regions were under their control.

In another argument for the near guaranteed success of the new colony, the Trustees reasoned that Georgia would benefit from its proximity to
South Carolina, where supplies and provisions could be easily acquired and
where expertise on how to plant and live in the climate was readily available.
Benjamin Martyn, the Trustees' secretary, wrote that despite difficult initial
challenges, Virginia had succeeded; surely, then, Georgia was "more likely to
succeed."[45]

The Trustees solicited advice from a wide variety of people who had information about America. Egmont had long held a friendly correspondence
with Virginia's William Byrd II and inquired about climate, crops, and especially the opportunity for producing silk. The Trustees sought the advice of

colonial governors and maintained correspondence with Jonathan Belcher of Massachusetts, who eventually donated to the cause. Samuel Eveleigh, a Charleston merchant and Indian trader, provided the Trustees with insight into the types of products that could come from Georgia. Eveleigh reported that Georgia had "a vast Quantity of extraordinary fine Land."[46] He also informed the Trustees that the colony required enslaved Africans because Euro-Americans would not work in such hot weather; they chose to ignore that advice. Eveleigh corresponded with the Trustees through the 1730s and early 1740s and visited Savannah to report on its status. He even took up a collection among Charleston residents for the new colony, helping to raise over £1,165 in April 1734.[47]

As a group, the Trustees comprised men with a history of interest in the natural world and especially of America's environment. At least seven of the original Trustees were also members of the Royal Society, including Egmont, Robert Hucks, George Heathcote, Stephen Hales, James Vernon, Robert More, and George, Lord Carpenter, Second Baron of the Cape of Killaghy. Antony Ashley Cooper, Fourth Earl of Shaftesbury, was made a Fellow after his service as a Trustee. Together, they pursued natural or scientific information about Georgia. A long curiosity led Egmont to sponsor the 1722 voyage to America by Mark Catesby, who returned to publish detailed descriptions and paintings of the flora and fauna of the Lowcountry in his two-volume *Natural History of Carolina, Florida, and the Bahama Islands.*[48]

As part of their plan for Georgia, the Trustees hired Dr. William Houston to gather plants and seeds from the Mediterranean, Africa, South America, and the Caribbean to experiment with in the Trustees' Public Garden.[49] Houston died in Jamaica, but not before he managed to send several seeds to Georgia. These were planted in the ten-acre Trustee Garden in Savannah, which was intended to be both an experimental station and a nursery for settlers where they could get plants for free. By 1735 the garden already had bay, sassafras, evergreen oak, hickory, ash, laurel, and mulberry trees.[50] The Trustees instructed their garden caretaker to plant a number of European fruit trees, including apple, pear, and orange. The garden nurtured Mediterranean products such as olives, figs, pomegranates, and grape vines, while a section was set aside for products from the West Indies such as cocoa, cotton, and palms. It was hoped that at least some of these plants would prosper in Georgia and provide the basis for a thriving trade.

When donating to the Georgia trust it was possible to designate the monies for specific purposes. One of the funds the Trustees established was for "Encouraging and Improving Botany and Agriculture," which attracted the attention and monies of several Royal Society Fellows, including the well-known naturalist and collector Sir Hans Sloane.[51] Sloane was possibly the largest single donor, annually contributing twenty pounds for the first five years to the botanical cause. Later, in 1736, the Duke of Richmond (a Fellow of the Royal Society), Charles DuBois, Heathcote, Oglethorpe, the Earl of Derby, and "the Company of Apothecaries" all committed to additional two-year subscriptions to the botany fund.[52] This fund financed Dr. Houston's travels and collections. The best available scientific thinking indicated that climate and flora depended upon the latitude; as Georgia was at the same latitude as the northern edge of Africa, the Levant, India, and China, donors and the Trustees reasoned that similar plants would thrive.[53] For the Trustees the interest was not merely scientific, as they were looking for products for the British trade that would reduce England's dependence upon Spanish, French, and Italian merchants.

The Trustees' interest in botany is an example of their ongoing concern for managing affairs in Georgia. Their deep engagement could certainly be seen as paternalistic and overbearing, but there was also a positive side in that they displayed a sincere interest in hearing from colonists. After the first colonists arrived in Georgia, the Trustees showed a remarkable attentiveness to the needs of the settlers. The first few years of their meeting minutes are full of appeals for new tools, for different land grants, and for extra provisions; in most cases the Trustees did their best to satisfy such requests. As we will see, Salzburger pastor Boltzius made frequent requests of the Trustees, and those were often met favorably.

One area of frustration for the Trustees that impeded their management was the difficulty of getting detailed and accurate information about the progress of the colony. Originally, they had hoped that James Oglethorpe, who traveled with the first ship of colonists in November 1732, would function as their eyes and ears. But Oglethorpe was not a diligent correspondent, and the Trustees grew increasingly anxious for regular, reliable reports. To fill this need, in 1739 they sent William Stephens as colonial secretary to be their designated correspondent; later, he was made colony president. Stephens was charged with providing regular journals and reports on the state of the country to the Trustees, a responsibility that was especially important as they began to get complaints from some settlers.

The actions of the Trustees from the beginning and until the end of their government are of a group intent on success, on gathering the best information, and on responding to the needs of the colonists. They were very optimistic about the possibilities for Georgia; given the expense and effort involved in launching any colonial project, optimism was probably a necessary quality.

## Poor Persecuted Protestants

In the Trustees' marketing tracts and in Oglethorpe's longer treatise, another benefit for establishing Georgia soon appeared: the settlers would spread Protestant Christianity and convert Native Americans, a long-stated but rarely realized goal of British colonization. The Trustees had not focused on this possibility in their earliest meetings. Perhaps because it was such a commonplace notion that a colony in America would spread the right sort of Christianity, the Trustees included Indian conversion in their marketing as a potential outcome of their venture. Along with this, the pamphlets added the "poor persecuted Protestants" of Europe to the list of the type of people they hoped to send. Both goals were part of the notion that the British Empire had a duty to spread Protestant Christianity.

By the early eighteenth century Britons were convinced that they were the leading Protestant nation, charged with protecting the true faith against Catholic cruelty, especially that of Spain and France. The Trustees wrote that an important reason to support Georgia was that "the Protestant Interest in Europe" was in decline, attacked by Catholic governments in France, Poland, Hungary, and Salzburg.[54] Indeed, the Trustees stated as fact that all Englishmen agreed that since Queen Elizabeth I, the English Crown was "look'd on as the Head of the Protestant Interest in Europe."[55] A respect for Britain's historical role as well as a duty to the faith demanded the Georgia colony help European Protestants.

England did have a history of helping European Protestants. In the seventeenth century, French Huguenot exiles moved to several British North American colonies, from South Carolina to Nova Scotia. Governor Johnson of South Carolina tried to recruit some in the early eighteenth century because he thought they would know how to make silk. In 1708 and 1709 more than thirteen thousand Germans arrived in England after hearing a rumor that England would pay to settle them in America.[56] About twenty-two hundred of them were sent to settle along the Hudson and Mohawk river valleys in New York, with some of them later moving into Berks County, Pennsylvania.

The Trustees began to include Europe's Protestants in their plan when they heard about the Salzburger exiles. The exact date they became aware of the situation developing in Southern German lands is unclear, but accounts of the Salzburger expulsion were printed in London's *Gentlemen's Magazine* by early 1732. In March of that year the journal reported that the "British and Dutch Ministers" had presented memorials to the emperor in Vienna in protest of the treatment of the Salzburgers.[57] Further, the magazine stated that in Berlin Frederick William I had announced he would shut all Catholic churches in Prussia as a form of reprisal.[58] Since the Trustees used *Gentlemen's Magazine* to communicate their plans to the public, most likely they had also read the Salzburger expulsion news.

The Trustees viewed the Salzburgers as ideal colonists largely because they had proven themselves loyal to their Protestant faith by enduring the Jesuit inquisition and subsequent exile.[59] Suffering through this ordeal indicated to the Britons that these exiles were worthy poor—people who would be hardworking, morally upright, and valuable subjects in the colony. For the first group of Salzburger migrants, the Trustees agreed to pay for the entire journey, from Augsburg to America, while the SPCK agreed to fund a minister and a catechist to go with them.[60] By arranging to send clergy, the Trustees helped ensure the group would settle near each other and work together to build small farms. Too poor to engage in a slave plantation economy, the Salzburgers were the ideal immigrants.

Thus, from the near beginning of the colony the Georgia plan incorporated the goal to succor the "poor persecuted Protestants." In Trustee pamphlets and published sermons the religious exiles were always referred to as a great benefit to the colony, arguing that history had shown that Germans in the British Empire had "augmented the Numbers and encreased the Riches of the Kingdom."[61] By 1738, one sermonizer had forgotten the mission to save England's poor altogether when he declared that "had this rising Colony been planted on no other Account, than to affording a Place of Refuge to our persecuted Protestant Friends, it could not have been laid on a better Foundation, or more likely to Succeed."[62] The founders had closely tied the success of the colony to the saving of continental Europe's Protestants, and that alone made it a worthy project.

Settling the Salzburgers proved to be a good decision. Although the Trustees faced challenges from many of the English settlers, the Salzburgers became the strongest supporters of the Trustees' unique plans for the colony and the exiles' success became a symbol for the Trustees that their plans were achievable. Further, the Lutherans were often the loudest voices in support of the Trustees in the fight over slavery that erupted within a decade of the first settlements.

## Challenging the Plan

To ensure that only the right sort of people went, the Trustees interviewed all people who wished to migrate to Georgia, whether they traveled at the expense of the trust or paid their own way. While this policy certainly demonstrates the scale of Trustee paternalism, these interviews also meant that at least one Trustee had met face-to-face with all the settlers of early Georgia, making the venture an extremely personal affair. When the Trustees contracted ships to send the settlers, they were careful that there was adequate food, reasonably clean quarters, and a doctor on board. They seemed to have tried to think of everything and were willing to adjust to meet contingencies. Reading their meeting minutes and Egmont's personal journal, one is struck by the Trustees' willingness to answer complaints and their sincere desire for success, not just of the colony overall but of specific individuals. It is somewhat surprising, therefore, that they did not anticipate the labor shortage so common in the American colonies. After complaints about the lack of labor (tied to the desire for enslaved workers), the Trustees instead responded by recruiting skilled craftsmen to send to the colony. Because the Trustees recognized most poor settlers in Georgia could not afford labor, the charity made indenture contracts with Germans to be servants in the colony. The Trustees' evident care for the well-being of the colonists helps to explain why they were so surprised, and so dismissive, when they started to receive complaints.

The rumblings began in early 1735, when Patrick Tailfer wrote a long letter to the Trustees asking them to allow slavery in the colony. Egmont, who read the letter in August 1735, characterized Tailfer as a "proud, busie fellow," and the request was dismissed.[63] Tailfer quickly became a leader of the discontented, most of whom were, like him, Scottish or Scots-Irish settlers in Savannah. They had the support of some South Carolinians who had long envisioned expanding their plantations south of the Savannah River. Tailfer's group met at a tavern in Savannah and discussed ways to change Trustee policy. They spread stories of how poorly the colony was performing and created their own marketing campaign in the Lowcountry and in London to change policies. Egmont labeled the group the "Malcontents," and the name stuck. The Trustees battled the Malcontents from the late 1730s until they surrendered their charter in 1752.

The main grievances were related to the two core principles of the original plan—the very practices that the Trustees believed made Georgia a unique place that would benefit the worthy poor. Settlers wanted to own the land free so that their daughters could inherit, and they wanted to be able to accumulate much more than fifty acres. Importantly, they wanted the right to enslave people. Other grievances, like the ban on rum, were characterized by the Malcontents as signs that the Trustees were overly controlling, while the intertwined issues of land and labor were at the core of the battles. To Egmont, Oglethorpe, and the original Trustees—particularly those who had been part of Bray's Associates—these issues were nonnegotiable. They believed that the Trustees' whole vision for a charitable colony to create a moral society for the poor, which also strengthened the empire, would be lost if they compromised on these issues.

By the late 1730s some of the Malcontents had left the colony, yet they continued to lobby for change. They were joined in their fight by Thomas Stephens, the son of the Trustees' newly appointed man on the ground, colonial secretary William Stephens. The younger Stephens traveled back home to London, where he circulated a tract he had written about Georgia's impending failure. In November 1739 he passed the pamphlet to Thomas Bramston, an MP for Essex, and by so doing involved Parliament, sharply raising the stakes of the debate.[64] Stephens skillfully lobbied Parliament, hoping to undermine the Trustees' authority by eliminating public funding grants for the colony. Tailfer and the younger Stephens reasoned that without government money the Trustees would fail and be forced to change policies or surrender control. In fact, this is what happened.

To counteract the Malcontents, the Trustees' appeals for parliamentary funding almost abandoned the charitable and commercial benefits of the colony and emphasized the critical importance of Georgia for overall colonial defense.[65] October 1739 marked the beginning of the War of Jenkins' Ear, which was fought on the Georgia-Florida border, and this was no time to weaken the colony. In 1740 Parliament agreed and granted Georgia £4,000, their smallest allotment yet.[66] By this time the Georgia project was completely dependent upon government funding. By about 1737 the initial enthusiasm in England over the new charity had waned and charitable donations had suffered a sharp decline. Historian Paul Taylor calculated that by then the Trustees had collected 90 percent of all they would get from philanthropy, receiving only £2,400 more over the next fifteen years.[67]

The parliamentary debates over Georgia's funding only increased in the period 1741–1743, largely because of skillful lobbying on the part of the Malcontents. Their campaign for looser land policies and legalized slavery was conducted through pamphlets that were distributed in England and the American colonies.[68] The 1741 parliamentary debate shows just how persuasive the Malcontents had been. Sir John Cotton said he "should be against granting any [funds], believing it of no advantage to England, tho' it had some private advantage to some."[69] Given the Trustees' emphasis on personal disinterest and ban on gaining from the venture, this comment must have stung. Echoing the Malcontents' argument that the colony was completely deserted due to bad Trustee policy, Lord Gage "wondered that any gentleman should think of giving a farthing more to support a colony where there is not a man left to be supporting, they being all gone away, and to the utter ruin of many who carried substance."[70] Fortunately, in 1741 the Trustees had the support of Robert Walpole, considered the first prime minister, who returned with the king's approval, ensuring that the Trustees' petition passed, and they were given another £10,000.[71]

The Malcontents had more success in 1742 when they were allowed, once again, to present their case to Parliament. Egmont felt that they praised the possibilities in Georgia but attacked the character of Oglethorpe and the Trustees.[72] The Malcontents' intent was to show what was possible in the colony if only the Trustees' rules could be overturned. The Trustees responded with their own report, drawing upon the accounts of William Stephens, who described success in the Salzburgers' settlement in Ebenezer and also in a community settled by Highland Scots called Darien. The Trustees argued that the Malcontents failed in Georgia because of their weak characters, not the colony's rules and regulations. That year the Malcontents won the debate and Parliament refused to grant funding to the Trustees.[73]

The Trustees fought against the Malcontents' publicity by issuing their own pamphlets extolling the success of their non-slave colony. Egmont took Tailfer's 1741 tract *A True and Historical Narrative of the Colony of Georgia in America* and replied to all the charges point by point, often using extracts from the Salzburger diaries and letters to support his argument.[74] The Trustees also issued their own *Account Shewing the Progress of the Colony of Georgia in America*, which refuted some of their opponents' claims and garnered enough support in Parliament to receive additional funding.[75]

The battle with the Malcontents drove the Trustees to a firm commitment to support the Salzburgers, who had mostly followed the Trustees' rules and were succeeding, building a community that was never very wealthy but was modestly sustainable. For the Trustees and their supporters, the Salzburgers' achievements were a clear sign that the original plan was beneficial for all. In a sea of conflicting reports coming out of Georgia, the Trustees' official responses chose to weigh the Salzburgers' experience favorably in part because both groups believed strongly in the notion that small farming families were more moral, and thus better, members of the community.

The Trustees themselves were divided on these issues, and it was really only Egmont, Oglethorpe, and some of the early founders who were firm in their antislavery stance because they were the ones with the stronger commitment to Agrarian Law and small family farms. The split in the Trustees might have been foretold, as they did not agree about the goals for the colony from the beginning. Those Trustees who were merchants were less concerned with building a moral society of family farms, and it was easy for them to compromise on slavery. The Trustees did change land ownership rules, so that anyone could inherit. But slavery was nonnegotiable until after 1742, when Egmont resigned from the Common Council, the powerful subgroup of Trustees who made controlling decisions. He had been the first president of the Trustees and one of the most consistent attendees at their meetings, working in London to keep the colony functioning. By 1742 he was in poor health, and he had already resigned from Parliament in 1734 in favor of his son. It is also possible that he hoped others would resign with him in a show of support for the original policies, but no other Trustees followed him. The Trustees' council continued to debate the slavery issue and in 1750 asked Parliament to repeal the law and to allow residents to import Africans as slaves beginning January 1, 1751. By this time Egmont had died and Oglethorpe was not heavily involved in the colony. Despite successes in the Salzburger community, the original ideal of creating a unique and moral colony had died, as the door was now opened to a slave plantation society.

The battles with the Malcontents, the difficulty in continuing to fund the colony, and the strain of running the trust wore on the Trustees. When Parliament refused to grant another round of funding in 1751, the remaining few Trustees began working to surrender their twenty-year charter before its expiration at the end of 1752. Antony Ashley Cooper, the Fourth Earl of Shaftesbury, had become a Georgia Trustee in March 1733 at the group's first annual meeting. Since then he had been a tireless supporter of the Georgia project. By the late 1740s he was one of the most active Trustees, and it was he who negotiated the end. At the last Trustee meeting in June 1752, only four were present, including the Salzburgers' steady advocate James Vernon. Their final action was to surrender the charter and deface the seal.[76]

For all of the criticism about their paternalism and naïveté, the Trustees did establish a colony. They failed to keep control largely because the English-speaking colonists did not accept the plan of small family farms.[77]

These agitating settlers successfully lobbied Parliament such that eventually it was thought easier, and possibly less costly, to bring Georgia in line with most of the other British American mainland colonies and establish a royal government. The Malcontents' lobbying had severely tarnished the image of Trustee rule. Further, British American colonies seemed a little safer after the 1748 Treaty of Aix-la-Chapelle, which ended the War of the Austrian Succession, known as the War of Jenkins' Ear in America. The defensive purpose for the colony no longer seemed imperative to the British Parliament, which had always provided most of the financing. The Malcontents had challenged Georgia's economic viability, the second goal for the Trustees.

The first, and primary, goal of the original Trustees was to have a colony that would save the poor, a place populated by industrious, religious, and morally upright subjects. In that endeavor they largely succeeded with the Salzburgers, who benefitted from the additional assistance of the SPCK and the German Pietist community.

# CHAPTER 3

# Protestant Philanthropists

From the earliest days of the Salzburger exile Protestants in Europe and Britain recognized this as a chance to put their faith into practice. As Augsburg's Lutheran minister Samuel Urlsperger shared with the Society for Promoting Christian Knowledge (SPCK), the Salzburgers' "great distress will give all good Christians a fair occasion of exercising a Practical Relief of one of the Fundamental Articles of the Christian Faith: The Communion of Saints: by contributing to the Necessities of their Suffering Brethren."[1] Protestants on both sides of the English Channel also believed the whole affair provided tangible evidence to all the world of the cruelty and error of Roman Catholicism, having faith that the Salzburgers' example of patient endurance would be a tool of conversion.[2] Those two strong forces—doing good works while also harming the enemy—pulled Protestant philanthropists in Britain and Germany into a union to assist the Salzburgers and settle some of them in America. Although enthusiastic about helping the "poor persecuted protestants," the Georgia Trustees could not have supported the Salzburgers' move and colonization without substantial support of religious philanthropies. As we have seen, the SPCK, headquartered in London, was an important go-between for the initial aid to the exiles. The institution worked in partnership with a group of Pietist German Lutherans who were associated with the Francke Foundations in Halle. Although separate organizations, both the SPCK and Francke had a history of cooperation and mutual respect that made it natural for them to come together for the Salzburgers. Without understanding these philanthropists, it is not possible to fully appreciate the Georgia Salzburgers. Indeed, the settlement at Ebenezer probably would have suffered a fate similar to the English at Savannah were it not for the religious, moral, and material aid rendered by these two Protestant philanthropic groups.

## Francke Foundations

Although the Salzburger exiles were not associated with Halle directly, their form of worship was heavily influenced by Pietist thought, such as that by Schaitberger. Further, the two ministers who accompanied them to Georgia both came out of Halle as Johann Martin Boltzius and catechist Israel Christian Gronau were working as teachers at the Francke Foundations' school when they accepted the call to America. Because of this association, the Georgia Salzburger community took the form of an outpost of Halle Pietism, a mission for a certain type of Protestantism in the battle against Catholicism and Catholic empires.

August Hermann Francke's Foundations (the Franckesche Stiftungen in German) began in 1695 when the Lutheran pastor established a school for the poor in Glaucha, an impoverished suburb of Halle on the Saale River, in Saxony (part of Prussia beginning in 1701). That same year he built an orphanage associated with the school, with the goal of improving education and developing a community of Christians. The Francke Foundations grew to include a printing house, a hospital, and a global pharmaceutical trade and quickly became a nearly self-contained institution with a farm and skilled craftsmen.[3] The charity had the support of Prussian king Frederick I, likely because Francke taught that believers should sustain political leaders, as Martin Luther had written.[4] The Foundations' printing house published thousands of books and tracts, including over 850 theological texts written by Francke himself.[5] The fame of Francke, the orphanage at Halle, and the Foundations quickly spread, and donations from the king and others poured in to sustain the charity.

Francke's Lutheranism emphasized the need for a personal conversion, repentance, and holiness. While he agreed with Luther that one could not earn a spot in heaven through good works, he was convinced that true Christians would live lives evident of their inner faith and conversion. His life's work was to instill that deep personal faith and Christian living in others, and that mission was the driving force of all he did. He believed this could be accomplished only by caring for the whole person, and not just ministering to spiritual needs. Within the first decade of establishing the charity the

Francke Foundations had become a center for German Pietism and the focus of social reformation. Generations of Pietist Lutheran pastors trained at the nearby University of Halle, where Francke was also a professor of theology.

Francke's theology had been inspired by the writings of Pietist theologians Johann Arndt (1555–1621) and Philipp Jakob Spener (1635–1705). Spener was one of the foundational theologians of Lutheran Pietism, and from 1691 until his death he served as the dean of the Lutheran clergy and pastor of St. Nicholas Church in Berlin.[6] Under Spener's influence, King Frederick III/I chartered Halle University in 1694 and supported Halle's brand of Lutheran Pietism. In the 1690s Frederick I wanted to establish Berlin as an important European capital, with a social and intellectual population. In short, he worked to strengthen Lutheranism to signal his own role as protector of the faith and to centralize authority away from local elites who supported Calvinist Protestantism. Frederick I's patronage of Halle Pietism helped him achieve those ends, as it made the religious leaders somewhat dependent upon him. In turn Spener, Francke, and the Halle Pietists had royal support in their theological battles with Calvinists.[7] King Frederick I's support of Halle Pietism elevated Francke's standing among the German elite, and he placed Pietist clergy with several German Lutheran aristocratic families.[8] When Lutheran aristocrats desired the services of a new minister, they often turned to Francke for recommendations.

The combination of Hohenzollern royal support, the Foundations' fame, and Francke's influence in Lutheranism led to the Palace of St. James in London in the early 1700s. When Prince George of Denmark moved to England to marry Anne, daughter of James II and later Queen Anne, he established a Lutheran chapel in the city. Despite his wife's status as head of the Church of England, Prince George remained a Lutheran.[9] In 1705, in need of a Lutheran minister, Prince George turned to the Francke network and to Anton Wilhelm Böhme, a Halle-trained Pietist Lutheran scholar who agreed to serve in London; it was he whom Samuel Urlsperger was sent to assist in 1711.

Böhme was instrumental in popularizing Lutheran Pietist ideas in Anglican England, beginning with a translation of Francke's book *Pietas Hallensis*. The *Hallensis* laid out much of Francke's thinking about caring for the whole person, the need for personal conversion, and the importance of creating a society in accord with the principles of Christianity. This royal connection between England and Halle, between Church of England and Lutheranism, helped prepare the ground to support the Salzburger exiles in the 1730s.

## The SPCK

In London in 1698, just three years after Francke founded his orphanage and school at Halle, Dr. Thomas Bray established the Society for Promoting Christian Knowledge (SPCK) for the purpose of helping Anglican ministers in England and in the British colonies. The original intent was to send libraries of religious material at very low cost, or even free of charge, to impoverished clergymen.[10] Bray also founded the SPCK's sister organization, the Society for the Propagation of the Gospel in Foreign Parts (SPG), which had a royal charter to promote the Church of England abroad by providing Anglican missionaries in the king's colonies. The SPCK's original vision quickly expanded to include establishing charity schools throughout England; in doing so, the group self-consciously pointed to Francke's school in Halle.[11] Just as Francke had done, the SPCK created a publishing arm and began distributing religious books and tracts throughout England and also Ireland, Switzerland, Holland, and New England.[12] Unlike the SPG, which was focused on supporting the Anglican church, the SPCK promoted ecumenical projects in support of Protestants worldwide.[13] Just two months after its founding, the SPCK voted to have "an account" of Halle's school reported to the organization and invited Francke to be the first corresponding (i.e., overseas) member.[14]

Robert Hales, brother of Georgia Trustee Dr. Stephen Hales, spent the first fifteen years of the eighteenth century in Europe devoted to serving the SPCK. Tasked with expanding the SPCK's network among continental Protestants, he distributed tracts and recruited corresponding members throughout central Europe. Hales also worked as the intermediary to make the Society aware of continental Protestants in need of aid.

Indeed, since the end of the Thirty Years' War in 1648, official Protestantism was on the decline in German-speaking lands. In the Holy Roman Empire Protestant rulers were outnumbered by Catholics and the Catholics were gaining ground, possibly as much for political reasons (the emperor was Catholic) as for personal religious convictions. The result was that the SPCK found a steady stream of Protestants in continental Europe in need of support. The charity raised money for the Bohemian Brethren in Poland, Protestants in Lithuania, and other Lutherans.[15] One of their most ambitious collaborations began in 1705, when the SPCK worked with Francke to fund Halle-trained clergy at the Lutheran mission in the Danish colony at Tranquebar (modern Tharangambadi) in modern-day India.[16]

By the time the Salzburgers streamed out of the Alps in the early 1730s, the SPCK was experienced at raising funds, publishing tracts about Catholic abuses, and distributing Protestant information. The Society had close contacts with the Francke Foundations and a network comprising Halle-trained Pietist clergy and philanthropic German aristocrats. When Francke died in 1729, his son Gotthilf August became head of the Foundations and maintained the network with the British. The Francke Foundations and the SPCK were, in fact, the perfect places to start looking for aid for the Salzburg Lutherans. And, it turns out, they were ideal partners for the Trustees for Georgia. Without the SPCK and the German Pietists the Salzburgers likely would not have established their settlement or been able to develop self-sufficiency as quickly as they did.

Samuel Urlsperger, the Augsburg Lutheran minister who received the exiles and arranged for their support, was connected to both of these Protestant philanthropic groups. Another important node in this ecumenical network was Friedrich Michael Ziegenhagen. A Halle-trained ordained minister, he was Böhme's successor in 1722 and became the king's Lutheran chaplain at the Palace of St. James in London.[17] Ziegenhagen spent the rest of his life in London, dying in 1776, and was an active member of the SPCK. These two Germans, Ziegenhagen in London and Urlsperger in Augsburg, with connections to the Crown, the British and German aristocracy, the Francke Foundations, and the SPCK, were instrumental in sending the Salzburgers to Georgia. The Georgia Salzburgers referred to these men, along with Gotthilf Francke, as their Reverend Fathers, as they provided physical and spiritual aid and comfort to the colonists throughout the eighteenth century.

## Sending the Salzburgers to Georgia

When the SPCK, Francke, Urlsperger, and the Georgia Trustees quickly developed a close working relationship to help the Salzburgers settle in Georgia, the first need was to raise money. In 1732 Urlsperger supplied numerous accounts of the persecutions, which the SPCK translated into English and published as *An Account of the Suffering of the Persecuted Protestants in the Archbishoprick of Saltzburg*.[18] The hundred-page tract included nine letters and testimonials about the suffering of the Salzburger exiles as they traveled, in the winter, from their homes in the Alps. Readers learned that these Protestants had been expelled so quickly that they arrived in Bavaria with few clothes and possessions but brought with them a deep commitment to their faith. The marketing materials always emphasized the piety of the Salzburg-

ers as a way to encourage support and donations to aid the "worthy poor" of
Europe. The tracts asserted that the Salzburgers were model Christians, who
were "modest, humble, peaceable, contented with, and thankful for whatever
was given them," and that they had the "greatest Delight in praying, singing of Psalms, and reading good Books."[19] This pattern of emphasizing religious devotion and personal piety continued in the Salzburgers' reports
from America, while omitting any hint of conflict or bad characters. The
SPCK printed three thousand copies of *An Account* and distributed them to
all the SPCK members, numbering about four to five hundred; the last page
was an appeal for donations.[20] This tract was so successful that the next year
the group printed another, *A Further Account of the Sufferings of the Persecuted
Protestants*, distributing it in the same manner.[21] The SPCK sent additional
copies to individuals who were not official members of the charity, as when
the group sent one dozen of each to Lady Dolius to distribute to her acquaintances.[22] In October 1732, the SPCK created a subgroup, the Extraordinary Committee for the Salzburgers, to manage the fundraising and to determine the best course of action for helping these exiles.[23] This committee
of five members included Ziegenhagen and the Georgia Trustee James Vernon and may have been created in response to a request from the Trustees.[24]

In August 1732 the Georgia Trustees decided that they would offer to
send three hundred Salzburgers to the new colony and began a special fund
for that project.[25] Rather than contact Urlsperger directly, they asked the
SPCK to notify Urlsperger. For the next several years, the SPCK—and particularly Ziegenhagen—served as the Trustees' intermediary with the Pietist network on the continent. This was partially because of his contacts,
and partially because he (or his aides) served as translator between German
and English to facilitate communication. Urlsperger was the main recruiting agent for German Protestants going to Georgia and helped negotiate
the terms of the migration between the Salzburgers and the Trustees, using Ziegenhagen and the SPCK to transmit information.[26] Urlsperger also
helped the English locate suitable commissioners, who were men charged
with escorting the exiles from southern Germany to Rotterdam, on to England, and then to America. After the Salzburgers arrived in Georgia, letters
and goods sent between the English and Germans on both sides of the Atlantic also frequently passed through the SPCK, Ziegenhagen, or Urlsperger.
For example, when the first transport arrived in Georgia in March 1734, the
Salzburgers' minister Johann Martin Boltzius and other exiles sent letters
of thanks to the SPCK and the Trustees, but the more detailed letters were
sent to Urlsperger. Letters addressed to Urlsperger traveled on an English

ship from Georgia to London, where, most likely, Ziegenhagen forwarded them to Urlsperger. Later in the fall, Urlsperger wrote to England describing the first group's arrival, sending a letter to London to the SPCK, which had someone (most likely Ziegenhagen's secretary J. C. Martini) translate it into English.[27] The SPCK then took the translation of Urlsperger's letter to the Trustees to be read at one of their meetings.[28] This multistep process seems unwieldy to modern eyes, but it apparently worked because, until the Seven Years' War interrupted Atlantic shipping, almost all letters to and from Germany passed through Ziegenhagen before reaching the Trustees or the SPCK members.

The three groups—the Trustees, the SPCK, and the German Pietists—never permanently formalized responsibilities but approached each transport (group of Salzburger migrants) and each request for aid in an ad hoc fashion, depending upon who had the money available to help. When the Trustees decided to send clothing and food to the Salzburgers, often it was the SPCK that actually fulfilled the need and arranged for transportation. Conversely, while the SPCK outfitted a ship to transport the Salzburgers along with their supplies, they relied upon the Trustees to arrange for the royal passport needed for the commissioner's travel. In some cases expenses were split evenly, as in February 1735 when the SPCK agreed to fund 149 Salzburgers out of the 300 the Trustees intended to send in the third transport.[29] Thus, in this planned ship of 300, one-half were to be supported by Trustee funds and one-half by the SPCK.

Altogether, this network of philanthropists sent four transports of Salzburgers to Georgia; the third and fourth groups did not have enough Salzburgers, as the majority of the original exiles had found refuge by that time, so Urlsperger included some other "persecuted Protestants," who came mostly from Austria to the east of Salzburg and from Carinthia, the territory just south of Salzburg. Three other groups of migrants, which historians have labeled the Swabian transports because most of the people came from near Ulm, traveled at their own expense or with the help of wealthy Augsburg banker, philanthropist, and Georgia supporter Christian von Münch. Nearly all of the Swabians joined the Salzburgers at Ebenezer or their surrounding communities. Table 3.1 shows the transports and which group paid for the travel and initial provisions.

As can be seen in table 3.1, none of these seven transports was financed exclusively by the Trustees. Without the aid of Protestant philanthropists in Britain and Europe, the hoped-for community of Germans on the Savannah likely would not have happened. For the first transport, the SPCK

TABLE 3.1. Salzburger Transports to Georgia and Their Funding

| Arrival in Georgia | Transport Group | Funding Organization |
| --- | --- | --- |
| 12 Mar 1734 | 1st Salzburgers | SPCK to England; Trustees England to Georgia |
| 28 Dec 1734 | 2nd Salzburgers | SPCK |
| 27 Feb 1736 | 3rd Salzburgers, Austrians, and Carinthians | Trustees and SPCK |
| 27 Jun 1739 | Sanftleben party* | SPCK, Germans |
| 2 Dec 1741 | 4th Salzburgers, Austrians | Trustees and SPCK |
| SWABIAN TRANSPORTS | | |
| 29 Oct 1750 | 1st Swabian | Own expense, Germans |
| 23 Oct 1751 | 2nd Swabian | Own expense, Münch |
| 23 Nov 1752 | 3rd Swabian | Own expense; recruited by Urlsperger per Trustee request |

*Georgia Salzburger Georg Sanftleben returned to Europe to retrieve his sister and some young single women, then returned to Georgia in 1739 by traveling with English settlers.

agreed to pay all travel expenses to Rotterdam and the Trustees paid travel and provisions expenses from there. The second transport was funded completely by the SPCK, with some help from Francke, while the third and fourth were joint ventures with the Trustees. The second Swabian transport in 1751 was financed partially by Christian von Münch, who sent his own representatives to Georgia possibly to help establish a transatlantic trading business. In 1749 he had sent a long questionnaire to Johann Martin Boltzius enquiring about the Georgia social, political, and business environment, to understand the possibilities for investing in the colony.[30] Included in that 1751 group of migrants was Gerard de Brahm, who was appointed official surveyor of Georgia. De Brahm's group joined the Salzburgers and settled north of Ebenezer, creating a new town called Bethany. Although the third Swabian transport arrived after the Trustee period, it had been assembled by Urlsperger at the Trustees' request.

One of the many ways the Trustees relied upon the German and English philanthropists was in arranging the details of travel for the Salzburgers. The first transport was conducted to Georgia by a young Hanoverian nobleman, Philip Georg Friedrich von Reck, the nephew of Baron Johann von Reck, King George II's envoy at the Holy Roman Empire's Diet at Regensburg. (George II was also Elector of Hanover.) The Trustees appointed the younger Reck at the recommendation of Gotthilf Francke and Urlsperger. The Trustees used Reck again to be the commissar for the third transport in 1736.

To fully understand the interwoven ways the Georgia Trustees, the SPCK, and German philanthropists worked together to aid the Salzburgers, it is instructive to look more deeply at the second transport, which arrived in Georgia in December 1734. The idea for this group began in the summer of 1734, after Reck returned from his trip to Georgia with the first transport, giving a favorable report. He painted such a glowing picture of the potential for success in America that the SPCK decided to pay all the expenses for the second group, and the Trustees, nearly always short of funds, agreed.[31] That is, although the SPCK needed the Trustees' approval as owners of the colonial charter, the British and German private philanthropies decided who to send to the colony and when and paid for the transport and for the ongoing provisioning expenses. For this transport the Trustees were not really managing their colony at all but simply approving the plans of the SPCK. It should be remembered though that some of the original Trustees were also members of the SPCK, including Egmont, Vernon, and Oglethorpe, which may explain their comfort with delegating authority.

The way the charitable organizations arranged the monetary affairs for this second transport also shows how they worked together in support of sending the Salzburgers. Rather than pay all expenses directly out of their own accounts, some of the SPCK money was funneled through the Trustees. For example, in late 1735 the SPCK paid £196 to the Trustees to cover the costs of the Salzburgers' journey from southern Germany to Rotterdam.[32] A little over two years later the SPCK paid the Trustees £287 for one year of provisions that had been promised to the second group.[33] In both cases the SPCK was reimbursing expenses incurred by the Trustees on behalf of the Society. When the SPCK wanted to send money to Germany, the group worked through Augsburg. Samuel Urlsperger was generally in charge of dispersing funds to pay for supplies, lodging, and travel expenses for the transport. He received the SPCK's money by using the Augsburg banking house of Christian von Münch, who was an early donor to the SPCK's fund for the Salzburgers and had sent £50 to London in June 1732.[34] He proved himself a faithful backer of the Salzburgers and the Georgia project, providing support for decades. Münch was the preferred banker for all continental affairs relating to the Salzburgers, as he had promised the English and Urlsperger that he would always exchange money at the most favorable rates and also did not accept the normal banking exchange fee.[35] In this manner, he helped Urlsperger have access to the most money possible to help the refugees. Funds collected by the Francke Foundations were also routed through Münch, as when Francke paid 302 florins to Ziegenhagen, via Münch's Augsburg bank, to pay for the travel expenses of the second transport from southern Germany to Rotterdam. It is unclear if Francke's donation was the source of the £196 that the SPCK transferred to the Trustees or if it was additional money.

Because the second transport was their project, the SPCK had to arrange for the travel, which included finding a commissioner to lead the Salzburgers on their journey. The group recruited Jean Vat, a Swiss Protestant who had lived in England and was experienced with colonial projects, although he had not been to America.[36] The SPCK asked Vat, who was living in Switzerland at the time, to accompany the Salzburgers on their journey to Rotterdam. At the same time, Reck, newly arrived home from his first trip to Georgia, was in Germany putting together a transport. In the end the SPCK let Urlsperger decide which man should be the commissioner, again bypassing the Trustees, who had the nominal say.[37] Vat took the group that had been assembled by Urlsperger and Reck to England, unsure if he would oversee the transport all the way to Georgia. Once in England he received a commission to America. Actually, he received two commissions—one from the Trustees and one from the SPCK—because of confusion over who had ultimate authority for this voyage. This ambiguity caused problems for the Salzburgers in Georgia in the future.

It was important to have an experienced commissioner escort because as the Salzburgers traveled down the Rhine to Rotterdam they passed through several different states. Each polity had the right to collect tolls and to demand transport papers. At the urging of the SPCK, Münch helped secure travel passes for the transport.[38] The commissioners needed individual passes, and the SPCK worked through Ziegenhagen to have those issued by King George II.[39] Even with the passes the transport was delayed along the river in Catholic states. In a report to the SPCK, Vat noted that the Salzburgers had been stopped, held, and required to pay "unjust" and "arbitrar[y]" fees at Mainz, Coblentz, and Kaiserswerth.[40] Fortunately, at Protestant Ruhrort and Wesel the group was allowed to freely pass. In Rotterdam, an SPCK corresponding member helped arrange a ship to England at reasonable rates.

The second transport of Salzburgers arrived in England in October 1734 and the SPCK arranged with the Lord Mayor of London to have the group travel up the Thames to visit.[41] In London, they attended church services in Trinity Lane, and Germans living in London donated £47 to help the new emigrants.[42] After leaving London, Ziegenhagen, with some of the SPCK members and Trustees, met the second transport of Salzburgers at Gravesend and gave each of them some money, from "the German Congregation at St. James's."[43] Jean Vat was awarded a very generous extra 60 guineas, equal to £63, for his services in leading the group to England.[44]

Once the Salzburgers arrived in England, they had to be outfitted with supplies for Georgia. Here again we see how the three philanthropic groups worked together. The Trustees contracted the ship *Two Brothers*, which was headed to Georgia in the late fall 1734 and was also taking back Tomochichi, the Yamacraw headman from Georgia who had visited England at James Oglethorpe's behest.[45] Although the Trustees chartered the boat, the SPCK paid the captain for the Salzburgers' transportation plus all their baggage. In addition to provisioning the second transport, the Trustees, the SPCK, and the German Pietist community used this second transport shipment to respond to requests from Boltzius, Gronau, and other members of the first group in an attempt to improve their conditions in Georgia. Thus at the last minute the SPCK spent money from Urlsperger and Francke to buy and send two good mattresses for Boltzius and Gronau.[46] Included in the extra baggage were one hundred books from Francke and a large chest of Halle medicines for use by Andreas Zwiffler, the apothecary who had traveled with the first transport.[47] The SPCK sent more books, the workings for a still (including iron bars), and an herb press.[48] There was so much extra baggage that the ship captain complained he took a loss of £105, when he should have gained £200, and that he had to take out beds and cabins to make room for it all.[49] The copious provisions imply that the journey was crowded for the Salzburgers but are evidence of the extra support they received compared to English colonists.

In total, the SPCK spent over £1,100 sending the second transport and providing supplies for their first year in Georgia.[50] This was a very large investment, estimated to be equal to about eleven thousand days of work for a skilled tradesman in the 1730s.[51] That figure does not include cost overruns, money sent by Francke or Münch, or Trustee funds that helped pay a part of the costs for the *Two Brothers*. Sending the Salzburgers to America was expensive, but in helping the group emigrate the philanthropists had also promised ongoing support that had to be sustained for many years to come.

## Supporting the Salzburgers in Georgia

Despite their good intentions, the Trustees never had enough money to meet the needs of the colony, and their funding from Parliament was subject to political debate.[52] Without the extra aid from the SPCK and the Pi-

etists, the Salzburgers likely would have had as much difficulty as the English settlers did in creating a stable settlement. This was, in fact, a common
complaint by the Malcontents, who argued that without all the extra aid the
people at Ebenezer would be clamoring for slaves. The network of Protestant philanthropists helped the colonists by paying the ministers' salaries, by
sending material aid, by functioning as a conduit for Boltzius to the Trustees, and by providing moral support in times of hardship.

The largest ongoing commitment made by the SPCK was for ministerial
salaries. While recruiting the first group of Salzburgers to settle in Georgia,
the Trustees promised that the exiles would be sent with Lutheran clergy,
sending Johann Martin Boltzius, the thirty-year-old teacher at the Foundations' orphanage school, and Israel Christian Gronau to serve as a catechist. Once again the Trustees relied upon the SPCK to execute the plan.
Initially the Trustees promised to pay the clergymen's salaries and pledged
to use £1,250 collected specifically for the Georgia Salzburgers to establish a
clergy fund.[53] It is unclear why, but five months later, the Trustees asked the
SPCK to pay for the minister. Eventually, the Society agreed to pay £50 per
year to Boltzius, £30 per year to Gronau, and an additional £10 to Christopher Ortmann, who was appointed schoolmaster for the Salzburgers by the
Trustees.[54] Gronau's salary was raised to £40 in 1735.[55] The Society sent six
months' salary with the first transport and arranged through the Trustees to
make future payments annually. Ziegenhagen met the first transport in England before it left for America, and he used some SPCK funds to give Boltzius a "proper chalice" and paten for offering Holy Communion.[56]

The Trustees and the SPCK thought they would pay the wages only for
the first few years, until a glebe plantation could be established to provide
for the ministers' support. But one of the challenges in early Georgia was
getting land surveyed; another was finding labor to establish a new plantation. In the end, Boltzius did not get his glebe lands until the 1750s, and he
dedicated much of that land to public use. Even then Boltzius was ambiva-
lent about owning this land. Gronau never did have a full plantation because
he died in January 1745. His replacement, the Francke-appointed minister
Hermann Lemke, also received an SPCK-supplied salary. Neither Boltzius
nor Lemke made much effort to profit from the glebe lands, although they
both did eventually receive patents for five-hundred-acre plantations. Boltzius had little interest in establishing a farm that took him away from his
work, and he accepted the land grant mostly to prevent undesirable British
people from Carolina from buying the property and settling near the Germans.[57] The SPCK continued to support the Salzburgers by paying the sal-

ary of Christian Friedrich Triebner, the Halle-trained pastor who arrived in Ebenezer after Boltzius died in 1765 and Lemke died in 1768. The accumulated expense of funding the transports and paying the ministers' salaries drained the SPCK's resources, and in 1740 they printed in their annual report that they were down to their last £55.7.3 in cash.[58] Fortunately, the Society had invested £2,500 in annuities to stabilize their fund, but that money was not easily accessible. So they published more accounts of the Salzburgers' success in Georgia and urged more donations. They appear to have always found sufficient resources to maintain their commitment to pay for two Lutheran ministers in Georgia.

When the Georgia settlements grew after the arrival of the Swabian transports, the Francke Foundations agreed to pay the salary for a third minister because the SPCK was unwilling to take on this additional expense. Working through the Society to make arrangements within the British royal colony, in 1752 Gotthilf Francke sent Christian Rabenhorst with the third Swabian transport. Rabenhorst, like Boltzius, was a northern German who had studied and taught at Halle.[59] The Francke Foundations raised money for a plantation for Rabenhorst, which would be sufficient to provide his support and obviate the need for a salary.

Besides the salary commitments, the majority of aid sent to the Salzburgers by the Society and the Francke Foundations was ad hoc. Reflecting its original purpose of providing a library to the clergy, the SPCK sent hundreds of books and pamphlets to Ebenezer. In just one shipment in 1735 the Society sent three hundred copies of a tract comparing Protestant and Catholic beliefs, along with a hundred each of *A Short Refutation of Popery*, *Questions and Answers about the Two Religions*, and *Dialogue between a Protestant Minister and a Popish Priest*.[60] It is difficult to know what Boltzius and Gronau did with these six hundred English-language anti-Catholic tracts, as they lived in a remote village with a group of German Protestants who were ejected from a Catholic principality. Boltzius did not even have a solid house built when these books arrived. Yet he was suitably thankful, so the support continued. Probably more useful to the group were the large quantities of German-language books and tracts sent by the Francke Foundations, including religious writings, hymnals, schoolbooks, medical instruction books, newspapers, and enough Bibles for each person in the community to have their own copy. Halle's leaders kept sending books, for free, even after the American Revolution. The Foundations' records from 1759 to 1810 show that they sent over a hundred books nearly every year, even during the Seven Years' War when shipping goods to America was difficult.[61]

For the first ten years of settlement the list of basic supplies the Salzburgers needed was large. After leading the second transport to Ebenezer,
Jean Vat reported that they needed seeds, shoes, leather, clothes, earthen-
ware, pots, casks, saws, and tools.[62] It was primarily the SPCK and the Pietist
network that responded to the settlers' needs, not the Trustees. James Vernon, the SPCK member and Georgia Trustee who was the most involved in
working for the Salzburgers, personally sent clothes to the group.[63] Banker
Christian von Münch in Augsburg sent linen.[64]

Münch's linen is an interesting example of the way charity and commerce
could mix in the eighteenth-century British Atlantic. Following the requirements of the Navigation Acts, the linen was sent through London and the
Trustees to Georgia as a charity good. Münch's idea was that in America the
Salzburgers could sell the linen for a profit, thus making it a trade good. Although in practice there was very little linen sent and it did not carry a large
commercial value, the same scheme applied to the shipping and selling of
Halle medicines. The Francke Foundations had built a reputation for having the most effective and consistent medicines in Europe. As part of their
charitable support of the Salzburgers they sent boxes of medicinal chemi-
cals to Georgia every year, even into the nineteenth century. The Salzburgers used most of these medicines for their own community, but the doctor
there was also expected to add to his living by selling some of these blends
in the colony. Francke used charitable donations from German Pietists to
pay for the Halle medicines and to ship them to Georgia via London. The
Salzburger doctors, as well as Boltzius, used the free product to generate income in America.[65] The Salzburgers, Francke, and Münch benefitted from
the structures of Britain's colonial empire to create their own trading opportunities. Britain and the Trustees provided the shipping, the customs, and
the necessary ports and warehouses in England and America to sustain the
German trade. Because of the British infrastructure the Germans could experiment with potential trade products without a significant initial cost.

Just as important as the physical shipments of charitable donations was
the role that the German Pietists and Ziegenhagen played as conduits for
Boltzius to the Trustees. Boltzius wrote the Trustees often, but he was more
direct when writing the Germans. In 1738 he wrote to Ziegenhagen asking that the Trustees send a shoemaker, men with skilled trades, and un-
married women "of the same Country," meaning German-speaking Lutherans.[66] Ziegenhagen took this request to the Trustees, and the group voted
to allocate a hundred pounds to send the desired people. When Boltzius
wanted something extraordinary, such as funding to build a more substan-

tial church or mill, he worked through the Germans in England and continental Europe.[67] When he wanted to complain, without seeming ungrateful, he sent a letter to Ziegenhagen or Urlsperger, asking them to intervene. This is most evident in the 1736 struggle over moving the town closer to the Savannah River, discussed in chapter 5. In another instance Boltzius wanted plows for Ebenezer to make the farm work easier for the Salzburgers. He wrote to Francke and to Ziegenhagen, asking that they present a request to the Trustees. In the end the Trustees agreed to send the plows.[68]

Francke acted as the go-between for Pietist Germans such as Münch and the Georgia Salzburgers. The Francke Foundations' archives today refer to letters that had been forwarded through Halle to Georgia, and vice versa. After Gronau died in 1745, it was the Francke Foundations that arranged to send his heirs the monies from his estate; the actual funds were transferred from British Georgia to Ziegenhagen in London, then forwarded to Francke in Halle, and finally reached Gronau's brother.[69] Even after Ebenezer became self-sufficient and less dependent upon donations, Boltzius communicated with other Germans through the Francke Foundations. For example, at the request of Francke, Boltzius sent American seeds to Baron von Münchhausen in the early 1750s and Münchhausen sent some German seeds in return.[70] The Münchhausen family had long been supporters of Francke and had donated to the Salzburgers, but this new exchange was about increasing knowledge and collections and was not a part of sustaining the exiles.

The Reverend Fathers—Ziegenhagen, Francke, and Urlsperger—served an important role for the Salzburgers as their moral support in difficult circumstances. While communications between Georgia and these three men often contained some discussion of meeting physical needs, the bulk of the letters concerned matters spiritual. Francke proved to be a sounding board for Boltzius as he worked to shepherd his flock. Boltzius asked about proper discipline and how to bring his people to repentance, and he looked to Francke for theological discussions. All three ministers periodically wrote letters intended to uplift the whole community. These were read aloud during worship services and passed from house to house among the Salzburgers in Georgia.

Without the SPCK, the Francke Foundations, and the donations of other German Pietists, the Salzburger settlement at Ebenezer may have failed. Despite receiving large funding grants from Parliament, the Trustees simply did not have enough money to support the colony, and these Protestant philanthropists stepped in to meet the need. They not only paid transit costs but continued to supply much needed provisions. Importantly, they also provided the cultural artifacts that helped the town feel like a community. They sent books and religious material that would link the Salzburgers to their home culture. The stream of encouraging letters from the Reverend Fathers provided the emotional support Boltzius, Gronau, and the others needed in a difficult American wilderness.

In return, it was necessary that communications from Georgia to Europe position the Salzburgers as behaving in line with the religious ideals of the SPCK and Francke. That meant demonstrating that the community was sufficiently pious, was experiencing a Pietist inner devotion to Christ, and showed sufficient respect for the secular authority of the Trustees. The community's dependence upon not just the Trustees but also the philanthropists meant they had strong reasons for aligning with Trustee programs and goals. In practice, though, the Salzburgers could have "voted with their feet" and left Georgia if they disagreed strongly with the programs. Only a few ever did, indicating general support for building a society that conformed to Trustee plans and served as a model Protestant mission in the empire.

# CHAPTER 4

# The Good Forest

The first task for the Salzburgers in America was to assess and understand the Lowcountry environment. The Georgia coast's relatively flat landscape, hot weather, and unusual plants and animals would have seemed quite foreign to new arrivals from alpine territories. To successfully settle, the Germans first framed the new environment in religious terms, viewing themselves as similar to the biblical Israelites wandering in the desert as they prepare to meet God. At the same time, they took a pragmatic approach to developing gardens, fields, and orchards, which depended upon a careful study of America. In so doing, they became experts and collaborators in an epistolary network that craved information about the new colony and the opportunities available there.

One thing was clear: the American woods could be dangerous. On July 4, 1734, Andreas Zwiffler, the Salzburgers' apothecary, walked into the forest near Ebenezer and did not return. Less than four months earlier, the Hungarian-born, German-speaking Zwiffler had come with the first transport of settlers, selected and sent by the Trustees to be the chief provider of medical care for the Salzburgers. Forming a search party on July 5, Minister Johann Martin Boltzius recruited some local Yuchi Indians to help, counting on their skill at navigating and traveling in the difficult terrain.[1] As native-born people, the Yuchi were more familiar with the woods, and Boltzius periodically drew upon their expertise during the first period of settlement. After days of searching without success, all assumed Zwiffler was dead.

Zwiffler may have been the first, but he was not the only Salzburger lost in the forest. In August 1735 Margaretha Schweighofer and Mrs. Eischberger became lost in the woods and spent an anxious night outside. Andreas Resch was part of a party sent to look for them, but he never returned, while the women were rescued by another Salzburger.[2] Eight people searched for Resch for a week, hoping to help him find the way home by lighting a tree on fire and marking a path on tree trunks. Despite this effort, he never returned. After a year of waiting Resch was declared dead and his wife remarried.[3]

Upon arrival in Georgia in March 1734, Boltzius and the first transport's commissioner, Philip Georg Friedrich von Reck, quickly identified the American forest as a dangerous place, primarily because it was so difficult to find one's way. In Reck's otherwise glowing report of the new colony, he noted that "in this country, one must take great care in the forest as one gets easily lost."[4] Even after living in Georgia for twenty years, Boltzius was still wary of the forest, warning of the animals and people one might encounter there.[5] And despite generally good relations initially with the local Indians, he wrote that meeting them in the woods could be dangerous as they were capable of being "like the highway robbers in the Thüringer Wald," referring to the German woods with a reputation for danger and for sheltering thieves.[6]

Led by their pastor Boltzius and the Bible, the Salzburgers understood this expansive spread of bewildering flora as a type of biblical wilderness that presented physical tests yet also offered spiritual redemption and reform. In the Old Testament God tests, refines, and saves the Israelites through their wandering for forty years in wilderness. The New Testament also treats the wilderness as a place to come closer to God, where John the Baptist was "crying in the wilderness" for a coming Messiah and where Jesus overcame Satan's temptations at the end of his forty-day fast.[7] We know that Boltzius intended this biblical metaphor in describing the moist swamps and lush forests of Georgia because he used the German word *Wüste* and not *Wildnis* (wilderness) to describe America.[8] To describe the land of Canaan the Luther Bible uses *Wüste*, a word that is usually translated into English as "desert," meaning a desiccated place, bereft of life-sustaining resources. That the 1615 English King James Version uses the word "wilderness" to describe the same place can be misleading to modern readers as today the term denotes a place of wild nature. In the seventeenth century, however, the English wilderness held the meaning of wild, desolate, barren, waterless, and treeless, conveying the same idea in the English Bible as *Wüste* did in the German.

When Boltzius described the lush American landscape as a desert, he was seeing it as a metaphor for a place where the Salzburgers would be both tried and saved by God, not as the moist, forested land that it was. This Christian view of the landscape framed the challenges of colonization for the Salzburgers, as all setbacks were seen as tests from God. Georgia was simultaneously held as a place that saved and protected them from the reach of the Catholic leaders who sought to prevent them from practicing the true religion. Staying in Catholic Salzburg would have imperiled their souls, but America could save them.

Life in the Georgia woods presented the Salzburgers with several case studies in understanding God. On July 15, 1734, eleven days after Zwiffler disappeared, Salzburger Jerg Schweiger "was moved to go into the nearby woods . . . in order to pray" and stumbled upon the half-starved, half-naked apothecary.[9] Zwiffler was brought safely home, back into the shelter of Salzburgers, where he could recover physically and spiritually from the terrifying experience. It was clear to the people at Ebenezer that God had protected him. Zwiffler recounted how he had quickly become lost in the woods but had eventually been led back to Ebenezer by a vision in which he "could see Senior Urlsperger and two pastors . . . who showed him the way."[10] Since Senior Pastor Samuel Urlsperger had acted as the group's host, guide, and protective father in German lands, it seemed entirely appropriate that a vision of the religious leader would guide Zwiffler to safety, just as God had inspired Schweiger into the forest to find him.

When groups or individuals seemed to be lost or were known to be traveling from Savannah to Ebenezer, the settlers made a habit of lighting fires and firing off guns as a way to direct people toward the safety of the community. Always keen to draw religious lessons for lived experiences, Boltzius reminded his people that the flash of firelight providing physical rescue was a practical reminder of the light of Christ enabling spiritual rescue. When Reck directed a portion of the third transport to Ebenezer in March 1736, the group became lost in the forest within close range of the town. As night overtook them, Reck fired his gun and the Salzburgers, led by Pastor Boltzius, came with their torches out into the "quiet wilderness" to rescue them.[11] The whole experience of being saved by a religious leader, the lit torches, and God's "bright moonlight" was "in every way moving" to a spiritually sensitive Reck.[12]

The hazards of wandering alone into the forest, separated from the community, served as a ready metaphor for the graver spiritual dangers of removing oneself from the community of believers. Even as Boltzius was arranging help to find Zwiffler, he was equally worried that the apothecary might be spiritually lost and unprepared to meet God.[13] To help explain the events, Boltzius turned to scripture, comparing Zwiffler's miraculous recovery to the Old Testament Joseph, who was believed to have been devoured in the wilderness but eventually was found to be alive.[14]

Ebenezer was in a region of Georgia where at least three different types of forest converged. Depending upon where they wandered, the Salzburger colonists could find themselves in dense forests of oak and hickory, with ferns and shrubs underneath, in thick canebrakes, or in regions of densely packed longleaf pines.[15] Not only was this biome completely different from that at their alpine homes in Europe, but these Georgia woods were expansive, spreading for miles near Ebenezer and presenting a confusing similarity that made it easy to become disoriented.

In addition to the forest, the Salzburgers also resided near Lowcountry swamplands and canebrakes, which also formed part of the American wilderness. This land was dark and dangerous, difficult to travel through, where cattle and people could easily become lost. Boltzius had familiarity with the problem of swamps as dangerous places in his native land, having been born in Forst, located along the Neisse River, not too far from an area of natural swamplands in the Oder River basin. These German swamps were known to be perilous as they were frequently populated by deserters and thieves; living things quickly decayed, and the air was full of "unhealthy miasmas."[16] Thus, although the Georgia climate was wholly unlike that in central Europe, Boltzius and the Salzburgers carried with them definitive moral ideas about the types of terrain they encountered.

## The Good Forest

Fortunately, the American wilderness was not only a place to become *lost*. Just as Andreas Zwiffler had experienced divine intervention to save his life, the wilderness was also a place where one could be *found*. In the Bible, the wilderness is the place where God led his chosen people and where prophets, apostles, and even Jesus went to be tested and to commune with God. It took no great leap of imagination for Boltzius also to see the wilderness surroundings as a physical and spiritual opportunity. In this, the Salzburgers were following a long line of European thinking about America, including that of Massachusetts Puritans and Quebec Jesuits, in which settlers tended to compare themselves to the Israelites, whose utter dependence upon God in a brutal wilderness eventually worked to their good. God's people in the wilderness, such as the Salzburgers, would be tested and refined, becoming a moral people, strong in their faith.

To the devout Salzburgers, the forest, swamps, and canebrakes and even the entire American continent composed a place where people had to depend on God for physical sustenance, just as the ancient Israelites did. This difficult physical challenge had the benefit of helping individuals find communion with God. This was such a common conception of a way to understand the natural world that the word *Wüste*, the biblical desert, became a sort of shorthand for Boltzius to represent the works of God in an individual's life. By 1740 Boltzius marveled that God had done "great things in this desert" (*Wüste*) in shaping the lives of the Salzburgers.[17]

Boltzius also emphasized to his flock that the Georgia landscape was where God intended the Salzburgers to be and therefore that he would bless them, just as he had blessed the Israelites in Canaan. In worship services, Ebenezer's soil was declared to be "as fertile as the land of Canaan."[18] During the group's daily evening prayers, as well as during Sunday services, Boltzius taught that God had promised that if the people were pious he would bless them and the land. In fact, Boltzius went further when he mused that for one to think ill of the American landscape was to show "a contemptuous attitude toward God and His Word."[19] It was spiritually weak and dangerous to question the value of the land, and by doing so one doubted the holy promises given to the settlers. By 1750 Boltzius was grateful that the Georgia landscape had been so thickly forested and swampy because its reputation as a difficult wilderness kept it from "being inundated with all kinds of people . . . and being spoiled." Rather, the difficult terrain had been saved for "honorable people," that is, devout Lutherans, to "settle here pleasantly."[20] Here we see Boltzius's strong desire to keep his group separate from others who could threaten their peaceful and religious community, thanking God for the physical difficulties that kept English people away.

The framing of the Georgia forest as having the power to save set the Salzburgers apart from other early Georgia settlers, particularly the English-speaking Malcontents who traveled to Georgia chiefly for economic reasons and were anxious to replicate South Carolina's plantation-based economy. The Salzburgers' views also more closely aligned with the Trustees' vision of the American colony as offering moral reform and regeneration for the British nation. This shared understanding that Georgia would be a suitable en-

vironment to challenge and strengthen people is one reason why the Trustees found such strong allies in the Salzburgers as they sought to implement
the original colonization plan.

Many of the founding Trustees—those who served on the parliamentary
Gaols Committee and who conceived of the colony—also held views about
the possibilities of the American environment in shaping mankind. Their
colonial plans assumed a moral redemptive power of the American (Georgian) wilderness, and it is in this belief that the Salzburger community and
the Trustees aligned. The Trustees' mission always had moral overtones, as
they expected the colony to create morally upright people out of the worthy
poor who had would learn to be "careful and industrious" by living in America.[21] Indeed, the earliest marketing tracts to solicit donations for the colony
spelled out that they intended to save the poor and persecuted "whose Light
is extinguish'd" by circumstances that keep them needy. Sending people to
Georgia, the Trustees argued, would save them from fear of want, from languishing out a miserable Life, from the humiliation of begging, from idle-
ness, and from even suicide, which was considered a sin.[22]

The Bible provided numerous examples to support this idea, and the
SPCK and the Georgia Trustees also made frequent references to the Christian notion of wilderness as a place to be saved. A 1736 Trustee publication
on the Georgia project used Psalm 107:35–37 as its main text, comparing the
colony to the scripture. The verse reads in part, "He turneth the wilderness
into a standing water . . . and there he maketh the hungry to dwell. . . . He
blesseth them also, so that they are multiplied greatly."[23] The Georgia landscape was again conceived as a place for people to be protected and blessed
by God in a 1738 sermon published by the Trustees that quoted Isaiah 41,
which declares that the Lord will make the wilderness a "pool of water" (in
a desert) for his people "that they may see, and know, and consider, and understand together, that the hand of the Lord hath done this, and the Holy
One of Israel hath created it."[24] Unlike the biblical Israelites, the people in
Ebenezer suffered from an overabundance of water. The swamps were difficult to pass; the Savannah River and Ebenezer Creek regularly overflowed
their boundaries and flooded the carefully planted gardens. Regardless, the
metaphor was the main point. Just as God made a garden out of a desert
wilderness for the Old Testament people, he would make a garden out of an
overly moist wilderness in Georgia. And while physical transformation of
the land into something useful for human life was an expected blessing, the
important idea was that people would come to know "the Living Water" of
the gospel of Jesus Christ.[25]

## Naturalist Perspective

The Salzburgers' move to Georgia coincided with important changes in the way Europeans thought about the natural world. People searched for ways to collect and categorize the things of the earth and to explain natural phenomena through experimentation and deductive reasoning. Linnaeus developed his categorization system in 1735, right as the Salzburgers were settling. Several botanists and naturalists traveled throughout the world on the hunt for new and interesting curiosities for collections in Europe, including important journeys to the little-understood regions of the Lowcountry and Caribbean. By the early eighteenth century, European and American naturalists and philosophers held a conception of the earth that might, at first glance, seem in opposition to a religious and folk understanding of the world. Men in Germany, England, and elsewhere in Europe found ways to reconcile their naturalist study of the world with the spiritual implications for the soul. Twenty-first-century people often think of "objective science" and "religion" as opposite ends of the spectrum of ways to learn truths. In the eighteenth-century Enlightenment, religion and naturalist science were not rivals. The Christian doctrine, which held that all things of the earth and heavens were made for man's benefit, had the effect of mentally removing him from the natural world, placing man above nature and below God. This mindset enabled a naturalist observational perspective in comprehending the earth.[26]

We can see this blend of religious and naturalist views of the world in the Pietist teachings followed by Boltzius and the Salzburgers. Pietists in Germany, Scandinavia, and England, including the Salzburgers, were heavily influenced by Johann Arndt, whose early seventeenth-century writings were the most read and requested works, after the Bible, in Lutheran and Pietist homes until the nineteenth century.[27] Arndt's writings, gathered into four books under the title *True Christianity*, were first printed in the early 1620s, with numerous translations and reprintings. The first German book printed in America was a 1749 edition of *True Christianity*, printed in Philadelphia by Benjamin Franklin and his partner Johann Böhm, who knew a best seller when he saw it.[28] Arndt devoted an entire volume (Book IV) to explication of the natural world, and he believed understanding the environment was critical for the development of the Christian soul. He taught that the "invisible world" of God and spirit was made known to mankind by careful study of the "visible world."[29] Arndt's own life was an example of this, as he was a philosopher and pastor who kept a chemistry laboratory next to his study.[30] The sun, moon, stars, soil, rocks, rivers, trees, plants, and animals all evidenced God's works. Arndt especially noted the order that seemed to exist in nature and "the mutual relation subsisting between the different parts of created nature."[31] Elements, plants, and animals created a unified system that was "for the benefit of man"; and man occupied a spot in the middle, above nature and below God. Study of the earth, in all its wonderful order, would elevate one's soul to God. Boltzius and supporters in Germany made sure each Salzburger home had a copy of Arndt's work within the first few years of arriving in Georgia, as most households had members who were at least able to read and a few had completely literate members.

Because of the strong influence of Arndt, and perhaps due to Boltzius and Gronau's university training, we can see the combination of a spiritual interpretation of the world with a naturalist's curiosity and desire to categorize and understand the Georgian environment. Boltzius's diaries are full of reports on attempts to grow crops, to understand the soil, and to comprehend the Georgian weather. The Salzburgers had been told about the destructive winds of hurricanes but felt the people must be exaggerating, that is, until they experienced one themselves in 1736.[32]

Members of the SPCK shared similar beliefs, although the English Anglicans may not have been as familiar with Arndt's works. In a 1729 sermon that was printed and distributed by the SPCK, Rev. John Denne preached that the "inanimate and irrational Parts of the Creation . . . declare and show forth the Glory of God."[33] The plants, animals, earth, stars, and sun obeyed God's laws and were to be examples of the obedience expected from humans. Further, by their "excellent Variety, Beauty . . . [and] exquisite Regularity in all their Motions," they revealed God's "Wisdom, Power and Goodness."[34] Denne taught that men were supposed to observe the world around them to learn about God from their creation and use.

In the pursuit of knowledge about the land, flora, and fauna of Georgia, Salzburger leaders Boltzius, Gronau, and Reck were also feeding the interests of several of the Georgia Trustees. As described earlier, even before the colony received its charter, several Trustees had invested in acquiring greater knowledge about the American environment. Trustees Sir Hans Sloane and the Earl of Egmont (Perceval) were two of the twelve original sponsors of Mark Catesby's 1722–1726 journey to the American Lowcountry.[35] Catesby's voyage covered the Bahamas, Florida, and Carolina, including land that became Georgia, to bring back specimens and to publish detailed information about the natural world in the southern colonies. The trip provided the raw material Catesby needed to complete his *Natural History*, an expansive two-volume set of hand-painted drawings of specimens. A pre-Linnean work, Catesby's volumes placed birds and animals in the same frame as their plant surroundings, rather than by a strict categorization. The first volume was completed in 1731, with the second published in 1743; Trustees James Oglethorpe, Sir Hans Sloane, and Lord James Cavendish each subscribed to the works.[36] All these men, as well as Mark Catesby, were members of the Royal Society, a group focused on understanding the natural world.

The Trustees believed so strongly about the opportunity Georgia presented to gather more information about the American continent that they used the fund designated for Encouraging and Improving Botany and Agriculture not only to promote experimental work in Georgia but also to share information with the Old World. Dr. Stephen Hales, a cleric, a Trustee, and a member of the SPCK, contributed to the botany fund to support his long interest in understanding the natural world. In 1727 he published *Vegetable Staticks*, announcing the results of numerous experiments focused on the movement of nutrients and water within plants to stimulate growth. While James Oglethorpe was in Georgia, he took care to ship American specimens to Hans Sloane in England, sending him some tree bark in 1733 that was said to heal "all types of Defluxtions" (the flow or discharges from a cold or flu).[37] The Trustees corresponded with more botanists after the death of their hired expert, Dr. William Houston, to gather seeds and plants for Georgia and to fulfill the part of Houston's intended work after arriving in the colony, which was to document the "natural" world as well as to experiment with imported plants.

In line with the European fascination regarding the American natural world, Commissioner Reck kept and published a travel journal of his two trips to Georgia, made as the Georgia Trustees' appointed escort for both the first and third transports, in 1734 and 1736. Reck's journal is dominated by extensive lists of the flora and fauna found in Georgia. It is clear he was pleased with the abundance he found there, as when he noted that the Savannah River was filled with oysters, sturgeon, and many other varieties of fish. Further, he recorded that "great forests line the Savannah river" and carefully listed the large variety and quantity of trees in the forest, cataloging a long list of "pine, oak, bay-wood (good grain, heavy), cedar, cypress, walnut, mulberry (with juicy berries), wild orange (no fruit), laurel, white cinnamon," and something he called "cabitch trees," which he said had "leaves like aloe."[38]

Reck further documented the Ebenezer ecosystem—forest, animals, fish, fruits—taking care to list items that would provide for the material needs of the new colony. Myrtle bush with green berries, sassafras, ginseng, indigo, and wild grapes were found in abundance.[39] A variety of animals were available for the hunt: eagles, "Indian roosters" (turkey), deer, wild goats, wild cow, horses, hares, quail, and buffalo.[40] He was apparently unaware that the cows, horses, and goats were European imports that had gone wild, as he praised the "natural wilderness" of Georgia.[41]

With an overly optimistic eye, Reck attempted to understand and classify the Georgia soil, which he proclaimed fertile no matter the quality. He described four categories of soil, each of which would be useful for the colonists. Sandy soil, the type found in pine barrens and near the ocean shore, was considered best for use in the winter for roots (primarily potatoes), kitchen gardens, and tobacco crops. Loamy soil, described as thick and black, was "good for general agriculture and making bricks."[42] A so-called heavy soil was deemed best for Indian corn, grain, hemp, and flax crops, while the swamps were ideal for growing rice, the "most profitable and useful crop here."[43] In reality, the town of Ebenezer was originally established in a pine barren, a place that events proved was not at all fruitful or abundant. However, Reck's categories of soil led him to believe Salzburgers should be able to use the sandy soil for roots and kitchen gardens, a notion he clung to despite repeated crop failures during the first two years. Reck further commented on the specifics of the Salzburger land around Ebenezer, noting that the "forest was not as dense here, save the beautiful meadows."[44] These "natural" meadows were most likely the result of Indians' controlled burns, a practice that facilitated hunting and enriched the soil for Indian crops.[45]

On his second voyage as the Trustees' commissioner, when he accompanied the third Salzburger transport that arrived in 1736, Reck declared that he wanted to provide "ocular proof" of the bounty of Georgia for the benefit of recruiting more Germans to settle in the colony. Again, he kept a journal of his travels, which included not just his stay in Ebenezer but also a trip to the Altamaha River to where Oglethorpe was busy establishing Frederica, a new military defensive town. Reck made several drawings to accompany the journal, apparently planning to publish them in a volume similar to works by Mark Catesby and Francis Moore.[46] Of the forty-two preserved drawings, twenty-three were of the Georgia flora and fauna, with a focus on those he considered to be native to America. In one, he drew three nonnative and potentially profitable plants that seemed to thrive in Georgia: sugar cane, pineapple, and ginger root. This was to provide proof of natural fertility and economic potential of the Lowcountry environment.

Shortly after arriving in Georgia for the second time, Reck realized what

Boltzius had said after just a few months of living at Ebenezer: the sandy soil of the pine barrens was no place to live. It simply would not support crops of any kind and similarly did not provide adequate grazing for their cattle. Worse still, the community was too far from the Savannah River and Ebenezer Creek was generally not navigable, requiring all supplies to be hand-carried several miles over mud, swamp, and forest. Reck joined with Boltzius in successfully lobbying James Oglethorpe to grant the group permission to move the town to a place with better soil. The New Ebenezer settlement was built on a bluff where Ebenezer Creek joined the Savannah River, on a spot that promised better soil.

## Naturalists and Pragmatists

As permanent, long-term settlers, Boltzius and the Salzburgers approached the land with a different eye than the Trustees or even Reck. Following Arndt's direction, they studied the land for insights into the nature of God. They also needed practical wisdom about what would grow, where the best soil was, and how best to prepare the land for settlement.

Like Reck and other early Americans, the Salzburgers categorized soil by what was growing there, a practice that was well developed by the settlers. This categorization is perhaps most visible on William Gerard de Brahm's 1757 map of the American Southeast.[47] De Brahm, a German cartographer from Koblenz, joined the Salzburgers in 1751 when he established the Bethany settlement on former Yuchi Indian land just north of Ebenezer. In that village were Salzburgers as well as other Lutheran Germans from Swabia and the Palatinate, and he would have learned details about the soil from earlier settlers. In addition to political and plantation boundaries, de Brahm hoped to convey the quality of the land, and he did so by designating marsh lands, "oak lands" (dense soils in bottomlands), and "pinelands" (sandy soils in upland plains).[48] He also included the term "swampland" on his map, but Boltzius and the Salzburgers had learned in the 1730s that there were different types of swamps. Old Ebenezer lay in agriculturally useless swampland—areas of black water and cypress trees that Boltzius came to call simply "bogs." When the group moved to its permanent spot on the Savannah River, Boltzius recorded that the colonists now understood how to identify a useful swamp. It was characterized as "dry and low cane-covered regions and valleys in which water does not stand except when it is raining and from which it drains off quickly even then."[49]

Because the first settlers were originally assigned nonproductive pine barrens, the Salzburgers became adept at locating good soil using plants as a guide. One key, the group soon understood, was to look for the cane swamps. In the seventeenth and eighteenth centuries canebrakes—dense, tangled masses of river cane—covered at least ten million acres of land in the American Southeast, where the plant mass could grow to be twenty-five feet tall.[50] Like the forest, canebrakes could be both dangerous and life giving. They were known as places where runaway enslaved people and indentured servants could hide, and it was easy to become lost inside them due to their density. However, cane also proved to be excellent feed for cattle, and the Salzburgers' animals seemed to fatten up quickly on the plant. As Boltzius noted, "everybody would like to have" the type of canebrake swamp found at Ebenezer.[51]

Another sign of good land was oak trees. The presence of oaks and hickories indicated alluvial soil; not only was such soil good for planting, but these trees also signaled the soil could retain the moisture needed to grow a variety of European crops.[52] On January 28, 1736, two Salzburger men spotted "beautiful land" that was at least "two thousand acres . . . with oak, nut and other deciduous trees, as well as grape vines as thick as your arms."[53] This is where they wanted to settle the new town, away from the pine barrens of Old Ebenezer. The settlers were excited by this find, as they knew from Europe and from Georgian experience that oak- and deciduous-covered lands offered productive soils. This prime acreage, nicknamed the Blue Bluff, was north of Ebenezer Creek at its confluence with the Savannah River, and in 1736 this land still belonged to the Yuchi.

The Yuchi were a small tribe, a language-isolate people who by the 1730s were some of the remnants of what has been called the "shatter zone" of Native and European interactions in the American Southeast.[54] As tribes engaged in Spanish, French, and English imperial market economies, and specifically in the Indian slave trade to fulfill South Carolina's market for unfree labor, wars between Indian tribes erupted in the region in the late seventeenth century and early eighteenth. The surviving Yuchi, a people probably originally from the upper Tennessee River valley, moved to the Savannah River and aligned themselves with the Muskogee, in opposition to the Cherokee and Chickasaw. By 1736 only two significant Yuchi settlements remained, one far up the Savannah River on the Carolina side and another the colonizers called Mount Pleasant or Yuchi Town (often spelled Euchee or Uchee in the English sources).[55] Although Yuchi Town was about thirty miles upriver from Ebenezer Creek, all of the land between the creek and the settlement was affirmed by James Oglethorpe as belonging to the tribe.

As the Salzburgers were expressly forbidden by Oglethorpe from settling on Yuchi lands, they kept up the hunt for oak-covered lands, eventually finding some suitable patches on the south side of the creek. Though it was not as abundant as the Yuchi's land to the north, the Germans recognized enough good soil to merit removal to that new location. Later, partially as a result of an outbreak of war between the Cherokee and the Muskogee tribes, the Yuchi relocated their town to a location along the Chattahoochee River near the main towns of the Lower Creek Muskogee.[56] As a result, in 1749 the colony's president, William Stephens, gave Boltzius permission to settle some people north of the creek. This much-coveted spot of good soil became de Brahm's Bethany settlement and the location of some Salzburger plantations.

When the Salzburgers found good deciduous forests, their primary goal was to clear them of trees to prepare for agriculture. "We shall have soon purged the land of its many trees . . . and made it fit," declared Boltzius.[57] There was little musing about preserving forests for future generations or managing the forest for optimal productivity, as was common in a Europe that frequently believed there was a shortage of wood.[58] Although they did always preserve a few acres for firewood, the primary goal for the Salzburgers was to purge the forest of the trees that hindered their progress. They may have expressed this attitude in part because the American forest seemed so vast and unending. Seventeenth-century Anglo-American colonists in New England were noted for their enormous consumption of trees, a usage pattern that continued as settlers moved west into New York, Pennsylvania, and the Ohio River valley.[59] Like these Anglo-Americans, Salzburgers saw the trees as impediments to productive use of the land. There was no long-term benefit derived from preserving so many trees in and near their developing town; they thought nothing of chopping down an entire tree in order to catch a squirrel for soup, as Reck noted in his travel journal.[60]

The Salzburgers also brought with them from the Alps a tradition of clear-cutting large swaths of forest. As noted, the majority of the first Salzburger settlers came from mining valleys some sixty to seventy miles south of the city of Salzburg.[61] In these regions forest management regulations from the early sixteenth century to the eighteenth were centered on providing energy for the gold and silver mining industry, a practice that began as early as 1237.[62] The result was mandated clear-cut harvesting, as this method brought in the most energy (in wood) for the lowest transportation and logging costs.[63] Clear-cutting was somewhat sustainable for two centuries in Salzburg's Alps because so much of the land was agriculturally unproductive high-alpine forest. The lack of productive land meant villages tended to remain small, with outmigration relieving any growing demands for wood energy.[64] Further, taxation policies in Salzburg's small valleys discouraged placing marginal lands under production, which served as another check on excessive demands upon the forest for non-mining energy uses.[65] Thus, large sections of the alpine forest were available for clear-cutting to supply the mines.

Yet another reason for the Salzburger assault on the Georgia forest was that they believed it would be more healthful if the trees were gone. The hot, thick, humid air was taxing on the residents. Cutting down the trees, it was assumed, would allow more wind to pass through their settlement, lowering the temperature and cleaning the air. In his 1736 journal, Reck praised the Salzburgers who "had cut down an abundance of trees, in order to breathe free air."[66] A century earlier, English settlers had argued that cutting down the forest in Newfoundland would warm the climate and make the North more habitable.[67] Whether in the North or the South, the solution to creating a healthful and salubrious environment in the Americas was to thin the forest. It is interesting to note that both Reck and Boltzius were concerned with air quality and thought creating a breeze would improve it. Georgia was founded at the same time European natural philosophers were advancing new ideas about air quality. Specifically, Georgia Trustee Stephen Hales developed theories on the importance of air quality for human health that were the impetus for adding ventilation to ships and prisons.[68]

Upon arriving at Ebenezer, and later at New Ebenezer on the Savannah River, the Salzburgers set to felling trees. The first trees were used to build shelter, followed by determined cutting to create agricultural fields. Before the bulk of the group would move from Old to New Ebenezer in 1736, a group of men were sent to the new location to clear the forest. Reck drew a picture of these early stages of settlement, showing a tent and the beginnings of two large huts, which were to be temporary communal housing; all are nestled inside thick forest (see figure 4.1). After a few acres in the town proper had been cleared, the majority of the group relocated to New Ebenezer in late March 1736 and immediately began sowing sweet potatoes, pumpkins, corn, and beans in the newly deforested plots.

To prepare larger fields for planting, the Salzburgers split into work teams by their transport group and went to work clearing several small parcels on the northern and southern edges of town. According to the Trustees' plan, each family was to have a half-acre town site, a five-acre garden plot on the edge of town, and a forty-five-acre plantation beyond the town. In this,

FIGURE 4.1. *Die Erste Hütten und Gezelte zu Ebenezer* (The First Huts and Shelters in Ebenezer). Drawn as the Salzburgers were first building in their new location on the Savannah River in 1736. The thick forest surrounds the makeshift tent, and there is an implied forest (the faint lines) surrounding the two huts that are under construction. The men in the foreground are working with felled trees. (The Royal Danish Library, Copenhagen, NKS 565 4°: Von Reck's drawings, no. 46.)

Ebenezer was intended to be laid out similar to Savannah, with squares for public use and a property ownership scheme that encouraged formation of towns and communities, rather than plantations spread along rivers as was common in the Carolinas and the Chesapeake. Because there was not enough good land around New Ebenezer, the group decided to create smaller, two-acre plots for each family and asked for forty-eight-acre plantations.[69] This way, in theory, each family had enough cleared land near town to be able to grow food sufficient for their needs. The combination of communal labor with the careful distribution of some productive land to each family was unique among Lowcountry settlements. In Savannah, land was assigned based on rigid plot lines, regardless of the quality of land, and each family worked its own acreage. In Purrysburg, South Carolina, a few miles downstream on the Savannah River from Ebenezer and populated by both French- and German-speaking Swiss, families were left to their own devices to prepare the soil. Purrysburg settlers quickly spread out far from the proposed new town, creating plantations along the river in a settlement pattern similar to most of the British Colonial Chesapeake and Lowcountry. The result, to Boltzius's mind at least, was that Purrysburgers struggled to maintain a community and were too far from spiritual guidance to remain cohesive and thus risked losing their souls.

At Ebenezer, the group labored for months to clear land. The typical schedule that first spring and summer in the new townsite was to work collectively clearing plots around the edges of town from early in the morning until about nine o'clock, then on individual gardens or town plots until about two or three in the afternoon, returning to communal labors until sundown.[70] Through this diligence, by summer 1736 they had cleared three large plots, one for each transport group; individuals were then assigned acreage within these lands. Clearing all the trees from the surrounding area took several years, but the Salzburgers eventually succeeded. In contrast to Reck's 1736 sketch that showed many trees, a map of New Ebenezer published in 1747 showed the town surrounded by cleared land and orderly fields. Only the Yuichi land north of the Ebenezer Creek still showed forest. The famous Great Awakening figure, the itinerant Anglican priest George Whitefield, visited Ebenezer June 25, 1741, and reported that for "near four Miles did I walk in almost one continued Field," in a landscape that had been a thick oak and deciduous forest just five years earlier.[71]

As soon as fields were created, the Salzburgers constructed fences to protect them from wild animals. The Trustees' secretary, William Stephens, reported that the group had successfully fenced in the entire town and the two-acre lots to the sides in less than two years.[72] The area around Ebenezer was frequented by bears, deer, and wolves, all of which the Salzburgers considered to be nuisance animals. The wolves presented the greatest threat, as they regularly killed Salzburger cattle and pigs and were able to circumvent fencing with apparent ease. The sound of their howling haunted the Salzburgers at night, and they often awoke in the morning to find pig, cow, or chicken carcasses. In the first few years the group made a determined effort to effect the "extinction of such harmful animals."[73] Deer, which were hunted for food and skins by the Indians, were considered harmful because they ate sprouting household gardens. Despite times of near starvation in the early years, the Salzburgers did not hunt deer to provide meat for themselves. Periodically some Muskogee or Yuchi Indians brought a deer into Ebenezer, desiring to trade or sell it. Then the Salzburgers did eat it, but they generally preferred to wait for the meat from their cattle and pigs or for salted meat from the Trustees' storehouse in Savannah. One reason may be that alpine communities tended to focus on raising cattle because they lacked large areas of fertile land that were needed for cultivation. Cattle could graze in the high alpine meadows on land that was too steep for agriculture.[74] As a result, the alpine Salzburger diet centered on beef, not venison or other game meat.

The Salzburger settlers created their own knowledge of the landscape, combining notions from home with their practical experiences in Georgia. Surprisingly, they seemed not to rely too heavily upon or to trust other sources of useful natural information from their neighbors. Boltzius was very skeptical of any information they received from the English people living in Savannah, as he found them to be an unruly and disrespectful people, opposed to the pious ways of the Salzburgers. Thus, when English settlers told the group the land around Old Ebenezer was pine barrens and unfit for settlement, Boltzius thought them unchristian and ignored the advice. A small circle of Englishmen who proved themselves sympathetic to the Salzburgers gradually became accepted as reliable sources. This trusted group included Thomas Causton, the Trustees' appointed magistrate and storekeeper in Savannah, and John Wesley, the Anglican priest sent by the Trustees to minister in the colony, who would go on to found Methodism. The problem was that despite being judged as upright and good people, these men were not experts in the Georgia landscape or in best farming practices. Englishmen who could provide useful and practical information about the landscape—settlers in South Carolina—were viewed suspiciously because they favored large plantation-style agriculture. The Salzburgers did eventually produce some rice, using ideas developed in South Carolina, but on a very small scale. And they used this as an example to show that their way, without slavery, was sufficient and superior to the plantation system used across the Savannah River.[75]

Some useful information was gleaned from the fourteen enslaved Africans who were lent to the Salzburgers by Paul Jenys, the speaker of the Commons House of South Carolina.[76] The men were sent to help build the first few houses in Ebenezer in 1734, and they apparently also shared with the settlers some information about what would grow in the Lowcountry. From them Salzburgers learned about growing squash and watermelon, produce Boltzius thought most tasty. These plants were considered remarkable enough for Reck to prepare large drawings of them. The town tried their hand at beekeeping after the enslaved men showed them how to find and maintain hives.[77]

It appears from the diaries that these fourteen men began almost immediately trying to escape slavery upon arrival in Georgia. Enslaved people in South Carolina knew that Spanish Florida offered an opportunity for free-

dom, and being transported across the Savannah River would have been an
advantage in escaping. Boltzius reported that at least four of them escaped
for some period because he noted that they were recaptured and punished
with beatings, although it does not appear the whippings were administered
by Salzburgers.[78] In July one of the men committed suicide, an act to escape
slavery.[79] Because of their early experiences with these enslaved men, Boltzius and the Salzburgers were sympathetic and alarmed at the plight of the
enslaved, while simultaneously harshly judging them as lazy and dangerous.

We might assume that the local Yuchi, Yamacraw, and Muskogee Indians were reliable sources of information for the Salzburgers. Oglethorpe had
worked hard to keep good relations with these groups, and the Salzburgers were generally on good terms with them, although also fearful of them.
However, relatively early in the colonizing project Boltzius came to distrust
the Native Americans. The tensions came about because the Salzburgers settled so near to Indians; the official diaries report incidents of Indians setting up encampments in Salzburger fields, taking produce as they wished,
and once entering a home and threatening the residents. Boltzius and his
congregation responded mostly by allowing these "intrusions" for the sake of
keeping on good terms. In the first few years of Salzburger settlement, local
Indians periodically came into town, offering meat and corn for weapons or
money, and they sometimes stopped for a few hours or days on their way to
and from Savannah. One Muskogee man lived with the Salzburgers in New
Ebenezer for several weeks while his injured leg healed.[80] And in 1736 a curious Reck traveled to the Muskogee and Yuchi communities, spending ten
days with them to record the names of various plants and animals in their
languages.[81] Despite these early intercultural connections, there is very little evidence that the Salzburgers adopted Indian methods of agriculture or
hunting. For example, when many seeds from Europe did not perform well,
they preferred to wait to get more sent by fellow Germans living in Pennsylvania than to seek seeds from local sources.[82]

One area of Indian knowledge the Salzburgers did somewhat value
was medicinal herbs to cure American diseases and dangers. Boltzius, Andreas Zwiffler the apothecary, and Ernst Thilo, the Halle-trained doctor
who arrived in Ebenezer in 1737, looked to the Indians to provide information about American plants. This was consistent with European notions
that the cures to American diseases would be found in America. Similarly,
Reck learned from an Indian that "four stones or glands" from an alliga-
tor's head could "be pulverized and used as medicine against dropsy."[83] Despite these interactions, the search for Indian medicines did not range far,

largely because the premier supplier of medicines throughout Europe was the Francke Foundations in Halle. Their reputation for high-quality cures that behaved consistently was well known in Europe and traveled with the German missionaries who went to India, Russia, Poland, and North America.[84] A well-stocked medicine kit was part of the regular charity shipments sent by Halle to Ebenezer, and the Salzburgers preferred to rely upon this proven source than to experiment with American solutions. The Salzburgers received the first shipment of a large supply of Halle medical material on April 2, 1736, and they continued to receive them into the nineteenth century.[85] The 1736 package was especially fortuitous as many of the original group were quite sick, probably with malaria and possibly also with scurvy. Andreas Zwiffler, the formerly lost apothecary, expressed his joy at receiving Halle medicine as he believed it to be "the safest and most successful" for his patients.[86] Boltzius, Gronau, Zwiffler, and Thilo turned to Halle for the best information about medical treatments, rather than to local colonists or Indians. They particularly depended on the Halle-published guide *Die Höchstnöthige Erkenntnis des Menschen* (The highly necessary understanding of the body), which was written by Christian Friedrich Richter, the Halle professor who created many of the medicines.[87]

A tally of Halle's shipments to Ebenezer from 1749 to 1759 shows requests for over seventy-five different types of medicines.[88] Halle exported these shipments primarily through London as charitable donations and continued to do so long after the colony ceased to be run as a charitable operation under the care of the Trustees because the Navigation Acts required English transshipment. Even with control passing to a British royal governor, the medical shipments continued to forge another strong link between the Georgia settlers and their German sponsors.

In assessing local resources of information about the Lowcountry environment, Boltzius, and other Salzburgers, first judged the quality of the people as guides to whether their knowledge was truthful or valuable. With few exceptions, South Carolina planters were deemed lazy and too given to luxury to be good Christians. Therefore, their ideas about the landscape—what would grow, how to establish farms, which animals to eat—were largely ignored. The same is true of the English settlers at Savannah, who were generally considered irreligious by Boltzius. The Swiss settlers in Purrysburg across the Savannah River presented a mixed bag. The area was settled by Swiss Protestants, including both French- and German-speaking people. Some of them, such as Thomas Kiefer, were devout Lutherans who earnestly sought to meet with the Salzburgers and welcomed Boltzius and

Gronau when they came to provide services. Those people could be trusted, and Kiefer willingly shared his knowledge of how to care for cattle in the climate. The French-speaking Purrysburgers were seen as somewhat less reliable, in part because of the language barrier but mostly because they followed the Calvinist Reformed faith. It was the wrong religion for Boltzius.

## A Transatlantic Knowledge Network

The reluctance to accept information from other colonists meant the Salzburgers constructed a good deal of their knowledge experientially. We can almost hear Boltzius's sigh as he wearily writes, "Through practice we are gradually acquiring experience" about which types of landscapes are most fertile.[89] His cumulative experience and having the good fortune to live a long life meant that Boltzius became an expert representative for America as he participated in an extensive correspondence network. The exchange of information about natural America served to strengthen the British Empire by providing colonists with opportunities to participate in knowledge production while simultaneously giving English collectors the information they desired.[90] Boltzius's correspondence with the SPCK and the Georgia Trustees in England served similar social functions and more. His requests for assistance included important information about the fledgling colony, discussing the geography, climate, flora, and fauna of Georgia as well as agricultural practices, Indians, the Spanish and French threats, and slavery. Not only was this information crucial for the Trustees' decision making, but, more importantly, it was the raw material for their extensive publications.

Boltzius quickly became a preferred expert for Germans wishing to know more about colonizing America—not just in the Lowcountry, but anywhere in America. When Halle sent Heinrich Melchior Mühlenberg to Pennsylvania in 1742 to organize the disorderly Lutherans in the Mid-Atlantic colonies, he was instructed to first stop in Georgia to get advice from Boltzius. The advice Mühlenberg sought was pragmatic information about how to establish a home and a church and how to set up the homestead so that it supplied a sufficiency.

Because he was Halle trained, Boltzius was a member of the worldwide correspondence network of missionaries and pastors and was the central node in the web for insights into life in America. The Pietist German community in Europe was interested in America for both scientific and colonization purposes. Although no German polity had a colony in America, thousands of Germans were moving to British colonies, and the Pietists were enthusiastic supporters. As a result, Boltzius was asked about the people, the economics, and especially the character of the land, such as its soil and what would and would not grow. In 1751 he answered a very long questionnaire that was probably from Christian von Münch, the Augsburg merchant and banker who had fulfilled the Trustees and SPCK banking needs in Europe and was also an active Salzburger supporter.[91] Münch had already sent some items to the Salzburgers with the intent to sell them, and it is likely the questionnaire was intended to guide his further trading and colonizing investment. The questions dealt with slavery, plantation economics, and American plants and animals, addressing continuing European concerns about poisonous or noxious plants.

In 1756 an article written by Johann Martin Boltzius but published anonymously appeared in the *Hamburgishes Magazin*, a journal dedicated to printing "collected writings from the natural sciences."[92] The "Report and Remarks on the Plant Kingdom in Georgia by a Pastor of the Ebenezer Colony, 1752" detailed over eighty-seven species of plants found in the American Lowcountry, nine of which were not previously described in European literature.[93] Capable in English by the 1740s, Boltzius frequently reported to the English Trustees on the plants and animals in Georgia, with a particular focus on potential economic profits. He chose to circulate this more scientifically oriented 1752 article to his German contacts. We do not know how the work came to be published in the *Hamburgishes Magazin* or just who was the conduit for Boltzius, but we do know he maintained correspondence with men trained at Halle University. The fifty-page report details the characteristics of plants, those for economic purposes and those not. The economic plants are broken down into edible crops and forestry products. There is another categorization scheme: which plants flower in the spring and which in the summer.[94] Boltzius and the Salzburgers paid close attention to when plants flowered, for they were not merely signs of a changing seasons but also signals of when to plant certain crops. Folk agricultural practices as well as husbandry manuals sent from England and Europe to Ebenezer included helpful mnemonics of when to plant, weed, and harvest crops.

The people at Ebenezer approached understanding their new settlement with a mixture of folk wisdom, religious metaphor, and pragmatic trial and error in an effort to understand the Lowcountry landscape. As with the earlier Pilgrims in New England, the Salzburgers viewed the American wilderness with fear, respect, and awe. It was in this challenging and dangerous wilderness that they expected to find a closer communion with God and build a strong community. This idea—that the good Georgia forest had redemptive powers for the settlers—aligned the thinking of the Trustees and the Salzburgers.

Married to this mystic and folk view of the natural world was a pragmatic approach that led the Salzburgers to discover and experiment with native and nonnative plants that might help them sustain the community. We might not make much note of their efforts, except that their position within the Pietist network meant that their experiments in Georgia were recorded and communicated with other German settlers in America and with Europeans who were curious about the nature and structure of the world. Though they came to the new land with alpine and central European ideas about the proper use of the land, the Salzburgers quickly became reference experts for naturalists, scientists, and future colonists.

# CHAPTER 5

## Subjects

When the Georgia Salzburgers came to America they were not only adapting to a new natural environment but also adopting new loyalties as subjects of King George II. As a people who were nearly stateless, evicted from Salzburg, they quickly learned to value their new status in the British Empire. Despite their rebellion against the prince archbishop on religious grounds, in general the Salzburgers were deferential and compliant with the hierarchical power structures of the Protestant colony. They were wholly committed as new subjects of the British king and jealous of their newfound "English Liberties." Yet in the early years of settlement even they had to challenge and lobby their leaders and sponsors to shape outcomes in their favor. Their experiences reveal that there was considerable ambiguity over authority and responsibility in the early years of the colony, exposing a serious weakness in Trustee rule. The uncertainty was exaggerated by the great distance between the colonists and their European sponsors, which resulted in tangible hardships for the settlers. However, the ambiguity also presented opportunities for the Salzburgers to exploit to their benefit, all while they continued to present themselves as model citizens who were devoted to the Georgia Trustees.

### Subjects of the British Empire

When the first Salzburgers traveled from Bavaria and Swabia to the new colony of Georgia, they made an essential stop in England. At Dover on

December 21, 1733, they were met by Thomas Coram, philanthropist and an early Trustee for Georgia (as well as future head of the famed London Foundling Hospital) who oversaw an important ceremony. At the request of the Georgia Trustees, before the group could depart for America a proclamation was read to them, in their native German, which formed a contract between the Trustees representing the British state and the Salzburgers. The immigrants swore allegiance to King George II and agreed to "be subject to the English government"; and in return they were promised the full "enjoyment of their rights and freedoms."[1] The Salzburgers signaled agreement as a group with a "loud *yes*," then males filed past the document and touched it with their hand to signify their individual consent. Finally, they shook Coram's hand and were thus made subjects of Britain.[2]

Those newly granted rights and freedoms had been carefully clarified over the previous months in letters between the Trustees, the SPCK, and Samuel Urlsperger. An Atlantic crossing was dangerous, and Georgia was a new colony with just a few hundred residents, so it is not surprising that the Salzburgers received the offer of settlement in America with some wariness. They repeatedly clarified the proposed situation in the colony before accepting the offer. The Trustees and the SPCK were careful to communicate to Urlsperger, through the SPCK's secretary Henry Newman, that they did not want to encourage people to settle in Georgia if they were already settled in a principality or kingdom. It was important that the Trustees did not appear to be poaching subjects of a realm other than Salzburg. As the Salzburgers were essentially stateless, in the end the Trustees promised in writing, in German, that the exiles would have free and unencumbered land, freedom to practice their religion, and all the civil rights of "His Majesty's Natural Born Subjects."[3] One version of the Trustees' offer indicated the Salzburgers would become "Denizens, and have all the Rights and Priviledges of Englishmen."[4] It does not appear they were ever granted true denizen status, which was granted only through royal prerogative and was not part of the authority delegated to the Trustees, but it is clear that the Salzburgers and their British sponsors intended to extend all English liberties to the new colonists.[5] That is, the Salzburgers' new community in Georgia would be full subjects of the British king, a status wholly welcomed by them.

Their rights as British subjects were a point of pride for the Salzburgers and a significant benefit justifying their choice to live in Georgia instead of moving to Prussia with the majority of their coreligionists. The enjoyment of these English rights became a defining characteristic for the group as they set about establishing their community. In November 1738 Ebenezer colonist

Ruprecht Steiner wrote to his brother Michel in Lindau, a Protestant city at the foot of the Alps that had accepted many Salzburger exiles, urging him to come to Georgia. They had found good, free land with plenty of cattle available to make a living. Importantly, in Ebenezer they enjoyed "much freedom" under English rule and government.[6] Steiner's letter accompanied a community letter sent from Ebenezer to Germany intended to attract more settlers, which also touted the freedoms they enjoyed.

When they wrote of freedoms, the Salzburgers often referred to specific types of liberties that they valued most. The greatest of these was the right to practice Lutheranism unobstructed, and letters home reported that they "enjoy here all Christian freedoms in religion."[7] For a people who had left their home after resisting Catholic inquisitions into their faith, this was a prized freedom indeed. In the last few days of his life, after having lived in Georgia for just two years, Salzburger Paul Schweighofer testified that one of the greatest blessings God had given him was the gift to be "in America where he and his children could" worship in the Lutheran manner.[8]

Other rights were cited as part of the "complete freedom of the English" the group had acquired in North America.[9] Johann Martin Boltzius commented in 1738 that in Ebenezer they "enjoyed all of the freedoms that do not exist in Germany."[10] Those freedoms included property that was protected from authorities, without feudal-style labor requirements tied to it. Expressed another way, Boltzius reported one of the great "material benefactions" accorded the Salzburgers was that "no one demands anything from them, and they are no one's servant."[11]

The right to self-govern and to make decisions autonomously within the community was equally cherished. The Salzburgers lived under Trustee and English rules and laws, including common law, but as Boltzius noted, "All good regulations . . . are made with everyone's approval" within their settlements.[12] As expected, this was true for church matters, but also for civil affairs including land distribution. In one case, to ensure that each family had an equal share of good- and poor-quality land, three neighbors split their surveyed plots into thirds and redistributed how it would be planted. In so doing, Boltzius was careful to note that "they have not violated the plans and orders of the Trustees, since the old [survey] lines remain."[13]

Boltzius's comment about following the Trustees is significant, as the type of freedom they envisioned included responsibilities to the community and respect for authority. Liberty was not license. A. G. Roeber found that some Germans in America subscribed to this type of internal liberty that valued freedom of conscience but still envisioned allegiance to authority and responsibility to serve the community.[14] This definition of liberty held sway in Ebenezer as it reflected the teachings of the Halle Pietist August Hermann Francke, founder of the Francke Foundations, where Boltzius had been trained. Pennsylvania German settlers, in contrast, largely conceived of a liberty without constraints, a "libertarian" view that emphasized protection against encroachment from rulers and elites. Roeber describes this "libertarian" tradition as coming from the Swiss and Swabian settlers—people often called Palatinates by the British—who used civic structures and communities to fend off encroachments upon personal liberty. One might expect the Salzburgers, as an alpine people, to share the libertarian view in America, but their close-knit society and deference to their Halle-trained pastor Boltzius seem to have shaped the community toward the definition of liberty that emphasized shared responsibility.[15]

Belief in the duty toward community was put into practice in Ebenezer, where they established a poor box in the first month of arriving in the colony to care for less fortunate members of their group.[16] In contrast to Georgia's English-speaking settlers, they were unusual in their willingness to work together, and as a community they cleared forests and built fences. By 1737, just three years after arriving, the group founded an orphanage for Lowcountry German children that also functioned as a school and a home for poor widows and the aged. The orphanage was run by Ruprecht and Margaretha Kalcher, a Salzburger couple, who were paid a small salary that came out of charitable funds donated by Ebenezer residents and their supporters in England and Germany. In civic matters, Salzburgers showed their support for authority when they willingly served on Savannah grand juries, even though doing so created some degree of hardship as it required a journey of several days.[17] Although unnoticed by the Trustees as unique, it was this fundamental value that made the Salzburger settlements in Georgia align so closely with the original plan. The shared sense of obligation to the community meant the exiles prioritized unity and concern for all members over the naked pursuit of individualistic economic gains.

Boltzius frequently praised the "paternal care" of the Trustees, who considered themselves the "Guardians of the people," for their good care and plans for the colony.[18] James Oglethorpe, whom Boltzius frequently lobbied for concessions, was also particularly honored by Boltzius and the Salzburger colonists for his constant care and concern toward the Salzburgers. Oglethorpe has come down in history as paternalistic and overly involved in every detail of the colony, much to the frustration of some settlers, most notably the Malcontents. However, the Salzburger record shows that they—or at least their leaders who kept records—usually considered Oglethorpe their friend and welcomed his "paternal care." He is frequently viewed as an ally in Salzburger disagreements with English colonists, which is not surprising since the Salzburgers were strong supporters of the Trustee policies.

That the settlers at Ebenezer considered themselves loyal members of the British Empire is perhaps most evident in their efforts to find economic activities that would contribute to their own well-being and fit within the British mercantile structure. When questioned about opportunities to participate in trade, Boltzius's first response was that as an English subject each person in Georgia was "free to trade what he wishes," loading one's ships "with anything he wants, anywhere he wants" provided duties were paid.[19] Boltzius seemed to be reveling in the trade freedoms accorded them. He quickly noted, however, that some Dutch and German goods were contraband and trade in them was impossible. Boltzius's willingness to applaud British trade opportunities, even as many trade doors were shut in practice, is consistent with the loyalty he felt toward his adopted home.

Because the Salzburgers' conception of their British liberties envisioned a moral component that emphasized hard work and communal responsibilities, Boltzius considered people who held other definitions to be undeserving of English freedoms. In this context, Boltzius referred to a group of British colonists who opposed Trustee policies as "*foreigners*," in that they did not deserve access to full English liberties. The group who became known as the Malcontents was a prime example of this type of disloyal, undeserving subjects. In this way, then, Boltzius and the Salzburgers conceived of membership in the British Empire not only as coming from birth but also as a status earned upon fulfilling a sort of social contract. Some English settlers were found lacking by Boltzius, and he wrote that their version of freedom, which emphasized lack of constraint, ought to "be called more a misuse of freedom" that was "harmful" to people.[20] On visits to Savannah, Salzburgers observed that "no one heeds" Oglethorpe, a situation Boltzius described as a sin and a sign of moral decay.[21] Boltzius and the Salzburgers believed it was proper to discuss their needs with Oglethorpe, and to lobby for increased support or changes in policy. But outright disobedience was a sign of moral failing.

While Boltzius and to a lesser degree his assistant Israel Christian Gronau were willing to work within the ambiguities of the young colony to press for the needs of the Salzburgers, the community was still deferential to authority and to hierarchy. They were grateful for their opportunity to start over in British America, and especially jealous of their newfound rights as British subjects. Thus, they present a paradox: deferential to monarchy and social hierarchy as it represented the center of their civil rights, but also willing to lobby, complain, and challenge authority to meet their needs.

In Georgia's earliest years, there was considerable ambiguity over who held civil authority in the colony, largely because the Trustees chose to rule from London rather than delegate. Boltzius and the Salzburgers used that uncertainty and leveraged their relationships with the Trustees, the SPCK, and the German Pietists to agitate for their needs in ways that were not available to the English settlers. Salzburger access to the upper reaches of power and the uncertainty over policy and authority enabled the Ebenezer community to advocate for itself. Two intertwined cases illustrate this point. The first centered on the issue of moving from Old to New Ebenezer, and the second was over which of the Trustees' many appointees had true authority in the Salzburger community.

## Challenging and Asserting
## Authority in Georgia

In early February 1736 Johann Martin Boltzius confided in his diary what he believed was the root cause of many problems in his small community. "If we . . . knew where we stood in regard to governing the people, it would prevent many a misunderstanding."[22] Misunderstanding was an understatement, as at that time there were two officially appointed civil leaders in tiny Ebenezer, Georgia: the Swiss Jean Vat and the young Hanover noble Baron Philip Georg Friedrich von Reck. Each vied for power. The matter was further complicated, not resolved, by appeals to higher authorities in Georgia and England. This confusion over who governed contributed to the tribulations endured by Boltzius's Salzburgers in the early years in the new colony. In 1736 many were starving, struggling to survive on sandy, unproductive land, and denied many of the provisions that had been shipped to Georgia by their European sponsors. Boltzius's diary entry for January 1 noted that eleven children were born in the community in the previous year but only four were still living.[23] Further, twenty-one people in Ebenezer had died in that same year. The need for assistance was real, and as the group's leader, Boltzius labored, lobbied, and pressured to resolve the political issue of authority as well as to provide relief for the very tangible consequences of the power struggle.

In these early years, before they had developed sustainable farming and economic programs, the community struggled to establish themselves in Georgia and for the first few years was dependent upon their sponsors for even the most basic supplies of food, shoes, clothing, and medicines. Their physical dependence and their theological support for patriarchy and hierarchy resulted in many humble supplications for aid by Boltzius to his sponsors. Requests were often couched in a formal appeal flowing with the language of subservient praise and gratitude for the kindness, generosity, and worthy nature of the Trustees, the SPCK leadership, and the Pietist leaders in Germany. Oglethorpe, the only Trustee who was on the ground in Georgia when the Salzburgers arrived, was often singled out for his "fatherly care" in Boltzius's diaries and letters. Partially as a result of the language of these appeals, the Salzburgers have been portrayed as the community that "came closest to fulfilling what the [Georgia] trustees desired of all immigrants" because they were "devout and hard-working small farmers who earned their bread by the sweat of their brows" and who opposed slavery.[24] Despite their experiences defying Catholic power in Salzburg, as good Lutherans the group "tended to uphold authorities and to agree with St. Paul's admonition to the Romans: 'Let every soul be subject unto the higher powers.'"[25] However, behind the formality of subservience, we see in the tactics of Boltzius a skilled lobbyist and negotiator who succeeded in forwarding the needs and desires of his congregation through a variety of means.

Within the first months of their arrival the Salzburgers discovered the land they had been assigned by Oglethorpe was sandy and unproductive. Knowing the news would reach both Urlsperger in Augsburg and the SPCK in London, Boltzius began laying the groundwork for relocating the town in the official diaries, the *Detailed Reports*, with entries describing the very poor quality of the land. Boltzius gave the first indication that the soil around Ebenezer was unsuitable with his August 17, 1734, entry in which he described the surroundings as "swampy and waterlogged" and noted that "there is much beautiful level land on both sides of the [Savannah] river" better suited to be the Salzburger settlement.[26] Because of the poor land, within just a few months of arrival Boltzius had members of his community looking for better land than that assigned to them by James Oglethorpe. He thought they had found it in a spot on the Savannah River known locally as Red Bluff and Indian Hut. Boltzius appealed to Thomas Causton, Savannah storekeeper, magistrate, mayor, and local agent for the Trustees, to help get approval to settle on the more advantageous site. Causton and the official surveyor Noble Jones "went up and found a small tract of land" near Ebenezer that would suffice.[27] Shortly afterward the catechist Gronau asked Causton to allow some "Settlers under my Care to build a hutt on the . . . Land for working there jointly."[28] Lacking authority to distribute land, Causton was hesitant to approve the new settlement, and thinking he could not override Oglethorpe's choice, he deferred to the Trustees. Causton did, however, add his voice of support for Boltzius in lobbying London for the Red Bluff location.

Boltzius also coordinated with commissioner Jean Vat, who had arrived in December 1734 with the second transport, to urge a new location for the Salzburgers.[29] In August 1735 the SPCK received a detailed report from Vat on the quality of land in Ebenezer and of the urgent need to relocate the settlement. He noted that the agricultural yields "confirm the . . . dismal Accounts given by everybody concerning Pine-barren Lands!"[30] Vat urged the SPCK to arrange for another location, blaming the unhealthy and unproductive site for many premature births among the Salzburger women. Indeed, Vat argued, the very ability to continue a settlement at all was in doubt, unless the community was allowed to resettle to better land at Red Bluff. On January 15, 1736, the SPCK received a letter from Savannah's Anglican minister Samuel Quincy, written at the request of Boltzius, noting the Salzburger settlers complained of the "Badness of their Lands, and that Mr. Vat and Mr. Boltzius have a great Deal to do, to persuade [the Salzburgers] to stay on the Place."[31] In his quest to move Ebenezer Boltzius had recruited the primary holders of official authority in Georgia to his cause: Thomas Causton, the Trustees' official agent, magistrate, and keeper of the stores in Savannah; Jean Vat, the appointed commissioner of the second transport; and Samuel Quincy, the Trustee-appointed Anglican minister for the colony. Each of these men lobbied both the Georgia Trustees and the SPCK in support of the Salzburger request to relocate. Of course, the SPCK had no authority to distribute land or to approve the move, but Boltzius knew that communication with the sponsoring organization could help bring pressure upon the Trustees.

No radical, Boltzius continued to press for official permission to move to the Red Bluff rather than risk moving his people without permission. When James Oglethorpe returned to Georgia in 1736, Boltzius took advantage of the opportunity for a face-to-face appeal, quickly traveling to Savannah to make his case. Oglethorpe agreed the Salzburgers could move but insisted they could not resettle on the Savannah River as it was "against his instructions," presumably referring to the Trustees' orders for him when in Georgia.[32] Not satisfied, Boltzius continued for several weeks to pressure Oglethorpe to allow the Salzburgers to settle at Red Bluff and Indian Hut. His chief arguments were that the land along the river was best for agriculture and transportation. Oglethorpe eventually relented, with the caveat that the Salzburgers had to leave all buildings in Old Ebenezer (i.e., they could not reuse the sawn wood) and had to name the new location New Ebenezer, possibly to protect Oglethorpe's image as a wise colonial projector and to provide continuity in marketing the Georgia Colony as a success.[33] Over time, nearly everyone associated with the colony dropped the New and called the location Ebenezer; they maintained the name "Old Ebenezer" to describe the deserted inland town, which the Trustees repurposed as a cowpen for Trust-owned cattle.

Boltzius succeeded in part because of his ability to exploit the ambiguity surrounding authority and responsibility in early colonial Georgia. As noted, the Salzburgers had three main sponsoring groups: the Trustees, the SPCK, and the loose network of German Pietists centered in Halle. Each had a financial and emotional stake in the exiles' success. The result was somewhat fluid lines of responsibility and authority. The Trustees, for example, were a private group with a royal colonial charter who were awarded public funds by Parliament to establish the colony. They were responsible to the English government for the administration and planting of Georgia and for the wise use of public funds. The Earl of Egmont recorded several instances of political maneuvering, often appealing to the British need for defense in the American colonies against a possible incursion from the Spanish in Florida, to get needed funding for the colony from Parliament.[34] This political accountability forced the Trustees to maintain a focus on the goal of colonial defense. However, they also solicited private donations to support the benevolent program for the colony, making them accountable to the charitable donors for maintaining high ideals of a slavery-free, independent farmer settlement that would help the poor.

In addition, as noted earlier, although the Salzburgers were officially sponsored by the Trustees, the SPCK paid many of the expenses. In turn, the SPCK and the Trustees solicited funds and material from the German-led Pietist network in order to provide the level of support the Salzburgers in Georgia required. The result was that the responsibility to care for specific needs of the Salzburger emigrants was addressed in an ad hoc fashion, depending on whether the Trustees, the SPCK, or the Germans had available resources. Capitalizing on this ambiguity, Boltzius and the Salzburgers appealed to all groups when they needed additional clothes, food, books, seeds, or other provisions.

Part of the reason for the blurred lines of responsibility and authority in Georgia between the SPCK and the Trustees was that many of the same individuals sat on the councils for both. To individuals such as James Oglethorpe and the Earl of Egmont, each a prominent member of both organizations, which of the two societies carried out the mission of the colony may have seemed a minor point. Yet the secretaries for these organizations had very clear understandings of the scope of authority for each organization. For example, the SPCK's secretary Henry Newman forwarded all land-oriented requests to the Trustees, while the Trustees forwarded requests for clothing and books to the SPCK. In their correspondence these secretaries regularly explained to supplicants exactly which group held the proper remit for the requests, as when Newman wrote in August 1734 that "I serve as Secretary to a Voluntary Society . . . who concern themselves only as Sollicitors of Charity . . . it is not in their Province to address the Court here for any Civil or Military" matters.[35]

Despite the efforts of the various secretaries, Boltzius continued to make his reports and appeals to Pietist leaders in Germany, the Trustees, and the SPCK without regard for divisions of responsibility. It does not seem likely he was merely unaware of their different roles. He knew, for example, that the Trustees alone were responsible for surveying and granting land. However, Boltzius used all three groups to argue for a new location for Ebenezer, as when Samuel Urlsperger, the Lutheran leader in Augsburg, relayed the need for better land to both the SPCK and the Trustees.[36] Boltzius was wise to have Urlsperger raise land issues to the Society; despite the fact that the SPCK was aware they had no legitimate authority to issue land grants, they took up the matter in their council meetings and asked the Trustees to quickly act on the behalf of the Salzburgers.[37] Put in simpler terms, Boltzius capitalized on blurred lines of responsibility to press for his causes.

For Boltzius to succeed in his campaign for better land, he needed to establish his own personal expertise, and that of his supporters, on the matter. Boltzius was a trained pastor and not an obvious agricultural expert, yet he drew upon his own eyewitness testimony as one means of sustaining his argument. He wrote of poor yields from his own small garden and of sandy soil that lurked a few inches below the topsoil. On August 22, 1735, Boltzius and one of the settlers "inspected the various locations and we find it impossible, also unnecessary" that the community settle in such a poor location.[38] Consequently, his expertise came not from book learning or theory but from actual experience—a notion that had gained currency in Enlightenment Europe. He had seen with his eyes the poor yields and the sandy soil. Further, he had seen enough bad soil to recognize the useful and fertile land just a few miles away at Red Bluff. His experience made his voice authoritative, despite lacking formal training.

The Salzburgers' neighbors served as another group of experts on the soil. Although they remain nameless in the official diaries because of their low status, Boltzius refers to his English and Scottish neighbors as "people who know this country" by virtue of having settled earlier than the Salzburgers.[39] Their own experience was called as a witness. Native Americans—probably Yuchi or Yamacraw—periodically visited Ebenezer, and in his appeals Boltzius noted that they told him the land around Ebenezer was long known to be "chiefly Pine barren, a sandy white Ground not above one Fifth or at most one Tenth Part of tolerable mould."[40] Corroborating evidence from the Indians was crucial as they were widely regarded as possessing unique expertise on the natural world. Eighteenth-century men of the Enlightenment believed "Indians . . . possessed a keener sensory and mental apprehension of the natural world around them."[41] Not just their greater experience on the land but also something innate in their character made Indians the most perceptive experts on the American natural world. Or, as one Englishman wrote in 1731, "No People have better Eyes . . . than the Indians."[42]

Boltzius broadened the grounds for the appeal by specifically targeting issues he knew would be important to the Trustees. Granting a removal to the Red Bluff location would help establish the colony because "many additional Salzburgers would . . . [come] to America and into the wilderness" if they saw the first group succeed.[43] Further, he noted not only the unproductive soil but the fact that Ebenezer was in a bad position for transportation, trade, and defense against the Spanish threat in Florida. Ebenezer Creek, the Savannah tributary upon which the town was sited, was not navigable most of the year, forcing the inhabitants to make difficult overland journeys for supplies, and potentially complicating any military defensive campaign. Although he was not, on paper, an expert on matters military and trade, Boltzius again relied upon his eyewitness experience of the unnavigable Ebenezer Creek and of muddy, impassable roads. Further, he asked the ship captains who had transported the second Salzburger group to report upon their return to London. Presumably the captains would be deemed reliable sources on the transportation issues, in addition to being eyewitnesses capable of a "faithfull Account . . . of this place as having both been here."[44]

In making these requests, Boltzius was careful to portray the community as obedient subjects who were working hard to implement the Trustees' plan for small family farms. The Salzburgers, he wrote, were deserving people who were the ideal settlers the Trustees wanted. Their "happiness requires that they be settled on a land where they will be able to eat their own bread through the work of their own hands, as they have long desired

to do."[45] These settlers were not freeloaders, content to live off their sponsors' provisions, but hard workers who wanted nothing more than to live up
to the Trustees' founding ideals. Boltzius was worried that the crop failures
might be blamed not on poor quality land, but on laziness. On several oc-
casions he took care to note how diligently the Salzburgers worked clearing and planting land, at one point noting he was "amazed that they have
been able to accomplish so much."[46] Further, Boltzius notes, the Salzburgers "had to drag their provisions . . . partly on their backs" throughout the
hot summer months.[47] They suffered with sickness and disease even while
they worked to clear Ebenezer Creek and plant crops. Truly, these Salzburgers were the right sort of settlers, and their hard work was reason enough to
ask for better lands.

Naturally, the great distance between Georgia and Britain and Europe
caused delays in resolving the appeal for new land. Although the Trustees
did establish a mail service between Savannah, Ebenezer, and Charleston,
South Carolina, regular communication was still slowed waiting for transatlantic travel. The Trustees and the SPCK urged their agents Causton and
Vat to be more diligent in sending regular reports, as the lack of information
made it difficult for them to govern from London.[48] As a result the Georgia Trustees had to rely upon their delegates on the ground to implement
their policies. On the pressing issue of relocating the Salzburgers to New
Ebenezer, Boltzius finally heard back from the SPCK in a letter sent June 3,
1736, which reassured him that the complaints had been forwarded to the
Trustees.[49] This letter was sent several months after New Ebenezer was established on the Red Bluff and the issue had been resolved by pleading with
Oglethorpe. It is also interesting to note that the SPCK, not the Trustees,
responded to Boltzius on this matter. The SPCK had no legal authority to
make land grants. This is yet another example of the vagueness of authority
that existed.

In Georgia distance could also be a useful political tool, functioning as a
ready excuse to explain actions. For example, Boltzius felt sure Oglethorpe
was using the distance of the Trustees as an excuse to prevent the Salzburgers from moving to the Red Bluff. Oglethorpe insisted the group must settle
a few miles inland from the shores of the Savannah River because the Trustees had not given him permission to allow Germans to settle directly on the
Bluffs. Boltzius never fully accepted this reason and confided in his personal
diary, "If only he [Oglethorpe] would no longer hide behind the pretext of
his insufficient authority and instructions" the group could settle where they
chose.[50] It is not clear what instructions the Trustees gave for settling the Sa-

vannah River, however their meeting minutes do not mention any restriction
to English colonizers. Boltzius was right in noting that Oglethorpe seemed
to have, or take, complete authority in Georgia when it suited his purposes.
Trustee instructions were not required when Oglethorpe originally directed
where the Salzburgers should settle. Further, Oglethorpe did not hesitate to
exercise power to service his projects. On the 1736 voyage he intended to establish a defensive settlement against the Spanish on the Altamaha River
and managed to direct all supplies for the third Salzburger transport to this
new location. This was expressly contrary to the arrangements established in
London by the Trustees and the SPCK and is an example of Oglethorpe taking advantage of distance to meet his own ends.[51] Boltzius was likely close
to the truth when he wrote that Oglethorpe was hiding behind the need for
Trustee approval—and the ensuing time delay created by distance to get that
approval—in the matter of settling at Red Bluff.

Oglethorpe finally agreed to allow the community to move to lands very
near Red Bluff and quickly left Ebenezer, traveling to his new settlement further south along the coast, near the Altamaha River. Boltzius continued to
lobby for the river bluffs through letters, but he also took advantage of the
distance, allowing the Salzburgers to begin establishing New Ebenezer before the final details had been resolved with the Trustees. At the same time,
Boltzius did not intervene when the settlers decided to lay out their new
town according to their own design. Oglethorpe had wanted a single fence
around the entire new settlement, but Boltzius noted that arrangement would
not permit the Salzburgers to keep their stock animals near their homes, as
was the custom in their alpine homeland. "It must be considered against Mr.
Oglethorpe's order," noted Boltzius, as he did nothing to stop settlers from
"fencing his own [individual] lot and hastily building something for his livestock."[52] Despite Boltzius's firm belief in divinely ordered hierarchical power,
he believed he would eventually succeed at convincing Oglethorpe; further,
the distance between Ebenezer and the Altamaha River meant it was quite
likely Oglethorpe would not undo a *fait accompli*. It was the same reasoning
used by Oglethorpe, as he counted on the Trustees to support his new Altamaha River settlement once the project was begun.

Salzburgers also ventured into the neighboring frontier to locate and map
out their own land, a task that was nominally the responsibility of Noble
Jones, the colony's official surveyor who lived in Savannah. They were able
to do this in part because of the multiday travel distance between Savannah and Ebenezer and the delay in communications between London and
Georgia. They continued to apply pressure for official survey plats to affirm

ownership of the promised fifty acres each, but the Salzburgers took matters into their own hands and initially laid out their own plots so they could begin building their homes, fences, and stables.

Boltzius succeeded in negotiating a better location for his people by pressuring the authorities and by taking advantage of the distances between Ebenezer and his sponsors. However, his skills were greatly tested when his own authority within the community was challenged by claims to power by Commissioner Jean Vat. Again, Boltzius felt he must lobby his sponsors and assert his own power for the good of his community.

## Who Is in Charge?
## Competing Authority in Ebenezer

Although Boltzius was able to make the inherent ambiguity of having three sponsoring organizations work to his favor in some cases, the uncertainty also had profoundly negative impacts. This is perhaps best illustrated in the dispute that arose in 1735–1736 between Commissioner Jean Vat, Philip von Reck, and Boltzius over just who had civil authority in Ebenezer. Soon after the first transport of Salzburgers was settled at Ebenezer in 1734, Oglethorpe and Reck returned to England. This left Boltzius as sole leader, responsible for the civil, physical, and spiritual welfare of his small congregation. Jean Vat, a Swiss native who had lived in London, came with the second transport, arriving in Ebenezer about nine months after the first group. Upon arrival, Vat announced he had a commission from both the SPCK and the Trustees to be the community's civil leader, which included responsibility for community defense as well as for safeguarding and distributing all supplies such as food, clothing, medicine, and tools.

Friction soon developed between Boltzius and Vat over when and to whom provisions would be distributed. Boltzius described Vat as having a "fantasy and imagined authority, which, according to his own assertion, is as great as that of the Trustees himself."[53] Vat further aggravated Boltzius by ordering members of the community to stop construction on a fireplace in the parish house and to perform military guard duty on the Sabbath. Vat gave this order based upon instructions sent by Oglethorpe, yet he insisted on exceeding the Trustees' requirements by requiring more guard watches and more service than Oglethorpe intended. Vat's manner of interrupting Sunday service to announce the new duties was clearly designed to communicate his power over Boltzius.[54]

Boltzius again enlisted the support of Thomas Causton, the Savannah storekeeper and magistrate appointed by the Trustees. Causton immediately sided with the pastor, writing that he "does not approve Mr. Vat's behavior but rather concedes [the Salzburgers] complete liberty" to arrange their own affairs.[55] Vat, however, stated he had greater authority than both men because Causton was appointed by just one organization (the Trustees) while Vat was the "delegated Commissioner of both Societies."[56] Despite this assertion, Vat traveled to Savannah to "complain very copiously to Mr. Causton" about Boltzius interfering with his orders.[57] Apparently, although Vat claimed the right to rule, both he and Boltzius recognized Causton's connections to the Georgia Trustees as a source of power.

The dispute over legitimate authority in Ebenezer escalated with the return of Philip von Reck as commissioner of the third transport of Salzburgers in February 1736. At this point both Reck and Vat believed they were the legitimate civil authorities in Ebenezer, Reck having been appointed by the Georgia Trustees. Once again, Vat claimed superior rights based on his commission coming from both the Trustees and the SPCK. Reck, in return, appeared to make a claim based not only on his appointment but on his status as a German nobleman. For his part, Boltzius was not satisfied with Vat or Reck and lobbied against both men in a letter to Friedrich Michael Ziegenhagen, the private Lutheran court chaplain to King George II in London. Ziegenhagen had been one of the Salzburgers' spiritual supporters, so it was not extraordinary that Boltzius would communicate with him. However, since both Vat and Reck had been appointed by the Trustees, the appeal directly to the king's court was one means of pursuing his case to the highest authority in Georgia's affairs, circumventing any ambiguity.[58]

This was not merely a personal squabble over theoretical power. Vat literally held the key to the storehouse and determined who in Ebenezer received corn, beans, and clothing as well as the sheep and cattle purchased for the community by the SPCK and Trustees. The nearest supplies were in Savannah, a difficult multiday journey for the Salzburgers; even if some settlers could make the trip, few had enough money to purchase all they needed in Savannah's stores. In these early years they were dependent upon the provisions sent by their sponsors. For reasons of his own, or perhaps at the instruction of the Trustees, Vat refused to offer supplies to members of the first transport. Vat may have considered the first transport no longer eligible for supplies since it had been two years since they had arrived in Georgia. However, we do not have Vat's account of the event. It must be said that the Georgia Trustees clearly intended to keep supporting the struggling community, but that information may not have been communicated to Vat, who had left

England some eighteen months earlier with the second transport. Even if we grant Vat this misunderstanding, his insistence that only he could distribute aid, coupled with his decision to refuse aid to the first transport, was alarming as Boltzius reported some settlers from this original group were very near starving. Given the material impact of this impasse, it is somewhat surprising the Trustees would send to the colony two individuals who were each appointed with civil authority over the community at Ebenezer.

Oglethorpe, upon returning to Georgia in 1736, could have personally intervened to clarify roles. The matter was certainly raised to him, and he was aware of the difficulties.[59] While he did intervene to correct some of the problems, as when he ordered supplies distributed and lightened the guard duty, he never resolved the core issue of who had the right to rule.[60] It is possible that Oglethorpe himself felt some requirement to consult with the full body of the Trustees. It is also likely that Oglethorpe preferred to keep some ambiguity so that individuals such as Boltzius, Reck, Causton, and Vat continued to consult him as the ultimate authority in Georgia. Boltzius persisted in lobbying London, sending reports to both the SPCK and the Trustees. The Earl of Egmont noted in the Trustees' minutes that Boltzius's letters "shew'd [Vat] to be a Silly busie and Domineering fellow."[61] Boltzius prevailed, possibly because of his longer relationship with the Trustees, and Vat was recalled.

Although at times Boltzius praised the character of Philip Georg Friedrich von Reck, he also expressed dissatisfaction with the young noble in communications back to Germany. Reck had cobbled together the third transport, which arrived in February 1736, with people who were not all Salzburgers. This group did not have the shared exilic experience, and Boltzius found it difficult to incorporate them into the culture. Because of Oglethorpe's Altamaha project, which redirected the transport's supplies, the third group had not received their food, tools, and clothing, placing an extra strain on the community just as they were starting over building a town at New Ebenezer. Boltzius lobbied all of his contacts for the promised provisions and for the Trustees to have their land surveyed. His official diary, which he knew would be sent to Urlsperger in Augsburg before being edited and translated into English, did not mince words. He complained about Oglethorpe and the Trustees' slow response, described Georgia's official surveyor Noble Jones as "lazy, selfish, and hostile," and placed the blame for everything on Reck.[62] Fortunately for Boltzius, after suffering sickness Reck became disenchanted with Georgia and left in late 1736. Boltzius had succeeded in removing both Vat and Reck from Georgia.

It is quite clear that Boltzius had real authority in Ebenezer far beyond his ecclesiastical duties, in large part because he had the trust of his people. They repeatedly came to him to solve disputes with Vat and Reck. When Vat insisted the Salzburgers sign a resolution in which they agreed to his leadership on several matters, including serving guard duty on the Sabbath, they came to Boltzius and "begged for good advice."[63] In this case Boltzius advised them to pray for guidance and reminded his followers that God would support them in their trials. They left, begging Boltzius "in a moving way to champion them as best I could before God and Mr. Oglethorpe."[64] This role as champion before Oglethorpe and the Trustees was one Boltzius had already assumed in the dispute over settling at Red Bluff, and he now extended it to deal with Vat.

As the struggle against Vat escalated and the needs of the Salzburgers became more desperate, Boltzius took a stronger stand against him. While Jean Vat was in Savannah and away from the contentious storehouse, Reck, taking advantage of the distance, "broke the lock on the store-room" and distributed some of the provisions stored therein.[65] Boltzius worried Reck did not have authority but admitted that "necessity required this, to be sure," and the minister's assent made it easier for the Salzburgers to go against the will of Vat.[66] Further, in at least one instance the people willingly chose to follow Boltzius over the wishes of Oglethorpe. In New Ebenezer, Oglethorpe intended the Salzburgers should work Trustee land before turning their efforts to individual plots. Trustee land would be used as a common store of supplies for the community, but Boltzius misunderstood and thought the land was reserved for the private use of individual Trustees. He refused to "consent to this and therefore none of the people will" work this common land.[67]

As the matter over Commissioner Jean Vat illustrates, in Ebenezer real power did not always coincide with appointed authority. Boltzius succeeded in having Vat recalled because he had the support of his congregation, and he was able to successfully lobby the colonial hierarchy. Similarly, he probably saved the settlement by petitioning all of the philanthropic sponsors and eventually persuading the Trustees to let the group move to the Savannah River, on land that was neither swamp nor sand. There is no indication that Boltzius was a power-hungry individual, and he preferred to use his ecclesiastical power to discipline rather than assume the role of civil magistrate. One of his tools was to withhold Holy Communion from community members who strayed, as he did in 1736 for some third transporters who were drunken.[68] However, he proved a skillful politician in lobbying and negotiation with the multilayered and somewhat ambiguous hierarchy that nominally controlled affairs in Georgia.

Boltzius and the Salzburgers lobbied the Trustees in London, their SPCK supporters, and colonial administrators in Savannah for the "rights and liberties of other Englishmen, as . . . promised to them orally and in writing."[69] Boltzius frequently reminded the European philanthropists of these promises in his efforts to secure land, provisions, tools, and the right to worship freely. When local leaders made requests that appeared to interfere with Sunday worship, such as formal guard duty or enforced communal labor, Boltzius vigorously complained that the demands were akin to treating Salzburgers "like Slaves" and not like "other free people in this colony."[70] Not only did he immediately send word to Oglethorpe in Georgia, but he also mindfully recorded these demands in his official diary whose audience, he knew, included King George II's Lutheran chaplain Friedrich Michael Ziegenhagen, the SPCK, the Trustees, and the Pietist Lutheran community in Halle.

Because the Trustees chose to keep the lines of authority murky, the Salzburgers carved out a space for their own system. In pushing for more aid or for policy changes, the Salzburgers were always deferential toward authority and made clear their appreciation for the new liberties they held as subjects of the British monarch. They preferred to have Boltzius function as their religious and civic ruler and relied upon his ability to lobby the Trustees, the SPCK, and the Pietists in continental Europe to address issues in Ebenezer. The willingness to go around local authority, exploiting their relationships with philanthropic sponsors to reach the Trustees, meant that the Salzburgers were active participants in shaping the policies of the British Empire while they also remained aloof from many of the English settlers in Georgia. The division between English and German settlers in Georgia was not merely because of language miscommunication; the Salzburgers had stronger connections to people in power in Europe through their philanthropic sponsors and exploited that to their advantage.

Over the 1730s and 1740s, with the growth of the Salzburger settlements to plantations and communities around the town of Ebenezer, Boltzius felt burdened by his civic duties. At his request, in 1747 the Trustees appointed a new conservator of the peace, Johann Ludwig Mayer. Mayer was charged with all civic duties. However, Boltzius remained involved in cultivating a strong sense of community in Ebenezer, and in nonreligious duties, especially in developing economic programs that benefited the settlement.

# CHAPTER 6

# Community

O ne of the distinctive characteristics of the Salzburgers was that the group had a strong sense of community based on their shared religion, which helped them create a settlement and flavored their interactions with the other people they met in Georgia. Boltzius and Gronau worked to make Halle Lutheranism central to the character of the town, and this helped the group maintain a sense of cohesion. Additionally, and unlike other early colonists in Georgia, they worked together and supported one another. The Trustees tried to enforce communal work at the beginning of the colony, but soon after arriving the English-speaking colonists complained and the idea was abandoned for the lack of support.[1] The Salzburgers also grumbled at being forced to perform communal labor, but they did so very frequently. In the early years they built homes for each other and helped fence the town. Later, they worked together on public facilities and helped each other when needed.

The first transports of Salzburgers, of course, had the shared experience of leaving their homes and traveling together. And they had a common alpine culture. But they actually came from several different places in the archbishopric. In the first transport the Gastein Valley had the largest contingent, but there were also people from Saalfeld and other valleys in the Pongau region. Subsequent transports brought religious exiles from many towns in the southern German states.[2] Religion and living in the Georgia wilderness were the common bonds. It was important to Boltzius that the group build a town and not just spread out into plantations along the Savannah River because in a town people helped one another. There would be a school and residents would benefit from having a church and a pastor nearby. For the Trustees and for Boltzius, South Carolina provided a ready example of the immoral sort of people who did not live in a town. The plantation owners lived in luxury, were focused on wealth, and did little work of their own. In Purrysburg, across the Savannah River, the people spread out in plantations, and Boltzius regularly described the residents as disorderly and full of "discord, hate, envy, and . . . intemperance."[3]

The Trustees also envisioned a colony of small towns for Georgia, and this was another point of agreement between the Salzburger settlement and the Trustee mission. Creating many small towns was partially a strategy for defense because a string of villages meant there would be clusters of militias ready to ward off an attack by the Spanish or their Native American allies. But there was a heavy moral component to the Trustees' urban planning scheme. In addition to avoiding establishing large plantations, they also did not want to create large urban centers in their plan to implement the ideas of Agrarian Law. Their plan for Savannah, which was also used for Ebenezer, featured a town of equal lots, bordered by gardens and plantations, with the idea that a town would be supported by the plantations around it. The plan for the towns included orderly neighborhoods and large public squares. The Trustees envisioned a society of farmers, who would come into the towns for the markets, school, government, and church. That the plantations abutted the town meant that once all of the planned lots were filled there was little room for growth.[4] Instead, a new town would be started a few miles away.

Under the leadership of Boltzius, the Salzburgers fashioned a vibrant community very similar to the plan envisioned by the Trustees. By the early 1740s they lived mostly on plantations surrounding Ebenezer, the heart of their settlements. Although Ebenezer never allocated all of its town lots, the expansion of the German community did follow the Trustees' plans. As plantations spread to the north and south of Ebenezer, new villages were established. Spreading out did not seem to change their sense of being one community, as the Germans' faith kept them unified, as it also kept them distinct from the colony's English and Indian residents.

## Religion and Daily Life

Religion structured the daily rhythms of life in Ebenezer, in large part due to Johann Martin Boltzius's determination to "fully convert" his congregation.[5] It may seem surprising that Boltzius would refer to some of his group as not yet converted; they were, after all, religious exiles forced out of their homelands by their commitment to their faith. Yet although the Salzburgers were Lutheran, they were not necessarily adherents to the Pietist brand of religion coming out of Halle. Accordingly, Boltzius sought to awaken his flock to an inner, heartfelt conversion to the gospel; he expected them to experience a new birth of spirit, which would be evident in their comportment and service to the community.

To work this conversion, Boltzius followed the same practices as at the Francke Foundations in Halle: he held frequent meetings, preached Christ in simple terms, and used hymns to help fix the message deeply into the Salzburgers' souls.[6] For the most part the Salzburgers were willing participants, at least for the first twenty years of the community. According to Boltzius's diary there were certainly individuals who were not religious enough for his liking, but they still came to church. Possibly due to strong social pressure, only a handful chose not to participate. The typical day started in Ebenezer with a communal morning service that included a hymn, a short discourse on a scripture, and a prayer. There was a similar service every evening, and sometimes at noon. Sundays were to be days of rest, when residents were expected to attend longer meetings in the morning and an evening service after dinner and to refrain from performing labor, unless necessary.[7]

In 1737 the people of Ebenezer built an orphanage to care for the orphans of Salzburgers and those of other Germans in nearby Purrysburg, South Carolina, and Savannah. Many Salzburger and Purrysburger families put their non-orphaned children in the school for at least part of each year to receive an education. The operations were funded by donations from the Salzburgers and from their supporters in Central Europe, so that Boltzius believed he needed to provide regular reports on the students' schedule and progress. As Boltzius had been a teacher at the Francke Foundations, it is not surprising that Ebenezer's orphanage followed the Halle plan and was similar in its regimentation around religious services and teachings. In 1738 Boltzius wrote that the children awoke before five, sang a hymn, read a chapter from the Bible, discussed the application of the scripture, kneeled to pray, and then recited a few versicles—a fixed call-and-response form of teaching. Next was some light housework, and then breakfast. School was held in the morning until the midday meal and included time studying the Lutheran catechism. After two to four more hours of school in the afternoon, the children performed some more work. For Boltzius, the labor was not intended to be difficult or draining but instructive, as it was necessary for all people to learn the value of work.[8] Another group prayer meeting took place around six in the evening, using a similar format as the morning service. Finally, the children were expected to give private prayers as they went to bed. During especially important religious periods, such as the week before Easter, the children might meet for their own evening service to gain extra instruction before joining the community prayer meeting.

The academic teaching materials included religiously themed messages. For example, we know the community at Ebenezer used ABC books from Halle because several hundred were shipped to them by the Francke Foundations; even as late as 1761, long after the Salzburgers were firmly established in America, the Foundations sent over a hundred ABC books to Ebenezer to be used in instructing the children.[9] The Francke Foundations' library in Halle contains several eighteenth-century ABC books, and they nearly all carry religious themes to teach the children the alphabet. A popular book, the *Biblisches A-B-C*, provided lists of example words for each letter. One list had the "virtuous" (*Tugend*) ABCs, and the next was the "sinful" (*Sünden*) ABCs.[10] For the letter "A" the child learned *Almosengeben*, meaning almsgiving, and the sinful word *Abgötterei*, idolatrous.[11] Virtuous words were love, mercy, faith, pray, heavenly, and hope. The child had four examples of sinful words for the letter "Z," including *Zorn* (anger) and *Zauberei* (sorcery). Another ABC book provided lists for the "children of God" (*Der Kinder Gottes*) and the "children of hell" (*Höllenkinder*).[12] Story books were also often religiously themed.

A defining feature of Martin Luther's teaching was the importance of hymns as part of instruction and devotion. From the early days of Luther's reformation, hymnbooks were designed for use in the home and by the congregation during services.[13] Boltzius was musically trained and had founded a singing club in Halle, which explains why his requests to the Francke Foundations were that each household have at least three vital books: the Luther Bible, the Pietist theologian Johann Arndt's *True Christianity*, and a hymnal.[14] Halle published its own hymnbooks that included newer hymns that the Salzburgers would not have had an opportunity to learn while living in a Catholic domain. As noted, the Salzburger exiles sang hymns on their exilic journeys in Bavaria, but Boltzius found that few of the exiles could read music, indicating they had probably learned the melodies by ear in their private household meetings. As a result, Boltzius and Gronau set to work teaching the Salzburgers hymns, first by reciting the words to the congregation. By February 1735, thanks to donations out of the Halle network of Pietists, most of the families had a copy of the Francke Foundations' most famous hymnal, that of Johann Anastasius Freylinghausen, who was well known in Pietist circles for his songs. Freylinghausen's first hymn-book was published in 1704 with 683 hymns and 173 melodies, 44 of which were his own compositions.[15] Freylinghausen's hymnal was a little less than seven by three inches tall and wide (about seventeen by eight centimeters), and about three inches thick (about eight centimeters), making it very portable for worshipers wishing to have hymns at their fingertips.[16] Most Salzburger adults attained some degree of literacy, despite being unable to read music, so the group was able to read the lyrics and to sing under Boltzius's instruction.[17] The pastor ensured that the students in the orphanage school learned hymns and continued to work with the settlers to teach them new songs. In 1740 the students learned twenty-nine new hymns in just the four months between Christmas and Easter. Apparently in the early going all of the Salzburgers sung the melody, but by 1740 they were learning four-part harmonies for each of these hymns.[18] One can easily imagine that the sounds of Ebenezer included many voices singing hymns, not just in worship but throughout the day.

The pervasive attitude of faith in the lives of the Salzburgers meant that everything was seen as under the control of God, a sign of God, or a rebuke from God. Even with this great faith, some things were difficult to understand. When members of the first transport had dysentery and "swollen feet," Boltzius could not explain it. "The people live[d] moderately and orderly" lives, governed by faith, and should have been protected.[19] "We cannot comprehend what the cause of such evil might be."[20] They continued using medicines supplied by Halle, read scriptures for comfort, and prayed. Especially in the early years before about 1739, which marked when the community had consistent food security, the Salzburgers relied upon their faith in God to fortify them in their difficulty. Nearly every week of Boltzius's official diaries recounts someone in the community expressing thanks to God for preserving them. During the War of Jenkins' Ear, all of Georgia worried about possible attack by Spain or by the Indians allied with them. When the fighting ended in 1742, the people of Ebenezer were grateful to have been spared. Upon hearing this news, Gotthilf Francke reminded them that "God [had] threatened them with the danger of Spanish invasion" so that they would evaluate their behavior and repent.[21] Boltzius's teachings always tied experiences back to the Salzburgers' relationship to God.

A casual read of Boltzius's reports might cause one to believe he was oppressive in his faith and controlling in his behavior. Certainly, Malcontent leader Thomas Stephens believed so, when he wrote of their "unworthy and base Minister" who had "made" the Salzburgers "belie both themselves and him" when they wrote to the Trustees of their success.[22] In 1743 Stephens printed a 127-page tract attacking the Trustees' policies. He included a letter from Ebenezer supporting the Malcontents' position, which also said that "Mr. Boltzius, our Minister . . . exercises an arbitrary Power over us."[23] It was signed by Christopher Ortmann, John Michael Rieser, and Thomas Bichler (sometimes written Pichler). Ortmann was not a Salzburger but a German who had served as a British marine and who was sent by the Trustees to be the schoolteacher in Ebenezer. He had had several disputes with Boltzius, mostly over the behavior of his wife, Juliana Ortmann, who ran off to Charleston and whom Boltzius characterized as given to drink. He wrote in his diaries that Mrs. Ortmann had scandalously spent time with an Englishman temporarily living at Old Ebenezer.[24] The Ortmanns had made motions to move away from Ebenezer in 1739 but eventually decided to stay, to the consternation of Boltzius, who saw them as liars and wrote in his diary that they spread false tales about him.[25] Boltzius generally viewed Juliana Ortmann as impious and not a true member of the community, and it is understandable that Ortmann was not pleased with life in Ebenezer under Boltzius's civil and religious rule. With regard to the second signer, Rieser, in 1740 Boltzius recorded in his journal that he had counseled Rieser's wife to "not take part in the sins" of her husband as he had traveled eight miles to Abercorn on the Sabbath rather than attend worship services.[26] It is easy to see that Boltzius's condemnation of Rieser's behavior seems a valid reason for his signing the Malcontent's complaint. In 1741 Rieser and the third petition signer, Bichler, expressed a desire to leave Ebenezer for Pennsylvania or New York, as their contract with the Trustees required staying in Georgia for only three years.[27] In the end, neither Rieser nor Bichler left the community, and later both were devout members of the congregation. Boltzius believed Ortmann was the one who facilitated the other two men in signing the letter, and he dismissed the schoolmaster and his wife, forcing them to leave Ebenezer.[28] Ortmann became the teacher at the new Georgia settlement of Vernonburg, something that was arranged by William Stephens, the Trustees' appointed president of the colony.[29] Ortmann reconciled with Boltzius in 1747 and returned to Ebenezer, living on a pension.[30]

This dissent by three residents is among the rare instances of public, documented complaints about the pastor and the religious tone of the community.[31] The year 1741 found a few families who expressed a desire to leave for Pennsylvania, such as Bichler and Rieser, in part because the community still suffered from malaria and other illnesses.[32] But for the most part the residents embraced their status as the pious, devout people the Trust-ees desired. Religion served as the carrot and the stick for maintaining com-munity harmony. As the community's religious leader, Boltzius counseled the Salzburgers and frequently reminded his congregation that God would punish the disorderly and defiant. For example, in just one diary entry he reported that on his rounds that day he gave the schoolmaster Ortmann and wife Juliana "very urgent admonishments" to repent, met with danger-ously ill Herr Kaesemeyer and urged confession of sins, and counseled Anna Margaretha Rieser (Michael's wife) against the behavior of her husband.[33] It seems clear that Boltzius believed he was keeping the community in the correct path, one that would bring eternal salvation and help ensure do-nations from British and German philanthropists, but that must have felt controlling or stifling to at least some community members, such as Maria Anna Rheinlander, a woman Boltzius harshly judged in his diaries. During Sunday worship in April 1741 her kitchen burned down. Because the people were all in town for services, they were able to put out the fire quickly and saved most of the contents, something Boltzius reported that the Salzburg-ers saw as "the special care of God."[34] But, he wrote, this Mrs. Rheinlander was a "rotten and hypocritical character." It seems that prior to the fire she had claimed poverty and taken aid from the church and from neighbors, yet when the kitchen erupted in flames she was concerned to save some money hidden in her bed. Boltzius's interpretation of events was that Mrs. Rhein-lander had more money than she had represented. A few days later, she came to Boltzius humbly; he wrote that he did help her but did not trust her re-pentance. Two months later, Mrs. Rheinlander complained about her ob-stinate son, and Boltzius told her it was because of her children's "miserable and wretched upbringing," laying blame at her feet.[35] Sadly, we do not have Maria Anna Rheinlander's voice to understand her feelings at the time. But it is not too hard to understand that a widow raising children, whose home was burned, desired more than a rebuke from her pastor. She also probably had very few options other than staying in Ebenezer.

There is no doubt Boltzius had a strong influence as both civil and eccle-siastical leader, but community members did have a voice in church affairs. Among the first documents written in Ebenezer was the *Kirchenordnung*, or the rules for governing the church.[36] It was modeled after a standard agree-ment that had been drawn up in London, and the document laid out the re-sponsibilities of the pastor and the congregation. Similar to the structure of Lutheran churches in Europe, the *Kirchenordnung* established a body of ves-trymen to control financial affairs and required regular service, home visits, and preaching from the pastors. On other issues, the church members made decisions and presented them to Boltzius, as in 1754 when settlers near Abercorn (about eight to ten miles south of the town of Ebenezer) elected three church elders and set aside land to meet for services.[37] They expected Boltzius or assistant pastors Hermann Heinrich Lemke (Gronau's successor after his death in 1745) and Christian Rabenhorst, who migrated later, to come preach to them on a regular basis.

The people at Abercorn were part of a set of expanding settlements, radiating out from Ebenezer. By the early 1740s most of the original Salzburgers had left the town proper to live on their forty-eight-acre plantations that surrounded Ebenezer. As more transports arrived, settlers searched out good land to the north and south of the original township. As a result, the Salzburger settlements spread for about twenty miles along the Savannah River, from Joseph's Town and Abercorn, about eight miles to the south of Ebenezer, up to Bethany, about five miles north of the original town. Bethany was settled last, in the early 1750s, by a group led by Gerard William de Brahm; this was the Yuchi land the first settlers had wanted for New Ebenezer but had been barred from settling.

Wherever the Salzburgers settled they built churches. The main church in Ebenezer was the Jerusalem Church, which was finally completed in 1743 at a cost of ninety pounds using donations from the Pietist network, the SPCK, and the Anglican evangelist George Whitefield, who had visited Ebenezer on his preaching tour and was impressed by the community.[38] Prior to that the Salzburgers met in a hastily built structure in the town or even outside in the open air in the earliest period. The same year they completed the Jerusalem Church, 1743, they built the Zion church near Abercorn for seventy-three pounds, using money on Boltzius's credit that the SPCK philanthropists eventually paid.[39] Boltzius and Gronau and later Gronau's replacement, Lemke, provided services at the Zion church every two weeks. By the late 1750s the settlers at Bethany had stopped meeting in the woods and had also built a church. The growing need for pastoral support is why Halle sent pastor Christian Rabenhorst in 1752 with the third Swabian transport; he eventually settled in the area around Abercorn.

As part of building their community the Salzburgers sought to incorporate like-minded religiously devout Germans into their settlements. Boltzius wrote in 1743, "As for our fellow-countrymen, we wish they were with us."[40] From their first arrival in 1734 the Salzburgers always wanted more Germans to live with them and wrote numerous appeals to have more come. But they had to be the right kind of pious Germans. The Salzburgers' Lu-

theran faith defined the community and brought a unity not found anywhere else in Georgia, so any newcomers needed to be the same sort of people in order to maintain cohesion. In 1738, thirty-six Ebenezer Salzburgers
signed a community letter sent to Augsburg with a specific list of fifty-one
friends and family members they hoped would be able to come to America.[41] The appeal held out promises of good land, plenty of food, and farm
animals, prebuilt homes, and the opportunity to live in "Christian freedom,"
"where most of the members will live comfortably together"—a reference
to their British liberties and the tenor of their community.[42] It was important to them that any new settlers fit within their deeply religious society.
Boltzius functioned as an amanuensis for some Salzburgers' letters home.
These, as well as his own diaries and letters, contained several appeals for
more settlers. The requests were all quite clear that they wanted only like-
minded, devout, serious Lutherans in their town. As in all of Georgia, there
was a sharp labor shortage, and Boltzius wrote to Samuel Urlsperger that
they desperately needed more people to work. But the "place would be settled with only such people whose highest priority was the salvation of their
souls."[43] They needed workers, but only those who put God first would do.

   Similarly, the town's bachelors and widowers pleaded for more women,
but it was crucial that they be "good Christian Women."[44] The religious lit-
mus test applied even to family members. In 1737 Boltzius's brother, a jour-
neyman shoemaker, wanted to come to America. On the surface, this should
have been a welcome choice because Ebenezer was in dire need of a skilled
cobbler and was dependent upon outside craftsmen for shoes. Yet Boltzius
told his brother that "he must first be converted" and suggested that he first
"go to Halle," presumably for religious training, before he considered coming to America.[45] The brother would be welcome only after he experienced
a pietistic change of heart and a full conversion. He never came to Georgia.

   The emphasis on creating and maintaining a like-minded, religiously
devout community is one key to the Salzburgers' success in Georgia. (The
other being the ongoing and prodigious charitable aid received from the
Trustees, the SPCK, and Germany.) They worked together to live harmo-
niously. This was unique in Georgia, where English settlers were assigned
land next to strangers and were left to build their own homes and farms after exhausting the two-year supply of provisions from the Trustees. Boltzius reflected on this in 1740, seeing clear material benefit to having such
a close-knit community.[46] He noted that in the rest of the colony people
who needed labor were forced to pay high rates and therefore usually had to
do without help. In Ebenezer, the Salzburgers worked for in-kind mutual

aid; one might assist to mend a fence and be reciprocated with help finding a lost cow. This saved the families significant expense in an economy
short of specie. Boltzius observed another advantage in the Salzburger settlements in that neighbors worked together to build fences or clear trees and
brush from each other's fields. When an English person was placed next to a
stranger, it was possible that the neighbor did not cultivate the same part of
the acreage, which meant no help with fences and uncleared trees along the
property line, which created shade and reduced productivity of a field. The
willingness to work with each other in building and maintaining the structures of the settlements was especially crucial for the Salzburgers, as the first
three transports had to do the work of building twice. Oglethorpe's requirement that the group leave behind their sawn wood when they relocated to
New Ebenezer meant redoing two years of hard labor to build the town and
plantations.

Ebenezer's solidarity was also uncommon for Lutherans in British America. Pennsylvania, which had the largest percentage of Lutherans in the colonies, was a factious place. According to one historian's calculation, by 1750
Germans made up about 50 percent Pennsylvania's population, and about
40 percent of those were Lutherans (i.e., 20 percent of Pennsylvania's total
population). The next largest group, at 30 percent (15 percent of the total),
was Reformed.[47] In eighteenth-century German territories there were two
main Protestant churches: Evangelische (Evangelical) were the Lutherans,
and the Reformierte (Reformed) were Calvinist. After receiving requests
for a trained minister from congregations at New Providence, Hanover,
and Philadelphia, Gotthilf Francke sent Heinrich Melchior Mühlenberg
to Pennsylvania to organize the Lutherans there. Arriving in 1742, he traveled first to Georgia to meet with Boltzius for advice on America and then
to Pennsylvania.

Mühlenberg is remembered today as the father of Pennsylvania Lutherans, with a college, a town, a hospital, several streets, and other place markers named after him. But when he arrived he found a vibrant religious environment that was divided by the colony's famous toleration and plurality
of religions, and he had great difficulty establishing the Halle version of
the faith.[48] He was, in effect, competing for souls against other Lutherans
out of Württemberg, Reformed (Calvinist) ministers, Mennonites, Moravians, German Baptists, and the Seventh Day Dunkers who created the
Ephrata cloister. Shortly after arriving in Pennsylvania, Mühlenberg sent
a long report to Francke in Halle and Ziegenhagen in London. He marveled that in one area there were so many other ministers, each represent-

ing their own version of Protestantism.[49] Although there are some notable exceptions, such as the Moravians, in practice most individual German settlers in Pennsylvania lived with German neighbors who practiced different versions of Protestantism. As a result, Pennsylvania German settlements have been described by historians as focused on the nuclear family with "no strong commitment to the communal mode" of settlement.[50] In the end, these Mid-Atlantic communities never achieved the type of solidarity found in Georgia.

## The Worldwide German Pietist Network

In addition to identifying themselves as Salzburgers, the Ebenezer community also claimed to be German and actively participated in a network of Pietist German Lutherans centered in Halle and Augsburg. This idea of being "German" more than a century before a German nation-state developed was based in a common culture and language rather than in citizenship in a specific state.[51] That is, in the minds of the Salzburgers and their leaders, Protestantism and Germanness were not tied to polities and transcended kingdoms and empires. Their common transatlantic bond as Germans overcame the fact that the Ebenezer community comprised the exiled people from Salzburg, their ministers from Halle (Brandenburg-Prussia), and later Lutherans from Swabia, Austria, and other culturally German states. This notion also enabled them to be both proud subjects of the British Empire and Germans, as King George II was also the Elector of Hannover and thus part of the Holy Roman Empire.

On March 22, 1734, just days after the Salzburgers arrived in Georgia, some Germans who had settled in Purrysburg, South Carolina, sought them out. Boltzius and his community were trekking to their eventual settlement and had stopped in the frontier town of Abercorn, where they were visited by the Purrysburgers who asked for Lutheran religious services.[52] Boltzius was "very happy at this request" both because it spoke well of these Purrysburgers, and also because he foresaw an opportunity to include the South Carolinians in the Ebenezer community.[53] Even at that early date he was already planning to build a school and hoped to attract German settlers' children, a plan fulfilled when the orphanage was completed.[54]

Purrysburg created an interesting challenge for Boltzius because the town had been settled by Swiss, some French-speaking, some German-speaking, some Reformed, and some Lutheran.[55] Although this town was across the Savannah River and about twelve miles south from Ebenezer, it was also their closest neighbor. When the Salzburgers lived in Old Ebenezer, provisions from Savannah could not be brought to the town via the river and creek, so Purrysburg became the supply depot. It also became a communications hub for the upriver community. This, and the shared language, helped the Salzburgers form relations with some of the Purrysburgers.[56] Boltzius, however, was concerned. He did not approve of the French-speaking residents, mostly because they were members of the Reformed faith. At the same time, he felt a responsibility to nourish all the Germans who lived there, and under his leadership the Ebenezer Salzburgers worked to incorporate Purrysburg residents into their sphere of community. Some Lutherans from the South Carolina side did eventually settle in Georgia; the best known of these was Theobald Kiefer, who wanted to live with the Ebenezer Salzburgers but appears to have owned enslaved Africans, so he remained on the Carolina side of the river. He was devoutly religious and a strong supporter of Boltzius, including having three children married in Ebenezer by the pastor.[57] He was so committed to Francke-style Pietism that in a June 1750 letter to Gotthilf Francke Kiefer asked if his son, Gotthilf Israel Kiefer (born 1744), could be a student at Halle.[58] The son did not go to Halle, and there is evidence he died at a young age.

Beyond Purrysburg, Boltzius and Gronau made it their business to extend their services to any German group in the Lowcountry that needed them. The Trustees began bringing more Germans, whom they usually called Palatines regardless of their original home, to Georgia to work as servants. Not only did this help populate the new colony, but bringing indentured servants was also a response to a labor shortage in the early colony, a way to provide workers without acquiescing to the desire for African slaves. The Palatines were particularly valued because of the Salzburgers' example; the Trustees believed these German Protestants made good colonists. The community in Ebenezer begged to have many of the Palatine servants settled with them. Ebenezer needed their labor, but they also wanted more Germans in the colony. Those Palatines who were not assigned to Ebenezer still benefited from the Ebenezer community, as Boltzius and others concerned themselves with the overall physical, moral, and spiritual welfare of all Germans in British America. Beginning in the late 1730s several Germans were stationed at Fort Frederica at the southern boundary of the colony, serving with Oglethorpe to protect against Spanish attack during the War of Jenkins' Ear. Boltzius worked to find them a minister and to ensure they had food, had clothing, and were kept in good health.[59]

The Pietist Lutheran faith provided another avenue for creating a broader community. In addition to caring for Germans locally in Georgia, the Salzburgers participated in an active worldwide Lutheran network that centered on Halle pietism. We often speak of Halle Pietists because Halle became the central education point for the group and thus their spiritual home. But Halle-trained clergy such as Boltzius and Gronau were spread throughout Europe and the world. Boltzius knew many of these ministers personally, and his correspondence web included individuals in Augsburg, Poland, Saint Petersburg, and as far away as Tranquebar, a Danish colony in modern southeastern India. The Georgia colonists were always anxious for news from "the missions" and were pleased to receive the Halle newspaper, the *Wöchentliche Relationen*, and other publications. As many of the Salzburgers could read, these newspapers, as well as letters from missions throughout the world, were shared from house to house within Ebenezer.[60] Although much of this correspondence has not survived in the archives, Boltzius's letters back to Germany contain several references to letters being shared with the community in worship services and being passed within the community from family to family.

As individuals and as a community the Salzburgers corresponded with Germany, ensuring their experiences were circulated among far-flung Pietists.[61] There was an especial bond between Salzburgers who settled in East Prussia, in modern-day Poland, and those in Georgia; the Prussians collected charitable donations and sent encouraging letters to Ebenezer, including a communal letter sent in 1742 and another in 1748.[62] Letters from Salzburgers in Prussia were particularly desired and passed through the community, in part because of the shared exilic experience. For example, in 1742 Boltzius wrote that a report authored by Herr Andreas Schumann "concerning the righteous character of the fine little crowd of Salzburgers in Prussia" was "circulating in our community."[63] The Georgians responded with similar letters, which included Bible verses and encouragement in keeping true to their faith. Boltzius often directed that his letters be forwarded to various individuals in the Pietists' community throughout Europe, in order to spread the word of their status. It was common for one letter to travel first from Georgia to London, where it was received by Friedrich Michael Ziegenhagen, the Lutheran minister at the Palace of St. James, a member of the SPCK, and a Georgia Trustee. Thus, he served as a crucial linkage point for information and goods traveling between Germany and America and vice versa. Next, per Boltzius's wishes, the letters would be forwarded to Lutherans in Augsburg and Halle, and on to Poland or Russia.

The emotional and spiritual sustenance provided by the Pietist network was enhanced by the very tangible material goods sent to Ebenezer by the Germans. As noted earlier, the Francke Foundations in Halle and Samuel Urlsperger in Augsburg worked to collect donations for the Georgia settlers. They regularly sent shipments of linen, tools, books, and medicines to the Salzburgers, a practice that caused the Malcontents to complain that the only reason Ebenezer succeeded at all was because they were "liberally supported both from Germany and England."[64] The complainers were probably correct, as the donations sustained the Salzburgers and supplemented the Trustees' shortfalls. Importantly, the Pietist network also sent money routed through London, which Boltzius used to fund communal economic projects. These economic projects were a way to keep Salzburgers employed within the community, and the developments worked to keep a strong sense of unity within the settlement.

The Salzburgers' faith and union also created challenges for the group, as it set them off from their neighbors in Georgia. Much of this separation was intentional, as Boltzius found the English settlers in the colony to be mostly irreligious and of poor moral standing. One way he enforced this during the early years of settlement was to instruct the schoolteacher Ortmann to teach only in German, although Ortmann was fluent in English.[65] This language divide, and Boltzius's animosity toward most English-speaking settlers, did create disharmony and an "us versus them" mentality in the colony. The greatest concern to Boltzius was that the group remain a strong community who helped one another and remained dedicated to the Lutheran faith. In that he and the Salzburgers succeeded. They worked, studied, and worshiped together and continued to participate in the transatlantic Pietist community through books, newspapers, and letters. The combined strength enabled them to survive during the difficult early years and was sustained as they incorporated new transports of Germans.

It was not until after Boltzius's death in 1765, and just before the American Revolution, that the group began to experience some fractures. By then Ebenezer was not just a "Salzburger" town but the center of a large German-speaking community in the Lowcountry. Most of the original exiled Salzburgers had died by then, so the community lacked that shared experience. Yet because Halle and the SPCK made sure they had Lutheran ministers, the German settlements along the Savannah River shared their faith, and most remained distinct from the English colonizers.

# CHAPTER 7

# A Moral Economy

Embedded in the Trustees and the Francke Foundations' policies for the Salzburgers were specific economic plans, designed to fulfill a number of goals, some explicitly stated, some not. Like for other British colonies, a large part of the marketing of the colony by the Trustees in England focused on the economic benefits that would accrue to Britain. The reality of any imperial colonization was that the economy had to work; Georgia had to at least be self-sufficient and preferably would add to the British Empire's wealth. As was true for earlier British American colonies, the Trustees believed that Georgia's location on Mediterranean latitudes meant the colony could provide a bounty of products that Britain was forced to purchase from the Italians, Spaniards, and French. At this time it was commonly believed that buying goods from other nations weakened Britain's power.

A second, equally important aspect to economic programs in Georgia was that they had to also meet the Trustees' goals of establishing a moral society. Early modern thinking about the economy did not separate one's economic life from that of ethics, morality, and religion. Indeed, these spheres were seen as tightly interwoven.[1] Cathy Matson notes that few clergymen "ignored the central role that material striving, commercial competition, labor systems . . . or imperial expansion had in the ethical and spiritual lives" of their followers.[2] The Trustees were not unique in linking commerce to morality. What was unique is that they had decided the moral society in their colony could not follow the same economic programs of other British American southern or Caribbean colonies and must succeed without using the labor of enslaved Africans and be populated by small family farms. The Georgia experiment was "widely seen as an alternative scheme for orienting work to society. . . . The aim was to ensure commercial ties did not displace social ones."[3] The life of luxury granted to large plantation owners elsewhere in the Americas seemed to the Trustees to be inherently immoral for the "worthy poor" common man in Georgia. These ideas might seem inconsistent, or even hypocritical, coming from the Trustees, many of whom were members of the aristocracy or gentry and had more in common with Virginia cavaliers than Georgia farmers. The Earl of Egmont lived in London off the rents derived from his Irish estates.[4] Several of the Trustees were involved in other colonial projects that did rely upon slavery, including James Oglethorpe, who owned land in South Carolina and was the deputy governor of the Royal African Company in 1732. (The Royal African Company was the major slaving establishment for imperial Britain.) However, the Trustees' ideas about work, economy, and society did not imply a leveling of social status or eliminating slavery throughout the empire. They believed in hierarchy, and as Oglethorpe argued, by working to bring about the colony the Trustees had done their part and "given up that Ease and Indolence to which they were entitled by their fortunes."[5] The people who were sent to Georgia were intended to be from the lower classes, the poor of Britain, and the "persecuted Protestants" of Europe. The Trustees' paternalism and utter conviction that God established the hierarchical society of Britain caused them to believe that the role of the poor was to work. For this reason, many of the earliest Trustee rules dealt with economics, such as bans on the acquisition of vast stretches of land and large plantations, the trading of harmful goods such as rum with Indians, and the use of enslaved labor.

The Pietist German philanthropic network who helped support the Salzburgers similarly saw economic schemes as tightly interwoven with the moral quality of a community. Just as at the Francke Foundations, they wanted the Georgia Salzburgers to be economically self-sustaining and work to reap the benefits of earning a living by the biblical "sweat of their brow," as God had instructed that all men must do when he expelled Adam and Eve from the Garden of Eden.[6] The Bible has more to say about work, enjoining mankind to enjoy the "labor of thy hand" and the "fruits of their labor."[7] The simple lesson derived from these verses was that God intended man to work for his subsistence and that doing so would bring happiness. Living from the work of others would bring unhappiness and was the mark of an ungodly life. In addition to the biblical imperative to work, pastor Boltzius quickly realized that a strong economy at Ebenezer would help keep the believers together under the care of trained clergy, rather than choosing to, or being forced to, look for work among the English.

Boltzius worked to find projects that would garner the approval and support of their philanthropic sponsors, while wrestling with Georgian realities. The primary means of support for the Salzburgers from their first arrival until at least the nineteenth century was farming a variety of crops and keeping a small set of animals, to provide food for the family and some surplus for the Lowcountry provisioning market. However, Boltzius sought to supplement family farms with communal economic projects that would provide meaningful work, bring some hard currency into the community, and keep the Salzburgers together. Boltzius saw that any Salzburger crops would not be able to compete on price with those grown on large South Carolina plantations with enslaved labor, so little effort was made to grow rice and indigo.[8]

The Salzburger approach was unique in Georgia and unlike that of other German settlements. The Moravians, who started in Georgia and resettled in Pennsylvania by 1742, "built one of early America's largest and most durable communal projects" in which ownership of all assets and all economic output were held jointly and dedicated to the proselytizing mission of the church.[9] Mainstream Protestant Germans, both Lutheran and Reformed, in the Mid-Atlantic did not typically create communal economic projects but rather preferred to settle on family farms.[10] In Georgia, the Salzburgers took a middle path. Families did own and focus on their small farms, while their income was supplemented by voluntarily participating in communal economic projects. Boltzius consistently sought funding from British and German supporters for community projects, and he invested those donations in capital enterprises—what we would call infrastructure today—to encourage individual family participation in schemes. In the official diaries Boltzius frequently mentions advising the residents about economic matters, such as "how our dear people should arrange their farming and silk."[11] Economy and spiritual lives were intertwined, and following the example at Halle, Boltzius saw encouraging projects to earn money as within his role as pastor to the people.[12]

Three case studies demonstrate how the settlers built the Ebenezer economy. Ventures in cattle, lumber, and silk reveal the ways the Salzburger community blended charity and communal work to improve their settlement's economic fortunes. Cattle and lumber production were mostly directed at provisioning the Lowcountry, as Georgia's restrictions on slavery and emphasis on small farming unintentionally steered the colony's economy to supporting the wealthier South Carolina market. This reality inevitably and ironically tied Ebenezer's fortunes to the plantation slave economy just to the north.[13] Boltzius and the Salzburgers' philanthropic patrons also looked to find products for the broader Atlantic imperial trade and placed their hopes in wood products for the Caribbean and silk for Britain. Investing and expanding the cattle and silk industry were pet projects of the Trustees that also garnered the enthusiastic support of the Germans at Halle and Augsburg. By aligning with these goals, Boltzius skillfully convinced these supporters to invest their charitable donations in Ebenezer's economic infrastructure projects, in some cases redirecting funds intended "for the colony" to specifically aid just the Salzburgers' settlements.

## Investing in Cattle

Just a few weeks after arriving in Georgia in 1734, the Salzburgers were given cows. At the time the strongest men in the group were with catechist Israel Christian Gronau and Commissioner Philip von Reck building communal huts to house everyone at the spot in the forest that was (Old) Ebenezer. The rest of the first transport of migrants, including children, the aged, and the infirm, were waiting with Johann Martin Boltzius at Abercorn, about eight miles south of Ebenezer by land. They had very few provisions, and a good number of the company were sick. Yet when they received thirty head of cattle, Boltzius's response was "God be praised."[14]

The Trustees were particularly keen to provide cattle to all Georgia settlers. James Oglethorpe, who was the only Trustee physically in Georgia in the 1730s, reported back to London that "this Countrey cannot be supported without Cattel."[15] But he was merely repeating their own beliefs, as cows were always a part of the Trustees' plans for Georgia. The Trustees knew from their communications with South Carolinians that cattle were abundant in the Lowcountry, and they believed that if each family had a few cows they would have better food security and possibly some income. Their first published pamphlet, designed to spur donations for the charitable colony, declared the Trustees would give the poor settlers "Necessaries, Cattle, Land and Subsistance."[16] Cattle were so central to the plan that the Trustees felt compelled to name them separately from other "Necessaries" and "Subsistence" items.

By the early eighteenth century cattle had a long history of being a measure of a good farmstead in Europe, and they were important to European farming practices. In German-speaking lands, farmers and cattle lived side by side, making cows a part of everyday life for most people. Cattle were so integral to life that a nineteenth-century lexicon listed over 634 German folk sayings about cows and another 185 about calves.[17] Some offered advice on how to care for cows, but most were directed at the people. "The old cow soon forgets she was once a calf" was used to describe an older person blaming the young for problems, and "the cow does not think of winter, when she is grazing in clover" was clearly directed at one who does not plan for the future.[18] These sayings reflect how central cows were to German lives.

In the northern alpine regions, including the former homes of the Salzburgers, historians have traced a shift from primarily raising sheep to a focus on cattle, which took place gradually from about 1500 to 1750. The higher proportion of pasture and meadow land in the Alps versus land suitable for farming helps to explain why there developed an "economy based on livestock and cheese-making, activities that promised a secure subsistence."[19] Because so much of the land in alpine regions was vertical, there was very little flat land at low enough elevations to have a suitable growing season for crops, while the meadows higher in the mountains were ideal for grazing cattle. The Gastein Valley, where many of the first transport of Salzburgers came from, is very narrow and surrounded by steep mountains. Bad Gastein, the main town in the valley, is so narrow that it is perched on the steep slopes on both sides of the Gastein river (a tributary of the Salzach), which creates waterfalls through the center of town. A large segment of the first transport also came from Saalfelden, a narrow valley similar to Gastein. A study of early modern practices found that "most mountain farmers were primarily engaged in cattle raising."[20]

Cattle raising determined the rhythms of life in the alpine valleys. On the official church calendars in the Salzburgers' homeland was the spring festival of Almauftrieb, which commemorated the day when the village herders would take the cattle to the high alpine meadows for the summer.[21] Each village hired men who would stay with the cattle all summer, promising to bring them back down to their owners in good health in the autumn. During the festival the lead cow would often be decorated with a flowered wreath, and the people celebrated this sign of spring by walking part of the way up the hill with the herders. Some villages celebrated a second event in the fall, Almabtrieb, when the cattle were brought back home fattened and healthy.

In the eighteenth century German Americans were known for carefully guarding or even creating meadows in order to have enough fodder for their cattle. A practice among Pennsylvania Germans was to negotiate inheritable water rights, which were used to sustain or build new meadowlands.[22] North

Carolina Germans in the Piedmont were so concerned about having meadows for their farms that one man's deathbed request was that his son have
four years' use of a meadow.[23]

Of course it was not just the Germans who valued cattle. In England
the wealthiest of aristocrats ate venison to display their access to the private
hunting parks. But beef was the food of the people. Roast beef became a
symbol of British pride beginning in the late seventeenth century, and it was
contrasted with the fussy sauces and dishes consumed by the French.[24] British beef pride can be seen in William Hogarth's 1748 painting titled *O the
Roast Beef of Old England*," which features a man carrying a large side of beef
to an English inn, surrounded by healthy Englishmen, standing together at
the gates of Calais.[25] In the foreground are weak, emaciated Frenchmen,
languishing on the ground. The painting's title is taken from a British patri-
otic song written by Henry Fielding, which similarly attacks the French as
weak and ineffectual.

It was natural, then, that English settlers would bring cows with them
when they colonized North America. The first colonists at Jamestown had
cattle.[26] Virginia DeJohn Anderson notes that when Edward Winslow
brought "three heifers and a bull" to Plymouth Plantation in 1624, it "marked
the end of the 'starving times' as dairy products and meat" became available.[27] Other European settlers also brought cattle early in their colonizing projects. French Acadians left behind numerous cows and bulls in Nova
Scotia, as they had averaged about twelve cows per household before leaving.[28] And, importantly for Georgia, cattle came with Spanish settlement
throughout the Americas, which led to a large number of feral cows in the
Atlantic Southeast.

The Trustees gave cattle to all heads of households in Georgia. The animals came mostly from South Carolina, where planters had amassed large
herds. In Georgia's earliest years the South Carolina Assembly voted to do-
nate cattle, at one point sending one hundred "head of breeding cattle" and
five bulls.[29] Most of the South Carolina cattle were not donated but purchased by the Trustees from plantation owners who drove the animals across
the Savannah River for the new settlers. Those very first cows for the Salzburgers waiting at Abercorn, though, had not come from the Trustees but
were probably donated by Jonathan and Hugh Bryan, South Carolina plantation owners who had experienced an evangelical conversion and actively
supported Christian causes including the "poor persecuted Protestant"
Salzburgers.

Like their English neighbors, the Salzburgers quickly accumulated cattle. In less than a year they were making butter.[30] When they moved from
Old Ebenezer to New in 1736, one of their first tasks was to build shelter for
themselves and for their cows. On the new half-acre town lots, each family built a little home on one corner and in another corner built "Stables for
the Cattle."[31] Three years after its founding Ebenezer had a surplus and sold
beef to Savannah residents; this trade in meat became a steady source of income. The community had such large herds that in 1741 Boltzius reported
that cattle breeding was half of the Salzburgers' living.[32]

The greatest challenge for keeping cattle in Georgia was the vast feral
herds that roamed the countryside. There were two types of wild cows, and
the smallest group were English cattle who had escaped Carolina by crossing the Savannah River. The vast majority of wild cows were large Spanish
breeds that had wandered north from Florida. When Patrick MacKay, an
early Georgia settler from the Scottish Highlands, traveled near the Chattahoochee River in 1735 he reported seeing "thousands . . . of wild cattle."[33]
One significant problem was that the tame cows would join the wild herds.
Georgians copied the Carolinians in practicing open grazing, meaning tame
cattle were allowed to wander in the forests, swamps, and canebrakes surrounding the settlements. The cattle favored the canebrakes because they
found the leaves fresh and nourishing. The cane was so thick in eighteenth-
century Georgia that cows that entered the brake were very difficult to see
or retrieve. When any of these open-range "tame" cows joined the feral herds
and hid in the canebrakes, it was nearly impossible to keep them domes-
ticated. English Georgians, most of whom were settled in Savannah, preferred to let their cattle range freely, periodically herding them back to their
settlements. This was a cost-effective practice because they did not have to
provide feed. The English chose to absorb the expense of losing some cattle
rather than keep them closer to home. The result was that the Ebenezer cattle could mingle with feral cows and with English property, and it was difficult to keep the groups separate.

The Trustees also maintained their own herd, which was intended to provide meat for their indentured servants and for the poor arrivals. To meet the
feral problem Oglethorpe and the Trustees established a cowpen for their
own cattle. After the Salzburgers moved from Old Ebenezer, the Trustees
set up their cowpen in the old town, right where Boltzius had planted his
first garden. Even this did not work because the hired cow keeper was not
very careful. The cowpen keeper's assistants were indentured German ser-

vants who were close enough to Ebenezer that they kept contact with the Salzburgers. They told Boltzius the keeper was using the allotted feed to fatten his own cattle and ignoring the Trustees' herd.

Another problem with wild cattle was that it was difficult to tell if a cow was the natural increase of someone's property or just a feral animal. The Trustees took the position that all cattle were owned by someone and that any wild cow was by default owned by them. They felt a captured wild cow could be slaughtered and used to feed the poor. This did not satisfy others, as Savannah residents pushed to claim wild cattle as their own. The Salzburgers suffered from this problem, as it was also impossible to tell their cows from the English cows or from the feral. Of course Georgians clipped ears and branded their cattle to help prove ownership, but the real issue was around calves and the increase, and this remained an ongoing issue for the colony for at least twenty years.[34]

The herds increased so much that they became a kind of menace, sometimes viewed as vermin. In the country around Ebenezer the wild cattle were particularly numerous, and the Salzburgers had difficulty rounding up their own. Compounding the problem, feral cows destroyed crops.[35] After some exchange of letters from 1746 to 1748, the Trustees had their president, William Stephens, arrange for a mass slaughter of the wild cattle in that region.[36] To facilitate the extermination the Salzburgers surrendered all claims to wandering cows; this made it possible for the hunters to kill without first determining ownership. That Boltzius and the town would agree to this gives an indication of how plentiful and problematic the cattle were. In the long term the presence of wild cattle remained a problem for Ebenezer. At the bottom of the 1766 probate inventory of Boltzius's estate a note mentioned that he owned "very few Cattle and 2 or 3 Mares in the Woods, but not knowing yet wither they will be got."[37]

The problems controlling the cattle and turning them into a profitable export for the colony have been cited by historians as an example of the failure of the Trustees' administration.[38] The argument put forward is that limiting land holdings to just fifty acres meant it was impracticable to establish a network of cowpens in support of open-range feeding, as had been done in South Carolina. While the Trustees had a cowpen at Old Ebenezer, needed for success was a series of them, spread out in the countryside, constantly gathering in the roaming tame cattle. Further, the argument goes, the colony needed enslaved Africans to herd the open-range cattle, as labor was too expensive for Euro-Americans to perform this task.

It is certainly true that cattle exports rose sharply after the Trustee period.[39] South Carolinians flocked to Georgia when it became a royal colony and established large plantations using enslaved labor. This raised the speculative value of land, which opened up credit and enabled landholders to invest in the economy, including cowpens and the enslaved people who worked them. The growth in population and the elimination of Spain as a threat at the end of hostilities in the War of Jenkins' Ear in 1741 also helped open up territory in the backwoods, making it safer to have a system of cowpens and open-range cattle.

The Salzburgers stand out for their success at raising cattle under the Trustees' plans. They worked to amass cattle holdings like the English settlers did, but their experiences were unique in the colony. They received more support from charitable sponsors, meaning they were able to accumulate holdings more quickly than other groups. This was partly because Boltzius was not reticent to lobby the philanthropists for more cattle. And, significantly, the Salzburgers took a communal approach to keeping cows, so that they were better able to manage the challenges of feral animals. By some measures cattle were the greatest source of long-term wealth for the Salzburgers. They accumulated large herds rather quickly. In 1738, just three years after arriving in Georgia, some Salzburgers wrote home to Lindau in Bavaria to encourage family members to come. As evidence of the great possibilities in America, they noted how many cows they owned. Ruprecht Steiner had five cows, Georg Kogler six, and Christian Riedelsperger five.[40] One year later Kogler had fourteen. Back home, these men would have had one to two cows as part of a small family farm. The town had so many cattle that a 1747 map of Ebenezer shows herds of cows surrounding the town on all sides. These cows represented a significant portion of their wealth. When Boltzius died, his twenty head of cattle equaled 30 percent of the value of his estate, and he had not devoted much energy to his personal farm or agriculture.[41]

The Salzburgers were able to develop such large herds initially through charitable donations given to them because of their special status as Protestant refugees. Although some animals were purchased for all new settlers with general Trustee funds, charitable donations to the colony could be earmarked by donors for specific purposes, and some were designated exclusively for Salzburger cows. For example, in 1737 the Trustees instructed their magistrate and storekeeper Thomas Causton to provide more cattle to the Salzburgers because they had received a "particular benefaction" to that end.[42] Unlike English and Scottish Georgians, the Salzburgers also benefited from donations from their religious supporters. In December 1735 the

SPCK donated thirty-six pounds to the Trustees marked expressly for "Cattle and Fowls supplied the Saltzburghers at Ebenezer."[43] This money may
have been used to pay for the thirty-five cows and thirty-five calves that
Hugh and Jonathan Bryan of South Carolina brought to Ebenezer in June
1735 as a gift from the SPCK, but the timing suggests the June donation was
separate.[44] The Salzburgers also prioritized purchasing cows, and although
they were regularly described as poor, they seemed to always be able to find
cash to purchase cattle.[45] Even in this they benefited from charity, as Bry-
ans are known to have also offered to sell cattle at reduced rates as a means
to help Ebenezer residents build up their herds.[46] The Trustees' 1741 defense
of the status of the colonizing project proudly noted that at Ebenezer "they
have great Herds of Cattle" and the town was "thriving."[47] The Trustees
equated settlement success with having a large number of cows, as did the
Salzburgers themselves.

Boltzius encouraged the Salzburgers to take a communal approach to
building the economy of Ebenezer. One way he did this was to use donated
funds to hire Salzburgers for town projects, like building the church and
mills and planting glebe lands. These had the triple effect of helping Salzburgers live morally by their own labor, bringing money into Ebenezer, and
making a more viable town. These projects were paid for by donations sent
by the Pietists in Germany, the SPCK, and the Trustees. In May 1738 the
group began clearing and preparing the land around the orphanage to plant
crops. Their work was compensated by donations from Europe, and the Salzburgers used that money to buy cows.[48]

The cows were individually owned, but the community hired a herder to
tend their animals as they grazed in the forest during the days and to help
bring them back home at night. In the early years most of the herder's salary was paid by the SPCK and the German Pietist network, but the community took over fully in the 1740s.[49] The practice of having a village herder and
of bringing their cows into their town lots and later to their plantations was
how they had cared for livestock in Salzburg and Germany. A piece of German folk wisdom held that "a good cow is found in the stall," indicating that
the best way to raise cattle was to bring them home at night.[50]

Other North American colonists hired herders; it was how early New
Englanders cared for their cattle, as they similarly hired a town herder for
the task.[51] But it was a unique practice for Georgia and South Carolina. This
method eased the individual burden to track cows and allowed the people
to add milk, butter, and cheese to their diets, where the English in Savannah did not have enough access to their free-range cows to do so. The Salz-

burger community expanded to the south near Abercorn in the late 1730s
and designated a portion of the lands there, which were not yet patented,
as a communal pasture. The territory was near Abercorn Creek and was described as swamp, pasture, and canebrake, the kind of place that cows loved.
These terms need not be conflicting, as Boltzius noted most English settlers
called canebrake swamplands, and cane leaves were the most nutritious and
plentiful source of food for cattle in Georgia.[52] Boltzius used Pietist donations to build a cowpen in the land near Abercorn and to fund the salary for
Michael Schneider and his wife Elizabeth, whom he hired as the herders of
the Ebenezer orphanage's cattle there.

Beginning in 1741 the Salzburgers also began to let some of their cattle range free in the forests, cane, and pastures. But they continued to bring
home some milk cows each night, and they continued to hire a community
herder. The result was that the community practiced a mixture of free-range
and home pasture cow herding, which was a blend of European and American practices. By 1750 the Trustees had decided to close their cowpen at Old
Ebenezer. Their herder had been dishonest; their cattle were not well fed and
were still joining wild herds. There also were not as many new transports of
poor people or Palatine redemptioners who needed meat from the Trustees.
The Salzburgers saw an opportunity and struck a deal with colony president
William Stephens to buy all the Trustees' cattle for £400, to be paid in full
by 1753. In yet another act of charity the Trustees decided to lower the price
to £350. In another benefit, rather than paying in hard cash the Salzburgers
were allowed to work down their debts from the silk production activities.[53]

Despite these many generous advantages from the Trustees to the Salzburgers, Boltzius was skilled at lobbying his supporters for even more. He
used a combination of obsequious flattery and direct demands to advocate
for his congregation. Typical of Boltzius's style is a 1738 letter in which he
thanked the Trustees for all "benefits, which are above seven years bestowed
upon us, I never will be wanting to beseech our merciful God for rewarding
the Honorable the Trustees and other Benefactors sevenfold for them."[54]
Further, in the same letter he writes of the Trustees' "generous and praise-
worthy Intention, which aims only at the promoting the true Happiness of
Sober & industrious people." However, when it comes to getting cows, he
was much more direct. As we have seen, the third transport of Salzburgers, who arrived in February 1736, did not receive all of their promised supplies. Oglethorpe wanted them to move south of Savannah, to shore up settlements there and protect against possible Spanish invasion. They insisted
they must be settled at Ebenezer with the others, as they had been prom-

ised in Germany by Urlsperger, agent of the Trustees. Eventually they were allowed to join the other Salzburgers, but their provisions were sent south. Even after supplies were delivered, the 1736 transport still did not receive their cows, which angered Boltzius. Cows were essential to long-term survival and wealth. He wrote several letters pointing this out, revealing his strategy and the approaches he took with different sponsors. To James Vernon, one of the Trustees, he wrote in a deferential manner, opening the letter with thanks and humility but reminding the Englishman that only ten of the new families had been supplied cows and the others are "destitute of them."[55] With his German supporters, Boltzius felt he could be more direct. He wrote two letters to them on the matter. The first letter was to Gotthilf August Francke, head of the Francke Foundations, asking him to intervene with the SPCK and the Trustees to have lands surveyed and to give cows to the third transport.[56] The second was sent directly to Friedrich Michael Ziegenhagen, the court chaplain in London, in which he complained that the Trustees were not keeping their promises, specifically around distribution of land and cattle to the third transport.[57] As Boltzius had hoped, Ziegenhagen in turn wrote to the Trustees that not receiving the cows was "so contrary to what . . . the Honorable Trustees Solemnly had promised them."[58] The third transport got their free cows.

In addition to receiving much more aid than English settlers in Georgia, the Salzburgers benefited from their remoteness, being nearly twenty-five miles away from Savannah, in that it helped protect their herds from the spread of disease. Cattle disease, what the English called "black water" disease, spread throughout the colony in early 1742 and into 1743. Black water was called such because of the dark-colored urine from the infected cattle; sick cows very quickly became dehydrated, causing death in most, yet some were able to recover. This disease tore through both Georgia and Carolina, in some cases taking a person's entire herd. Yet Boltzius noted that they had not felt the grave impact at Ebenezer, which was interpreted as an instance of "God's wrath" against the residents of Savannah.[59] Later that same year Boltzius recorded in the official diary that the orphanage at Ebenezer was able to provide meat for the whole year, while other communities in Georgia and Carolina "lost very many cattle because of an infectious disease, nonetheless, we in our place have felt not the slightest trace of it."[60] Some German indentured servants, who Boltzius felt were ungrateful toward the Trustees, had "felt the heavy hand of God through the death of their stock."[61] Just as with the Old Testament Israelites, God had preserved them in their remoteness. Sadly, the next year the disease had not abated and came to Ebenezer, killing several Salzburger cows.[62] Even then, their remoteness appears to have limited the spread of the disease, and a majority of the herd survived.

Remoteness also brought a challenge unique to the Salzburgers as they complained that Indians frequently raided their herds. As discussed earlier, the town of New Ebenezer was situated on the south side of the mouth of Ebenezer Creek, where it met the Savannah River. North of the creek was Yuchi territory, and Euro-American settlement there was prohibited by the Trustees until 1750. This meant the Salzburgers were building a frontier town in the European sense of the word: on a border with another nation. Despite early hopes for Pietist missionary work and Oglethorpe's efforts at maintaining good relations, affairs between the Yuchis and the Salzburgers had been cordial but cool. In 1736, just as the Salzburgers were establishing New Ebenezer, the Yuchis complained to Oglethorpe that some of the settlers' cattle had eaten the Indians' corn.[63] Oglethorpe pacified their anger when he informed Boltzius of the problem and extracted Salzburger promises to cease the raids. In 1741 Herr Schneider, the orphanage herder at Abercorn, reported that Indians came on horseback and "scattered the congregation's cattle" that were grazing in the common pastureland and at the cowpen. The Yuchi fought hard to maintain the right to their lands and to keep Salzburger expansion in check. Boltzius did not see things that way and while recording the incident in the diary called the Yuchi "these wicked people."[64] Salzburgers in the Abercorn area pitched in to round up the cows again.

Despite the challenges of feral animals, disease, and Yuchi disputes, the Salzburgers were very successful at raising cattle. They serve as an example of what might have been for the rest of Georgia. Perhaps if the English had received more support from the Trustees to pay for herders and to establish pastures and cowpens, they would have succeeded. However, the real key to success seems to have been the Salzburgers' willingness to remain a cohesive community, jointly hiring herders, working together to build fences, and forming teams to round up scattered cattle.

## Mills and Dreams of Caribbean Trade

Tuesday morning, April 27, 1751, was an important day for the Salzburgers. They came from the town and from their plantations and gathered at the edge of Abercorn Creek to marvel at the beauty of their new sawmill. A fifteen-hundred-foot-long ditch brought water from the dammed creek to the new mill, just as a similar parallel ditch brought water to the old gristmill nearby. The group admired the work from the exterior and then moved inside the mill, where the sawyer cut a straight and clean board, using the two new saws. After that satisfying display, the Salzburgers all took seats and consecrated the works. The meeting formally began with the congregation singing the hymn "My Hope on the Living God Standeth Firm" ("Meine Hoffnung stehet feste auf den lebendigen Gott"), followed by a prayer. Next, Boltzius preached a sermon using the theme that the mill had been "granted to us by our God . . . for the benefit of the whole community."[65] They prayed for forgiveness, for God's help, and "for our king, the Lord Trustees, the Society, and all known and unknown worthy benefactors."[66] With that they closed the meeting and production at the mill could begin.

This simple meeting reflects the Salzburgers' understanding that their economic lives were not separate for their spiritual selves. The holistic well-being of the community depended upon having success in their work lives, as much as it rested upon religious principles of repentance and forgiveness. This was not their first mill; mill building began with funds from the Trustees in the late 1730s. At that time the Salzburgers grabbed on to the idea of having a mill as important for their overall success. This 1751 mill was the most complex and ambitious they had built in the previous twelve years and was the fulfillment of Boltzius's dreams.

Boltzius's original reason for having a mill was to make life a little more tolerable for the Salzburgers. Milling flour, stamping rice, and cutting boards was very difficult work when done by hand. The Salzburgers needed cut boards for their homes and to create threshing floors for their grains. Grinding corn and grains with the hand mills they had received from the Trustees was difficult and time-consuming. In 1744 his idea was that, with the addition of a sawmill, they could sell some cut boards to other colonists in Georgia to generate enough income to pay for the "support of the rice and grist mill," including wages for the miller.[67] In this way the mill complex would be self-supporting and provide great labor-saving benefits to the people. By 1746 the dream had expanded; he and the Trustees wanted to sell lumber to a larger market: the West Indies.

The first Ebenezer mills were for grain. When the group first arrived in Georgia they were given iron hand-cranked mills to grind corn, and later the community added European grains like rye and wheat to their farms. These hand mills worked poorly, required a lot of labor, and produced very little flour. After a year in the colony Boltzius and Jean Vat, the Trustees' commissioner for the second transport, asked for grinding stones, which the Trustees sent a year thereafter, arriving in 1737.[68] The community built a small, hand-

operated mill for the new stones. While thankful for the new stones and capacity of the mill, they realized more could be accomplished if they built
a water-powered mill. Boltzius pointed out to Oglethorpe that the Salzburger settlements provided access to two good creeks, the Ebenezer and the
Abercorn. Oglethorpe was enthusiastic and donated twelve pounds of his
personal money to the cause.[69] In fact, before the Salzburgers settled there,
Abercorn Creek had been briefly settled by a Swede named Henry Parker,
who built a mill on the creek. He left, the mill flooded, and the millrace was
destroyed. Yet Parker's Mill, as it was called, suggested the possibility for
the Salzburgers. Boltzius's plan included using the skilled carpenter Georg
Kogler and the donated labor of town residents to build the new gristmill
and rice stamping mill. This was a common approach for the community:
Boltzius gathered charitable funds to pay for the materials, and the community worked together to complete the works.

About the same time that they were sending the first mill stones to the
Salzburgers, the Trustees had a sawmill built at the abandoned Old Ebenezer
site intended to benefit the whole colony. Because iron and sawn wood were
in short supply in Georgia, in 1736 they arranged for a Georgia mill, starting
by partially constructing one in London at a cost of five hundred pounds.[70]
This is a significant cost considering that the Ebenezer congregation built
a church for only seventy-three pounds.[71] The mill pieces were sent aboard
the ship *Two Brothers*, along with two men experienced in building mills. In
June 1738 the colony's newly appointed president, William Stephens, visited
the works, and what he saw should have signaled that Old Ebenezer was not
a good mill location. The water in the creek was running very low, and the
ditch to the mill was not very deep. Stephens questioned the man in charge,
named Cooper, who assured him the creek was lower than "was known in
the Memory of Man" and that all would be well.[72] There was so little water
that cut logs could not be floated to the mill, but Cooper assured Stephens
that it would work when the rains came. Stephens, a thorough man, also
asked if the works were strong enough for a rush of water, and Cooper was
convinced they were. Unfortunately, Stephens's suspicions were correct, and
all of issues he had noticed were indeed problems for the mill. When construction was complete in 1738, there was not enough water to float the logs,
so people hand-carried them to the mill. Then there was not enough water
to power the mill, so production stopped. Finally, in summer 1739 the creek
flooded and destroyed the expensive Trustee mill.[73]

Undeterred by the news the Trustees tried again. In March 1740 they informed Stephens to find a better location, a place that had "sufficient wa-

ter" and where timbers could be "floated down" to the works.[74] This appears
to be the point where the Trustees' project for the good of the whole colony became focused upon the Salzburgers. The group at Ebenezer, who already had two failed mills in the area, lobbied Stephens, Oglethorpe, and
the Trustees to have the new sawmill built at Abercorn. Since both the Old
Ebenezer Mill and Parker's Mill at Abercorn had been destroyed by flooding, it seemed obvious there was enough water. They reasoned that they just
needed better engineering to control the flow. They would reuse the iron
from Parker's mill and from the destroyed Trustees' mill. This Salzburger
proposal occurred at the same time that the Malcontents were beginning
to raise their dissatisfaction with Trustee policies. Stephens's reports on the
state of the colony had praised the Salzburgers as industrious, sober, and
hardworking. The combination of the two—complaining English settlers
and obedient German settlers—made it easy for the Trustees to decide to
place the new mill in control of the Salzburgers.

The Trustees at London ordered a new mill in March 1740, but the Salzburgers had already begun building before May 1740, surely before receiving word. They started with Oglethorpe's twelve-pound donation. Like with
other economic programs, Boltzius began the mill with this money and set
about working to get more. He encouraged the town to work on the mill,
with the hope of payment for their labors when more donations came in.

In late June 1740 work on the mill came to a stop as Kogler complained
about the wages for his work; he had stopped his farm labors to build the
mill so did he need the income.[75] Other workers similarly complained,
knowing that the price of labor in Georgia was higher than what they had
been promised. The problem seems to have been that Boltzius was building
the mill based on donations he had already received and on the hope of more
benefactions in the future. In short, he did not have the cash. Boltzius's response to the problem was to make the topic his theme in one of their prayer
meetings, thus linking the spiritual and the economic. He reminded them
that the money they were using was donated by German philanthropists and
urged the group to consider being similarly charitable with their labor. Further, the mill was for everyone's benefit, so all should contribute if possible.[76]
The argument that seemed to quell the discord was that he would keep track
of their time and pay them when he could, but not the exorbitant Georgia labor rates. The group returned to building the mill. This period of discord among the Salzburgers reveals how their community chose to deal with
the realities of the colony's economy. They knew labor was in short supply

and that they could demand higher wages; yet they ultimately chose to accept lower rates, paid at some unknown future date, for the good of all. This was the secret to the Salzburgers' success: charitable funding from a network of philanthropists, hard work, and free or low-cost communal labor on infrastructure projects. Fortunately, the Trustees decided their new mill project would be redirected to the Salzburgers' new mill project. They donated seventy-seven pounds, which combined with Oglethorpe's personal twelve-pound donation covered the eighty-nine-pound cost of construction.[77] The new mill was a success and by December 1740 made six bushels of flour overnight.[78]

The cost of flour came down for the Salzburgers, and the mill provided a means for the community to sell to the local market. In January 1741 the price of Abercorn mill district flour was six shillings per hundred pounds in Savannah, compared to the course rye flour sent from New York for eight shillings.[79] The mill was self-sustaining and provided an income to Kogler and the Ebenezer settlements.

The water ran quite high during the mill construction, which helped the carpenter Kogler to understand how to design a mill to withstand the floods. Or so they thought. The mill operated for three years, before it was destroyed in another flood in the spring of 1744.[80] Captain Joseph Avery, an English engineer appointed surveyor by the Trustees, proposed a new plan for a mill complex to Boltzius. He envisioned a new rice stamp as well as a sawmill, was certain that there would be enough water to sustain both, and promised that he could design a system to prevent flooding.[81] Avery told Boltzius it would be possible to operate the mill even with very low water.[82] Boltzius wrote to the Trustees, asking to use what could be salvaged from their destroyed mill at Old Ebenezer. Avery died before he could complete the new project, but he left solid plans that Kogler and others used to build it. The mill dam and millrace were already built, so this new mill complex was relatively quicker and less expensive to build than the first.[83]

The success of this third sawmill led Boltzius to think beyond simply supplying boards to the town. The sawmill was meeting its original goal of providing lumber to the residents at a modest price, but he began to write about sending lumber products to the Caribbean. Boltzius was thinking beyond his little community, beyond Georgia even, to engage in the Atlantic trade. Kogler thought he could do more, too. The region around Ebenezer had tall pine, cypress, and oak trees. He wanted to make furniture and other products from the mill and sell them within the colony. Boltzius was unsure because he thought the expense to move the trees to the mill made this "not a sound business proposition."[84] Although they do not appear to have sold furniture, the group did begin to ship cut boards throughout the colony.

The bigger dreams of Boltzius were partially fueled by the desires of the Trustees, as they wished for Georgia to participate in the West Indies lumber trade. In December 1745 Boltzius wrote enthusiastically to Francke in Halle, emphasizing the possibility of new income.[85] In February he wrote of an opportunity, brought to him by a man named Curtius, who said he was the son of a pastor from Württemberg. Curtius proposed that they produce boards for the West Indies and ship them through his cousin who lived in New York. Boltzius wrote to Francke seeking funds to help finance the project, hinting that perhaps the Augsburg banker Christian von Münch might have been willing.[86] Münch did lend Boltzius two hundred pounds for two years to finance the project.[87]

In June that same year prospects for a real economic benefit from the lumber trade seemed strong. Major Horton, the commanding officer at Fort Frederica, paid twenty-six pounds for some boards.[88] The money went to the mill fund, to pay for its upkeep and for Kogler's services. Boltzius began to encourage the people to make barrel staves and cypress shingles, as these could be sold in Savannah and to the West Indies.[89] The Trustees were interested too. As Trustee money had built the mill, they were quite keen to know the results. Boltzius reported that the new design, which featured two saws, could turn out more than a thousand feet of boards in one day.[90] The Trustees asked William Stephens to encourage the Salzburgers in the work, as it "may prove a very profitable Branch of Trade" to the colony if they could ship the boards to the "sugar colonies" in the Caribbean.[91]

Unfortunately, the grand schemes were short lived and came to a halt in August 1746 when Boltzius realized that Curtius was actually Kurtz and that he was "a liar and fraud."[92] Kurtz had insinuated himself into the community by saying he was religiously converted. Curtius is the Latinized form of his real surname Kurtz, and Latin names were supposed to be reserved for the clergy and aristocracy. By adopting this name he was projecting a status level to which he was not entitled. Kurtz was taken into people's homes, especially that of Salzburger Thomas Bichler. The scheme was relatively simple. Kurtz had the Salzburgers load up several wagonloads of lumber onto a boat in the Savannah River; they would be paid when he returned with either the proceeds of the sale to his cousin or goods brought from New York. They loaded the timber, yet he returned without any money or trade items. To satisfy their suspicions, Kurtz had Bichler and Pastor Lemke come with him to Charlestown, yet in that city he tried to get Lemke to authorize spending a hundred pounds on the pastor's credit. Lemke, finally, gave in to his suspicions and refused, but not before Kurtz had taken a load of Bichler's corn, charging transportation costs to Boltzius.

Although Boltzius was much more cautious about the possibilities of the Caribbean trade after this affair, the mill continued to benefit the community because the Trustees ordered boards for buildings in Savannah. Further, they still wanted to ship goods to the Caribbean, writing that they were "still attentive" to the idea and that the Salzburgers were the best option for bringing this to fruition.[93] To that end they ordered William Stephens to arrange for a landing spot on the Savannah wharves where Ebenezer lumber could be received. That is how it came about that when this third sawmill flooded, the Trustees funded a rebuild effort. Boltzius wrote in early 1750 that the sawmill greatly benefited the community, had provided good lumber for all of the colony, and still presented opportunities for a much broader Caribbean trade.[94] The German Pietists also contributed, paying the carpenters' wages so the mill could be completed more quickly.[95] This is the mill that was consecrated in 1751.

The 1751 Abercorn mill was the center of a robust industrial complex for the Salzburgers, which they now called the "mill district." Boltzius wrote a long journal entry, which he knew the German and English sponsors would all see, detailing the achievements in the region.[96] The mill dam now had several millraces powering a variety of machines. In addition to the gristmill and the sawmill, new resident Johann Paulitsch built a "new mechanism" that made it possible to make pearl barley, which the Salzburgers had wanted since arriving in America. The tanner, Neidlinger, built a workshop near the mill; he used tree bark to create the necessary lye and waterpower to pound the skins. The result was a much softer, higher-quality leather than could be had from Carolina, according to Boltzius, who may have been exaggerating a little for marketing. Further, Mrs. Kalcher established a tavern near the site, supplying beer and refreshments to all. Beyond simply subsidizing the cost of flour and lumber, the mills had become an important part of Ebenezer's economy.

In the spring of 1759 the new, robust complex and well-designed mill was again destroyed by flooding, with the building being under "very deep" water.[97] At the time the sawmill was working on boards for a new silk filature (factory), and that work came to a temporary halt. The mill dam began leaking in 1760, but as the whole complex was so critical to the community residents donated their labor and worked together to facilitate repairs.[98] Since the Trustees no longer controlled the colony, the royal governor, his assistants, the Assembly, and the Board of Trade and Plantations shifted the colony's focus to a variety of forest products, including naval stores (tar, pitch, and turpentine), barrel staves, oars, cypress shingles, and hoops (for barrels).[99] Finally, after years of effort, they had significant shipments to the Caribbean.

## The Allure of Silk

The official seal of the Georgia Trustees exhibited images of a worm, a mulberry leaf, and a cocoon and is just one indication of how important sericulture was to the new colony's founders. Silk has been called the "el Dorado" of North American colonies because the very notion of sericulture "lured the prudent and industrious" yet never seemed to fully succeed.[100] Silk dreams flourished from the first attempted British mainland colony at Roanoke. In 1588 Thomas Harriot, when describing the wonders and practical possibilities of an English colony in Virginia, included reports of silkworms "as bigge as our ordinary walnuttes," which led him to believe that silk will "no doubt . . . rise as great a profite in time to the Virginians."[101] It soon became clear these Virginia worms were the wrong sort and would never produce silk, yet the hope persisted. Silk schemes were launched and failed in Virginia, the Carolinas, and across the Mid-Atlantic throughout the seventeenth and eighteenth centuries. Although English colonizers overcame issues of finding the right worms and trees, the real problem was the lack of surplus labor in the colonies.[102] This did not deter the Georgia Trustees, whose faith in their plan led them to believe silk could succeed in the new colony.

From the beginning silk was promoted as an excellent product for Georgia and no other economic project received the same level of investment and commitment from the Trustees or later from the Royal Colony governors and British Board of Trade. By one estimate the Trustees spent over three thousand pounds in the early years of the colony alone, from 1734 to 1739.[103] Silk was always prominently listed among Georgia's possible products, and in 1741 the Trustees declared that "raw silk is the chief Article which the Trustees had, and have still in view."[104] At the founding of the colony Oglethorpe argued that the silk trade alone would support forty to fifty thousand people.[105] The Trustees believed the Salzburgers were ideal citizens for working in silk. Because the silk trade required skill, dedication, and intensive work, the Trustees felt the Ebenezer settlement would be ideal to carry out their plans. Their ideas were neatly summarized by Philip Bearcroft in his 1738 annual Trustees sermon when he proclaimed, "And now that we . . . [wish] to raise Silk in this Plantation, we are furnished with a fresh Supply of a very sober, industrious and religious Frame of Mind, that it looks as if Heaven . . . approveth."[106]

Sericulture had several properties that seemed to make it the ideal product for the colony. First, silk production could end Britain's dependence upon the Italians and other foreign merchants. The Trustees envisioned silk becoming a British export with which they could capture the revenue then flowing to the Italians and French merchants. In 1732 Oglethorpe estimated that Britain spent £300,000 on Italian silk and argued that Georgian silk could be produced at lower cost, undercutting European competitors.[107] More enticing than raw economic output was the notion that silk was inherently a morally good endeavor because it had been promoted by experts as ideal for small family production and was not a crop associated with enslaved African labor like sugar and rice. Further, sericulture could raise the productive capacity of the colony and empire, as the work could be done by the underutilized labor of women, children, and the aged. Thomas Boreman, an expert on silk referenced by the Trustees, reported that "one very great benefit [of silk cultivation]; that it employs a great Number of their industrious Poor; for not only Men, but Women, Children, and impotent Persons, may be of use in this Work."[108] The physical labor involved was "easy and pleasant, and performed in as delightful a Season [springtime] as any in the whole Year."[109]

Georgia's efforts at silk built on attempts by the South Carolina Lords Proprietor and later that colony's legislative Assembly and Board of Trade, which promoted the silk trade by offering production bounties and encouraging the planting of white mulberry trees, the vital food for the silkworms. One of South Carolina's founders was Anthony Ashley Cooper, the First Lord Shaftesbury; he is the namesake of the Ashley and Cooper rivers that flow into Charleston Bay and was the great-grandfather of the Fourth Lord Shaftesbury, a Georgia Trustee. The First Lord Shaftesbury sent his secretary John Locke to the silk-making region of Languedoc in France to spy sericulture practices, which resulted in a 1679 tract for Carolina that described the silk process.[110] That same year the Lords Proprietor of Carolina recruited Huguenot settlers who they believed had the necessary silk skills.[111] As hoped, this group spread enthusiasm for silk production among the Carolina planter elite.

Carolinians set out to prove that silk was a product that enslaved Africans could produce. Sericulture required a fine hand and delicate skill, particularly in unwinding the cocoon to reel the silk thread. Thus many argued that unskilled Africans could not perform the work. Yet in part due to incentives from the Lords Proprietor, Carolinians planted mulberry trees and set about producing silk using enslaved labor. In the early eighteenth century adventurers and planters alike found that silk was an ideal secondary product—a way to keep workers busy outside of the rice and tobacco crops, showing that sericulture was "compatible with slave labor and plantation production."[112]

The Georgia Trustees took a different approach. Although they certainly valued the economic potential of silk, the appeal was in their belief that sericulture was well suited to small family farms. A 1741 Trustees report boasted that silk and wine "do not require the Labour of Negroes," while other colonies that planted sugar, rice, and tobacco made slavery almost essential.[113] The Trustees were so committed to a society without slaves that they preferred to accept a lower economic production than in South Carolina, which, they acknowledged, having enslaved workers, "will soon be able to raise much more Silk" than Georgia.[114] Georgia's economic success mattered, but more important was that the colony's output proved sufficient for its settlers to "find a livelihood there."[115] Silk answered the call because people who were not considered economically productive members of society—the aged, women, and children—could reap the moral benefits of performing work. The Trustees followed the common belief that "Raw Silk requires very little Labour . . . [by] those chiefly who are of little Use in other Products, viz. Women and Children."[116]

The Trustees approached the project using the best current knowledge to help them establish sericulture in Georgia. Trustee the Fourth Lord Shaftesbury arranged for Locke's 1679 manuscript on silk to be printed in London and distributed to the British American colonies.[117] The Trustees also consulted experts, such as Thomas Lambe, the man who, in a bit of industrial spying, had copied a Piedmont "silk engine," a factory powering several machines with one water wheel. He brought it to England, for which he received a £14,000 award from Parliament.[118] Acknowledged in England as an expert, Lambe wrote a glowing letter predicting silk success in Georgia, based largely on assumptions about the colony being in the "proper Climate," which was thought to be like that of silk-producing regions at similar latitudes in the Mediterranean and China.[119]

In addition, the Trustees gathered climate and geographic reports from the American South. Recall that Trustees Lord Egmont and Hans Sloane had both sponsored Mark Catesby's naturalist voyage to Carolina in 1722 and had copies of his illustrations of America flora and fauna.[120] Significantly, one of Catesby's published drawings is of a snake wrapped around the branches of a naturally growing mulberry tree, with a cluster of ripe red fruit.[121] This was the American red mulberry, and its abundance in the Low-country seemed to promise an ideal climate for silkworms. Unfortunately, the Trustees and Georgians later learned this was not the correct tree, and it would be necessary to import white mulberry plants. Equally encouraging at the beginning and equally misinformed about Georgia was a correspon-dence between colonist William Byrd and Trustees such as Lord Egmont and Sir Hans Sloane, who enthused about the opportunities for silk in Vir-ginia and North Carolina.[122] In their enthusiasm for the possibilities of silk, both men seemed to ignore that Byrd's experience on the border of Virginia and North Carolina occurred over three hundred fifty miles north of Savan-nah and that there might be differences in soil, climate, and success.

Particularly influential with the Trustees and supporters of the Geor-gia project was a 1732 report from Jean-Pierre de Purry, a Swiss Protestant from Neuchâtel and founder of Purrysburg, South Carolina. Purry argued that the Savannah River was situated at the perfect latitude for humans and that a settlement there would produce a wealth of Mediterranean and Asian goods, such as wine, olives, and silk.[123] Purry had actually been to the Savan-nah River area as part of his preparations to build a town there, which gave his report a greater degree of certitude. James Oglethorpe was so impressed with the proposal that he gave Purry two hundred pounds toward his proj-ect.[124] Later, Oglethorpe quoted Purry as an expert source, providing evi-dence for the sure success of silk in Georgia.[125] When Purry established the town of Purrysburg he made sure to recruit some Piedmont Waldensians who were skilled in sericulture; these colonists were later crucial in helping the Salzburgers learn the craft of silk reeling.

The long-held dreams of British colonizers combined with expert opin-ions to fuel the Trustees' enthusiasm for silk. Included in the first set of rules for people who wished to be sent to Georgia was the stipulation that each person had to plant mulberry trees on part of their fifty-acre allotment; by the early 1740s the requirement was to plant one hundred mulberry trees for every ten acres of land.[126] Paul Amatis, an Italian silk maker, and his brother Nicholas (sometimes rendered Nicola) were sent by the Trustees in 1733 with some of the colony's first settlers to teach inhabitants proper methods and to oversee production.[127] Part of their contract with the Trustees stipulated that they would bring "2 Men and 4 Women who understand the whole of the Silk Business," with the Trustees paying ten pounds per person in wages, plus ten pounds more for tools and materials.[128] True to their word, the

Amatis brothers brought a "stocking maker" who could "draw & reel Silk," a "Silk Throwster" and his two apprentices, as well as Nicholas's indentured servant Giacomo Camosso and wife Maria Giovanna (often anglicized to "Camuse" in Georgia records) "both Winderes of Silks," along with their three sons.[129] Arriving in 1733, Paul Amatis went about planting and tending a stock of mulberry trees in the Trustees' garden to serve as a nursery for the colony. Settlers were given free trees to plant, and the first Salzburgers received theirs in early 1736, along with a promise that Maria Camosso would teach the trade to two Ebenezer women.[130]

Members of the German Pietist network in Europe were also enthusiastic about the possibilities of silk. Like the Trustees, they saw value in employing people who normally were not able to contribute economically to the community. It helped that Christian von Münch, one of the Salzburgers' chief supporters, had experimented with producing silk on his lands in southern Germany. In 1729 Münch purchased two villages northwest of Augsburg, including the former Fugger castle Ayestatt. As part of an expansion and reconstruction of the castle, he planted mulberry trees, built a filature (a silk factory), and imported skilled Italian silk workers.[131]

Although it took a few years to take hold, sericulture also appealed to Boltzius for reasons similar to the Trustees; he saw an opportunity to create a useful economic program that would enable women, children, and the elderly to contribute to the community. He set about persuading Salzburgers to plant mulberry trees and to participate in the trade. Boltzius's wife Gertraut Kroehr, a Salzburger from the Pongau region whom he married in Georgia about 1735, set the example as one of the leaders of the Ebenezer silk business.[132]

Producing silk required specialized training and demanded intensive focus during the spring. According to Thomas Boreman's manual, which was dedicated to the Trustees and copies of which were sent to Georgia, one started the work just as the mulberry tree was beginning to blossom. That was the proper time to take dormant worm eggs, called the seed, and place them in a linen pouch or warm box lined with paper to nurture them. Boreman recommended putting the linen bags of eggs inside one's clothing, near one's body, to keep them warm, until they hatched, which could be anywhere from three to six days later.[133] In his 1679 tract John Locke had reported this was the method the French used. Once the eggs hatched, the worms were placed in paper-lined boxes on shelves, which could be stacked several feet high and had to be kept in a warm, dry, protected, and airy location. Young mulberry leaves were laid on top of the worms for them to eat.

In Ebenezer picking the leaves was often a job for children, who had to be trained how to pick the young, tender leaves and limbs without destroying the tree. At this stage fresh leaves needed to be placed in the worm boxes every two hours. This is why Boreman's first word of caution was to be certain that there were enough leaves as the "worms produced from an Ounce of Seed, eat, in their whole time of Feeding, from two to three hundred Pound weight of Mulberry-leaves."[134] The leaves had to be kept dry and were best if gathered no more than four or five hours before feeding, although it was possible to use leaves picked up to two or three days earlier. Despite all the talk about easy work for the weakest in the community, it is clear that raising silk was a demanding, labor-intensive, round-the-clock project with the greatest demands coming during the spring planting season.

The silkworms changed skins four times before spinning a cocoon, and at each stage, which was called their "sickness," it was important to completely clean their boxes (without touching the worms) and to closely adjust the amount of leaves they were fed. About ten days after the fourth stage the worms spun their cocoon, and these were collected about fourteen days after that. Part of the skill in sericulture was learning when the cocoons were at their perfect, ripe stage, which was marked by the color and clarity of the ball as well as by the color of the worm inside. If the worker waited too long the worm would have already begun to change into a moth and may have destroyed the ball.[135]

To wind the cocoon balls into silk threads was an especially delicate task that took expert training and much practice and could not be taught from a text, but only by hands-on instruction.[136] The cocoons were first placed near an oven to kill the worm, then in a copper bowl full of hot water. The worker, who was nearly always a woman, next stirred gently to separate the strands. The most difficult task was gathering the threads and reeling them into a fine string of consistent weight with an even texture. A skilled worker, who had picked her cocoons at the proper time, could turn eight pounds of balls into one pound of silk thread. The whole process, beginning with the eggs in early spring until the reeling of fine thread, demanded intensive labor for two to three months.

The chief difficulty with silk production in America was that it depended upon a society where labor was cheap and available, as in portions of Britain, Italy, and France. The main argument in support of sericulture was that underutilized labor could help produce the cocoons. However, the colonies had the opposite problem: labor was in short supply and very expensive. When they first arrived the Salzburgers were so busy trying to create stable plantations that would feed their families that they were very reluctant to use family labor to tend silkworms. Children and wives were busy preparing fields and helping to plant at the same time the silkworms demanded attention. The result was the project languished in Ebenezer until the early 1740s, when the community had greater food security and the Trustees implemented bounties for cocoons. Despite the labor shortage, Oglethorpe convinced Boltzius to persist, and the pastor eventually became a strong advocate for sericulture in Georgia. He not only encouraged the Salzburgers but also lobbied the Trustees, and their colonial representatives, for them to offer price supports and bounties to develop the trade.

The process began in Ebenezer by planting white mulberry trees that had been given to them by the Trustees. Most of these trees were planted in the town rather than on the forty-eight-acre plantations simply because the larger acreage was slow to be surveyed and prepared for farming. Until about 1740 most of the Salzburgers lived in Ebenezer and traveled to their plantation to work. As a result, the town became heavily populated with the Trustees' free white mulberry trees. Salzburgers planted trees in their kitchen gardens, in the poultry yards near the vegetables, and along fences and streets as well as in the town squares reserved for public buildings such as the church and the school. Boltzius's official diaries mention very little about these trees in the 1730s, except when noting their potential value as food.[137] Apparently, in the early years the trees frequently did not bear much fruit, as Boltzius recorded that the mulberry's weakness as a food source was another reason the Salzburgers did not attend to the silk business.[138]

In 1740 James Oglethorpe visited with Boltzius and encouraged the Salzburgers to support sericulture. He again promised that Maria Camosso would come teach them how to "earn a good deal of money without difficulty."[139] At the same time Oglethorpe also sent along a copy of Boreman's silk-raising guide, which Boltzius noted was in English and which he did not yet have the "courage" to read. In late 1741 Boltzius, under Oglethorpe's direction, used five pounds donated to the Salzburgers to purchase twelve hundred mulberry trees, enough for twenty-two trees per family.[140]

Despite slow beginnings to sericulture, this last encouragement by Oglethorpe came to the Salzburgers at a time when they were able to take it on. The community's effort was centered around the orphanage, which Ruprecht and Margaret Kalcher had been hired by the community to run. At the urging of Boltzius the Kalchers began experimenting in sericulture in 1740. Frau Kalcher learned the craft from French-speaking Swiss Protestants who had settled in Purrysburg, possibly from John Lewis Poyas and his wife Susanne, who came with Purry in 1733 and taught sericulture to others in the colonies.[141] Two girls from the orphanage were assigned to pick the fresh mulberry leaves and to feed the worms. The results were modest but encouraging, as the orphanage produced hundreds of cocoons, with two hundred balls equaling one pound and worth four shillings in Savannah.[142] No one in Ebenezer was yet skilled enough to reel the silk into threads, but the Trustees ensured there was a market in Savannah for the cocoons, which gave a little extra income to the poor Kalchers. This encouraged Kalcher to propagate mulberry trees extensively on the orphanage property, which remained the focus of Ebenezer's silk industry. In 1741 two orphan girls earned £3.8.0 by selling seventeen pounds of silk in Savannah.[143] It is worth noting that the schoolteacher Ortmann's annual salary in 1745 (just a few years) later was £12, indicating the significance of the £3 silk earnings.[144]

About the same time as the Kalchers and the orphans began working in silk, Gertraut Boltzius and her sister, Catharina Gronau, also learned the art of sericulture. Catharina had married Boltzius's catechist Israel Christian Gronau, who died in 1745; she then married his replacement, Hermann Lemke. As wives of clergymen, the two sisters lived in the town of Ebenezer and had access to all the mulberry trees that had been planted and abandoned by Salzburgers who moved to their plantations. Clergymen's wives also needed money, as Boltzius's fifty-pound annual salary was always stretched thin since he often invested personal funds in community projects, such as the mills. The two women most likely initially learned the trade from the Purrysburgers and from Mrs. Camosso, although Boltzius complained that Camosso would only let students observe and not practice hands-on.

By 1744 the orphanage had outlived its purpose. The labor shortage in Georgia meant that Salzburgers preferred to take in orphans and widows on their plantations, where they could help as field workers and house servants. Boltzius, who had modeled the orphanage on Francke's beloved institution in Halle, was heartbroken but also saw an opportunity. He kept the Kalchers, had large racks built in two main rooms and the attic of the orphanage building, added some ventilation, and turned it into a facility for growing silkworms.[145] The orphanage was also where visitors stayed when they came to Ebenezer. It must have been quite an experience for springtime visitors to stay with warmed, growing silkworms in the building.

Boltzius and his wife experimented with production, so that in 1747 they began keeping worms at various stages of development to generate multiple cocoon crops in one year.[146] The church's glebe lands, which had not been patented until the late 1740s and were underutilized due to a lack of labor, were planted with four thousand mulberry trees to support the effort. About this time the sisters learned how to reel, which yielded a more valuable crop than just the cocoons. Gertraut Boltzius supervised the silk reeling for all of Ebenezer, which took place in the pastor's kitchen, a separate building behind their main house.[147] There was enough interest in silk production that Boltzius worried some experts might try to dominate the trade. So in May 1751 he arranged to send five apprentices to Savannah to be taught by the Trustees' experts.[148] As a result of the efforts of sisters Gertraut Boltzius and Catharina Lemke, Ebenezer's silk industry was centered on the orphanage and church properties until the American Revolutionary War. One small measure of the investment in sericulture comes from Boltzius's probate inventory. When he died in 1765 he owned 450 board feet of "silk worm shelves."[149]

Boltzius's commitment to silk production and the encouraging results by the sisters gradually brought more of the Salzburgers into the trade. Production grew so that in the spring of 1751 nearly all women in the Ebenezer community participated in the silk trade. In April 1760 all three schools in the town and surrounding settlements closed for two weeks so that the children could work the silk.[150] And they began to have some significant results. Although the data are incomplete, table 7.1 shows Ebenezer's rapid growth in silk production.

The community experienced this rapid growth in production during the three years from 1747 to 1750, and Ebenezer was regularly producing more than half the silk coming from Georgia. The 1759 earnings resulted in some Salzburger families receiving an extra ten to thirty pounds, which would be a significant contribution to the annual income, including for the Boltzius family. In a diary entry in April 1751 Boltzius expressed gratitude for the silk production, nothing that his salary from the SPCK was "not adequate for our meager support."[151]

The income from sericulture was a significant economic endeavor for the Salzburgers, and it is noteworthy that women were the primary producers. Both Renate Wilson and George Fenwick Jones argue that Gertraut Boltzius was actually running a *Verlag*, a German-style business that provided supplies to cottage industry workers and then acted as a wholesaler or distributor of the finished product.[152] Whether or not this is an accurate understanding of Gertraut's role, it is clear that she was a leader in the community and that silk production gave Salzburger women greater economic clout. It also provided one of the few opportunities for Ebenezer's women to interact with non-German settlers. For example, in March 1744 two Salzburger

TABLE 7.1. Ebenezer Silk Production by Year

| Year | Cocoons (lbs.) | Reeled (lbs.) | Value |
|------|----------------|---------------|-------|
| 1747 | 366 | | |
| 1748 | 437 | | |
| 1749 | 700 | | |
| 1751 | 1,500 | 100 | £99 |
| 1754 | 2,000 | | £200 |
| 1759 | 4,000 | | £650 |
| 1763 | 6,350 | | |
| 1771 | 6,570 | 438 | |

Sources: Compiled from *Letters*, 2:529; TNA CO 5/642/125; Renate Wilson, "Halle and Ebenezer."

women, including Anna Magdalena Ott, who spoke English "quite well," went to Savannah to learn reeling.[153] Frau Ott's having learned English indicates a level of interaction with the community far beyond the cloistered towns that are considered typical of German settlements in America.

Demand for skilled reelers in Savannah rose, and in 1751 seven Salzburger women went there to live for several weeks to work.[154] The group included three reelers and four apprentices. The reelers were paid one shilling six pence per day plus provisions, but the apprentices were initially offered six pence per day, a sum they refused. James Habersham, who was appointed to help manage the silk business, worked with the Trustees' silk superintendent Pickering Robinson to raise the offer to eight pence, and again the three women refused, aware that their skill was worth much more. Finally, they negotiated to receive one shilling per day's work, which was equal to twelve pence, or double the initial offer.[155] Habersham, who was generally a friend to the Salzburgers, was a little annoyed, but this small case demonstrates that the Salzburger women were capable of functioning in the world of English colonial business.

The silk enterprise in Ebenezer, which began about 1740 and lasted until the American Revolution, is a good example of the way Boltzius and the Salzburgers seized upon the Trustees' plans and used them for their own betterment. He fully accepted the Trustee idea that silk was perfect for the underemployed. For example, he was pleased to report that Georg Brückner and his wife, although suffering from "various physical afflictions" for several years, could contribute to the overall good of the community because they had wisely planted mulberry trees in their garden. "Making silk is an easy and pleasant work for them."[156] In another instance the pastor recorded in the official diary that he was pleased to see a young girl in town "carrying a little box" with twelve pounds of silk she had made.[157] Just as had been promised for over a hundred years in marketing tracts, young girls, the aged, and the infirm were able to produce silk cocoons and reap the benefits of their own labor.

As in the case of cattle and lumber, Boltzius used philanthropic supporters to fund the silk endeavor, and he lobbied them to influence government policies. His efforts made Ebenezer a successful silk producer, but it brought him into conflict and competition with English neighbors in Savannah.

Beginning in the early 1740s, after Kalcher's modest success at the orphanage, Boltzius began actively encouraging the Salzburgers to plant more mulberry trees on their forty-eight-acre plantations. In addition to the opportunity to earn some money, Boltzius emphasized that raising silk would "fulfill the wishes and intentions of the Lord Trustees."[158] Although his nature was to give deference to authority, Boltzius also understood it was important to keep their philanthropic supporters satisfied with the Salzburgers' efforts in Georgia. This respect and obedience to the Trustees' plan paid results a few months later when, in July 1741, Oglethorpe advanced the community a hundred-pound interest-free loan to build a mill, buy horses and cattle, and help in the "raising of silk by the Salzburgers."[159]

Oglethorpe's loan was the result of Boltzius's letter-writing campaign to garner greater Trustee investment in Ebenezer. Pleased with this, Boltzius maintained an active correspondence with the British and German philanthropists, asking for tools, supplies, and funds to expand the business. Really, this was a continuation of his efforts from the 1730s, when he wrote asking for food, clothing, shoes, and books. The difference was that now he was asking for resources to bring about greater long-term stability rather than just fulfill basic necessities. The silk work depended upon charitable donations used for capital investments in the industry and serves as an example of the ways Boltzius used philanthropy to create communal economic programs.

In the early years of production Boltzius requested, and received, the tools and supplies necessary to expand. He wanted to develop Ebenezer's capabilities beyond simply supplying the cocoons and move the community into the more lucrative task of reeling. In 1747 the rate for reeled silk was two pounds per pound, compared to the two shillings per pound for cocoons. There are twenty shillings to a pound, meaning the price for a pound of cocoons was just 5 percent that of the price of reeled silk threads. Eight pounds of cocoons, which is enough to yield about one pound of reeled thread, would have paid sixteen shillings, still just 40 percent of the value of the reeled silk.

To facilitate an entry to the reeling business, Boltzius sent a sample of reeled Ebenezer silk to London for inspection, asking for approval and for aid. The Trustees, who were actively encouraging silk production in the colony, approved of the scheme and sent reeling machines and copper boiling vats to Ebenezer in 1748.[160] German Pietist donations paid for the restructuring of the orphanage into a silk house and financed locally produced wooden reelers and worm covers. Christian von Münch personally paid for and sent the necessary copper bowls and silk winding cards.

Boltzius lobbied the Trustees and the German philanthropists to continue to invest in Ebenezer silk. In the late 1740s he sent at least three shipments of silkworm eggs ("seeds") to Halle to aid them in developing a silk trade under the auspices of Prussian King Frederick II, who promoted sericulture as part of his plans to modernize his eastern territories.[161] Boltzius was not simply aiding the Prussian king who controlled Halle's territory; a majority of the original Salzburger exiles had moved to Prussian territories in modern-day Poland. Seeing economic development as part of his ministering duties, Boltzius pushed to have a full silk factory, called a filature, placed in Ebenezer and garnered donations from Christian von Münch in Augsburg and other Germans as well as from the Trustees. A filature would help the Salzburgers keep the more lucrative part of the business, the reeling, in their control, rather than merely taking cocoons to Savannah. Finally, after five years of letters to the Trustees, in July 1752 the filature was complete, at a cost of one hundred pounds. Built on a town lot across from the parsonage, the two-story building was over 1,850 square feet, a rather large building in the colonial backcountry.[162] Rather than have Ebenezer residents jointly own or invest in the filature, this building brought jobs to the town. Using money donated by the Trustees, Boltzius hired Salzburger carpenters to build the filature, done mostly by Stephen Rottenberger, Georg Koegler, and Rupert Schrempff. After completion, the factory was available to all who wished to participate in the silk trade, just as the converted orphanage had been earlier.

A significant reason for the Salzburgers' focus on sericulture was the price supports and bounties offered by the Trustees and, later, by the British government through the Board of Trade and Plantations. Throughout the 1740s the Trustees continued to emphasize silk as a primary product for Georgia and offered bounties for raising the cocoons as well as for learning how to reel. In 1750 alone the Trustees paid two Salzburger women a bounty of fourteen pounds each to teach reeling and one pound each to fourteen apprentice reelers in Ebenezer. On top of that they awarded two pounds to ten families each for building cocoon storage huts and promised thirty shillings for each silk-winding machine they built.[163] This represented a significant influx of capital into the community, and Boltzius lobbied the governments in Savannah and in London to maintain, or increase, these supports.

In 1747 Boltzius had heard rumors that the Trustees were reducing their support for the colony overall, including cutting bounties and salaries for silk manufacturing experts in Savannah. He quickly wrote to his supporter, court chaplain Friedrich Michael Ziegenhagen, to express his grave concern and to emphasize the impact such a decision would have upon the Salzburgers.[164] It seems clear that Boltzius hoped Ziegenhagen's connections to the king, the Privy Council, and the Trustees would help protect the bounties. The Trustees were under financial stress, having lost battles in Parliament against the Malcontents. Finally, in 1749 silk bounties were lowered, causing hardship to the Salzburgers who were now heavily vested in sericulture. Boltzius reported this to his German supporters, aware that news would likely filter to England through Ziegenhagen.[165] He wrote to Francke that although "silk making is not hard, but to our dear residents everything comes hard," and they still desperately needed support from Germany and England and warned that silk production in Ebenezer could come to an end.[166] The Trustees extended bounties for one year on cocoons and reeled silk for the 1750 crop, although we do not know if this was due to Boltzius's complaints or the accumulated complaints of the Salzburgers and others in the colony.[167]

Yet another issue with pricing arose when the Trustees offered variable prices for cocoons based upon the quality of the balls. They ordered payments based on three different qualities: the "superfine," "second best," and "worst sort."[168] The practice began in 1749 and was not well received by the Salzburgers. In April 1751 Pickering Robinson reported to James Habersham that the people in Ebenezer were "entirely averse to having their cocoons assorted, as the Trustee directed."[169] The issue seems to have been that the Ebenezer settlers, rather than act as individual agents, pooled their results and divided earnings among themselves. Once the cocoons were pooled it was impossible to determine who had grown which of the three grades. Of course this could have been easily resolved by not pooling the cocoons, but the Salzburgers, probably under the direction of Gertraut Boltzius and her sister, refused to do so. Their communal approach, unique to Georgia, meant that all benefited because that year Robinson agreed to pay the first-quality rate for all Salzburger cocoons.[170] Later that month Habersham reported that the people at Ebenezer were "enraged" at the notion of sorting cocoons, and he worked to find more money to pay the Salzburger women the same flat rate for all of their production.[171] Boltzius again registered his discontent over the new policy with his German sponsors, but this was a time of transition for the Trustees, as they were in the process of relinquishing their charter back to the Crown.

After the Trustees ceded control to the Crown, the Board of Trade and Plantations continued to support silk production, and Boltzius lobbied them for their support of Ebenezer as he had the Trustees. In 1753 the Board of Trade sent Robinson's replacement, Joseph Ottolenghe, to supervise Georgia silk manufacturing. Ottolenghe recommended, and the Board agreed, to consolidate silk reeling in the town of Savannah, which meant that beginning in 1754 the Salzburgers were not allowed to reel. This was a problem for the Ebenezer settlement because it meant ceding the most profitable part of the business. Boltzius responded by asking to meet with the new governor, John Reynolds. In late 1754 Reynolds visited Ebenezer, where, it is assumed, Boltzius made his case. Reynolds left with a sample of Salzburger silk that he forwarded to the Board of Trade along with his consent that they should be allowed to wind silk.[172] This appeal from the governor apparently did not succeed because as late as 1761 Boltzius wrote to Samuel Urlsperger that he had worked with Reynolds and his successor Henry Ellis to change the policy.[173] He also turned to his supporters in Germany, hoping they would apply pressure to change the official policy. Although he did not prevail Boltzius continued to press the case for at least ten years. The debate over the right to reel silk thread at Ebenezer became moot after 1769, when a hard frost destroyed many mulberry trees throughout Georgia. By August 1770 Ottolenghe had left the colony to teach the art of silk in Philadelphia, and most of the Georgia colonists abandoned the trade in favor of rice plantations using enslaved laborers.[174] Boltzius had died in 1765 and Gertraut in 1766, which left Ebenezer without the leadership needed to rally the community after the frost. The Board of Trade ceased all bounties and incentives. However, the Salzburgers persevered and continued to be nearly the sole supplier of Georgia silk from 1770 until the outbreak of war. Johann Caspar Wertsch, a prosperous Salzburger, continued silk production on his plantation into the 1770s; in 1772 he reported that he sent 485 pounds of silk to London.[175] Although Wertsch was economically successful on his plantation, he held to the idea that sericulture was more important as a morally good activity, as he asked James Habersham to help find donations of supplies for helping the poor in the Salzburger settlements.

Boltzius's success at garnering charitable donations from England and

Germany as well as his persistent manner of lobbying to continue price supports and to change policy led to clashes with the English residents at Savannah. The financial and material aid from the German Pietist network was a particular sore spot for the English settlers, who felt the Salzburgers had been given great advantages by the philanthropists. The English had a good point. Though they had received sericulture supplies from the Trustees and had the benefit of a filature in Savannah, the Salzburgers received extra aid from the Germans in the form of supplies and funding.

The dispute over reeling the silk in Savannah instead of Ebenezer was particularly sharp because it represented a loss of income for the Salzburgers. It was also a means for Savannah merchants to exercise control over the trade. Boltzius's appeals to the Board and the Trustees framed the English merchants in town as focused on profit and driven by greed, while he described the Salzburgers' interest in silk as a means to aid the widowed, orphaned, and poor.[176] Neither view was completely true, although Boltzius may have sincerely believed them. One of the Savannah merchants who controlled the silk trade was James Habersham, who Boltzius acknowledged was a friend to the Salzburgers and had helped them get higher wages for their reeling work.

From the perspective of London the Georgian silk trade was never as significant as the Trustees had hoped. It certainly never employed the forty to fifty thousand workers they had dreamed of in 1732. However, from the point of the view of the Salzburgers sericulture was a significant economic activity. They, or at least Boltzius, agreed with the Trustees that silk production could be a morally good economic activity, as silk not only brought much-needed hard currency into the community but also employed the aged, infirm, and orphaned. Although probably not a goal of either the Trustees or Boltzius, women in Ebenezer gained some economic clout and were pulled into the broader colonial economy through their work in silk.

In 1762, almost thirty years after arriving in Georgia and more than twenty years after Ruprecht Kalcher had made his first successful experiments in silk at the orphanage building, Boltzius proudly looked back on their accomplishments. He was pleased to report that the Salzburgers "eat their bread by the sweat of their brow, and they are well satisfied with the necessities . . . through farming, cattle rearing, and the cultivation of silk."[177] This was the very definition of a successful venture for Boltzius, the German Pietists, and the Trustees.

Although it was critical that Ebenezer, and Georgia as a whole, have a self-sustaining economy, the goal for the Trustees and for Boltzius was always to do so within the bounds of creating a morally good society. It was not enough that the Trustees banned slavery; the settlers also needed to find products for the broader market using their own labor. The Salzburgers experimented with and found some success by pursuing a variety of projects, including cattle, wood, and silk, which enabled them to do more than mere subsistence farming and to participate in the Lowcountry provisioning market. Indeed, Boltzius lamented that subsistence farming was not sufficient to sustain their community, writing in 1751 that the land around Ebenezer was "not so convenient for agriculture as for cattle raising, silkculture," and forest products.[178] The Salzburgers built these industries by working communally, such as building the mills and silk filature and hiring a cattle herder, while Boltzius emphasized that these economic projects would facilitate a better quality of life for all and provide for the development of private property. It worked because the Trustees' economic plans fit well with the Francke Foundations' model of business for the sake of the soul. Boltzius believed his position as minister to the Salzburgers necessitated his active participation in economic projects. Strictly speaking, he had no authority over civil affairs, yet he functioned as the town's de facto mayor, promoter, and, for a time, judge. Neither he nor the original Salzburgers saw borders between religious and economic life, and they mostly followed his lead.

The Trustees used any economic success by the Ebenezer settlement as evidence that the original Georgia plan was viable. The Salzburgers did not need enslaved workers to sustain themselves, the argument went, so the Malcontents were simply lazy. The Trustees never seemed to acknowledge, or even to realize, that a significant reason for the Germans' success was the extra support they received from the SPCK and Pietist philanthropists. Preferring to believe their own narrative, the Trustees labeled the Malcontents who wanted slavery as morally lazy. Naturally, this line of argumentation did not help foster strong English-German relations in Georgia. Boltzius preferred it that way and counseled the Salzburgers to remain distant from their neighbors.

# CHAPTER 8

# Neighbors

As the Salzburger settlements worked to be economically self-sustaining and socially cohesive within the community, in fact they were also an important part of the broader Lowcountry society. The Germans had to travel to Savannah and Charleston for supplies and to market their products. We have already seen that Salzburger women traveled and worked in Savannah for the silk trade. Trips to Savannah, the center of the colony's government, were important for matters of justice such as serving on juries. News and broader geopolitics also affected Ebenezer, as the community braced in the aftermath of the 1739 Stono Slave Rebellion in South Carolina. As a node in the Halle Pietist mission network, Ebenezer's pastors had two missions: the first was to minister to the Salzburgers, and the second was to spread Christianity, which necessitated interacting with the local Muskogee, Yuchi, and Yamacraw people as well as other European settlers. All these forces pulled pastors Boltzius, Gronau, Lemke, and the Salzburgers into the broader colonial society.

## Native Americans and the Salzburgers

Just three days after arriving in Savannah and before the Salzburgers even had a place to live, Trustee James Oglethorpe encouraged Reverend Boltzius and Catechist Gronau to learn the local people's language and to teach them the Christian gospel.[1] As was true of nearly all British colonial projects, the

Trustees had advertised that one benefit of establishing Georgia was that it would "contribute greatly towards the Conversion of the Indians."[2]

The two pastors were excited by the possibility of spreading the faith and had also been asked to carry out this mission by their religious sponsors, the SPCK and the Halle Pietists. The SPCK had established a sister organization, the Society for the Propagation of the Gospel in Foreign Parts (SPG), for the purpose of missionary work throughout the British Empire. In addition, since 1705 the SPCK had an ecumenical partnership with the Francke Foundations in sponsoring a Lutheran mission in Danish Tranquebar (now Tharangambadi, India). The Francke Foundations considered Georgia one of their missions and categorized all their records and copies of communications as such; that is, the Georgia Salzburgers were one node on a worldwide network of Pietist missions intended to spread the Lutheran Christian gospel.

Among the first activities undertaken by the Salzburgers when they arrived in Savannah was to gather together in a crudely constructed church, read a New Testament verse, and thank God for having the gospel, "since we have seen among the Indians what a great pity it is not to have it."[3] They had just seen their first Indians, probably Yamacraws, and it moved them to sorrow. A few weeks later, Boltzius wrote back to Germany that he and Gronau "desire[d] that we might carry [the Indians] into His bosom" and prayed that God would help them "overcome all the difficulties in learning the Indian language."[4] Boltzius approached this task with enthusiasm, carefully trying to learn the language even before the Salzburgers had reached Ebenezer. While the group waited at Abercorn to complete their move up to Ebenezer for the first time, Boltzius met some local Native Americans. The Salzburgers showed the Indians objects and tried to learn the word for each item.[5] This may have been a useful way to begin to communicate; unfortunately, Boltzius seems not to have realized that he was operating on the borders between the Yamacraw, who lived to the south and who spoke a Muskogee language, and the Yuchi to the north, who spoke another language entirely.[6] At this time Boltzius seemed unaware of these differences, and naturally he would have had difficulty learning the names of items if he received different information depending upon which group of people he asked.

Following instructions from Halle and the SPCK, Boltzius initially wanted to be on good terms with his Indian neighbors, but less than four years later he described them as troublesome pests who, when they came to Ebenezer, were drunk. He wrote that the only English words they knew were "horrible curses, swearing and slanders."[7] By the late 1730s and early 1740s the Salzburgers were not frequently in contact with the Indians, and they preferred it that way. Boltzius, like many Englishmen who came to the American colonies, had given up on his goal to convert the Indians. He believed the poor example of English settlers and traders made it difficult to proselytize the Indian community, but he was also hampered by having only infrequent interactions with local Yuchi and Yamacraw people.

Of course the local Indians tribes had a much deeper history with the Europeans than Boltzius realized. Their first contacts had been in the sixteenth century, when they met Spaniards as De Soto's expedition traveled through the heart of what became Georgia, South Carolina, Tennessee, and Alabama. In the seventeenth century, after Europeans had a permanent presence in the area, the Indians suffered from the Great Southeastern Smallpox Epidemic, which spread from the Atlantic to the Mississippi River and reduced the population by 90 percent in some places.[8] The spread of disease and death led to reconfigurations, new tribal associations, and jostling for power and control among the surviving Native American populations.

The arrival of the British in mainland North America created significant challenges for the local people. In the early eighteenth century South Carolinians made a concerted effort to enslave Indians, with armies assembled in 1706, 1708, and 1711 for the express purpose of capturing Native Americans from deep in the southern interior, some as far away as Mobile.[9] Allan Gallay estimates that between four and ten thousand Muskogee, Cherokee, Savannah, and other Indians from the Lowcountry were enslaved.[10] If we include all southeastern Indians, such as the Choctaw, Tuscarora, Arkansas, and Westo, the number climbs to twenty-four to fifty-one thousand individuals taken. Most were sent to the West Indies.

The result of these interactions between British colonizers and Native American tribes has been effectively described as a "shatter zone": a place where the effects of war and disease left tribes and Indian towns depopulated, on the move, and at war.[11] These stresses on the Indian population, from disease, European colonization, and the Euro-American slave trade, came to a head in South Carolina with the Yamasee War of 1715–1717. The Yamasee, who lived in the Savannah River region, attacked South Carolinians in April 1715, and the war spread throughout the Southeast to include the Muskogee, Choctaw, and Chickasaw tribes. Hundreds of English and Indian people were killed before the colonizers eventually won the war. Many of the Muskogee and Yamasee retreated south and inland, leaving much of the lower Savannah River area unpopulated.

When James Oglethorpe arrived at the Savannah River fifteen years later, he was met by a small band of Muskogee Indians called the Yamacraw who were led by Tomochichi. Tomochichi's tribe and town seem to have been assembled from outcasts who had been banished from the main body of "Lower Creek" Muskogee towns on the Chattahoochee River.[12] It was the Trustees' policy to quickly establish good relations with the local Indians, and Oglethorpe proved to be skillful at negotiating during these first contacts. Tomochichi welcomed the English, most likely because he saw an opportunity to develop a powerful partnership with access to trade goods, a relationship that could help in his struggles with other Muskogee peoples. Oglethorpe believed that Tomochichi simply wanted his people to become Christian and more like the English, unable to see other motives. An important element of Tomochichi's friendship was that the English had been granted permission to settle on Yamacraw Bluff, the high, flat plateau above the river that became the location for the town of Savannah. Oglethorpe promised to educate the Yamacraws' children and to establish fair trading policies in the colony. It seems very likely that Tomochichi intended to benefit from the trading opportunities brought by this new colony.

Tomochichi's status as an outcast from the Lower Creek towns meant that he was actually subordinate to them. Fortunately for Oglethorpe the Muskogee headmen of these towns confirmed Tomochichi's grant to the English and also clarified the bounds of the English settlers' lands.[13] Muskogee leaders agreed that the English would be allowed to settle Europeans on the land from the Savannah River to the Ogeechee River up to the tidal line.[14] Tomochichi visited England in 1734, sitting for portraits and meeting with the Georgia Trustees and King George II. It was there that he signed a treaty, the moment commemorated by a painting with all the Trustees, Tomochichi, and other Yamacraws.[15] For the British, the treaty formalized agreements made in Georgia in 1733 between Tomochichi, the Muskogee towns' leaders, and Oglethorpe.

In addition to settlement rights, a second reason for the British to want good relations was for the defense of the colony. Oglethorpe wanted the Yamacraws, and the Yuchi who were further upriver, to be English allies in any battles with the Spanish or French.[16] In 1736 he succeeded in winning an alliance, an important move by Britain in the saber rattling between Spain and Britain over who had rights to the land north of the Altamaha River. Oglethorpe was wise to find Muskogee allies as a hot war with Spain— known in America as the War of Jenkins' Ear—broke out in 1739.

When the first transport of Salzburgers arrived in 1734, the good relations with Tomochichi and the Yamacraws that had been established by Oglethorpe facilitated their settlement upriver. Indian guides, presumably some Yamacraws, led the migrants to Ebenezer and in the early days helped them locate people and cattle lost in the forest. However, when the Muskogee agreed to let colonizers settle on their land, they had expressly reserved a large tract along the river, northwest of Savannah town, which was for John and Mary Musgrove. The Musgroves were each half-Muskogee, half-European and had moved to the Savannah River area to establish a trading post.[17] Good relations with the Musgroves was important for the British, as the couple frequently functioned as interpreters for South Carolina and Georgia officials and settlers. This reserved land meant that the Salzburgers' settlement at Ebenezer was separated from Savannah not just by the miles of river and rough trail but also by this tract of Musgrove/Muskogee territory.

Like many Europeans, the first transport's official commissioner, Philip Georg Friedrich von Reck, was fascinated with the American Indians and their culture. As part of his 1736 "ocular proof" drawings of the region, he produced several pictures of the local people, studying and observing them. In his notebook pictures of Indians are interspersed with those of birds, pumpkins, alligators, trees, and watermelon. It seems that he believed he was simply recording the "natural" elements of Georgia, whether vegetable, animal, or human, although he may have intended to publish his drawings to help market Georgia in Europe.

Reck was interested in capturing the details of Indian dress, jewelry, and hairstyle, which is similar to other European settlers who valued these differences as markers of class and status.[18] Recognizing social hierarchies in Indian societies was a way for Europeans to find similarities to their own cultures and to imagine the possibilities for "civilization" in Native American people. Reck's works provide some insight into how the Salzburgers initially viewed the American Indians they met. In general Reck's drawings are sympathetically drawn and display curiosity. Certainly there is no hint of fear or animosity—that came later, after the young commissioner had already left Georgia.

Reck's paintings are ethnographic, as each one includes a picture and some description of what he saw. Many of them include a notation of Indian words, indicating that Reck, like Boltzius, was trying to learn the language. In one painting of Kipahalgwa, who was probably the Yuchi Indian external or war chief, Reck shows a man sitting, hands clasped between his legs (see figure 8.1). He is wearing a European-style shirt and red leggings. His face

FIGURE 8.1. *The Supreme Commander of the Yuchi Indian Nation, Whose Name Is Kipahalgwa*. Kipahalgwa was probably a war chief of the Yuchis; here he is painted as if planning to launch a battle. (The Royal Danish Library, Copenhagen, NKS 565 4°: Von Reck's drawings, 16 recto.)

is highly decorated and painted red and black, which Reck noted was a sign that "they have done injury or want to do it."[19] We do not know if Kipahalgwa was preparing to fight, but he does look at the viewer directly and confidently. That Reck was not threatened, and Kipahalgwa allowed the image to be made, indicates a comfort between the two peoples in this early period.

There is some indication that by the time he made this drawing Reck may have understood a little of Indian leadership dynamics, where southeastern tribes often had an internal chief and an external, or war, chief. In his notebook he differentiated between Kipahalgwa, the "supreme commander," painted with warlike red and black, and the "Indian King and Queen." The queen has her back to the viewer and we see only her European-style blanket used as a cloak and the bottom of her skirt. The "king" is drawn standing upright, staring at the viewer, but does not have red and black face paint. Both the king and Kipahalgwa had similar tattooing on their face, neck, and chest, which Reck called burnt (*gebrannt*); they may have been the markings of leadership for the Yuchis. A painting of Tomochichi shows similar vertical lines tattooed on his chest.[20]

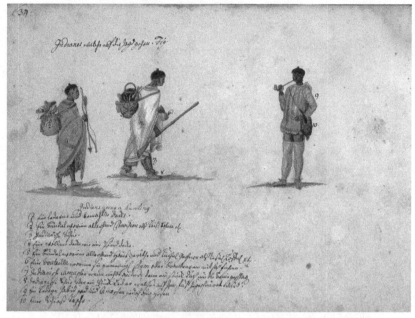

FIGURE 8.2. *Indians Going Hunting.* These Georgia Indians show a blending of Indian and European dress and tools. Note the iron pot in the middle person's bag, the European blanket as a cloak, and the gun. (The Royal Danish Library, Copenhagen, NKS 565 4°: Von Reck's drawings, 25 verso.)

Another painting is a composition of three Yuchi Indians who, Reck tells us, are dressed to go hunting. Unlike the images of the king and the military chief, this painting provides few facial or personal details. Rather, the focus is on their clothing and tools (see figure 8.2). There is much evidence in this painting of the long history of relations the Yuchis had with Europeans. One man is carrying a gun and another a shot pouch. The center person is carrying an iron pot, and another is smoking a European-style pipe. The person on the far left wears an Indian-style "painted leather blanket," the second wears a European blanket, and the third wears "a leather coat and gaiters, but no trousers." According to Kristian Hvidt, that leather coat is unusual and represents a combination of European styles (a coat or shirt) from Indian materials and sewing skills.[21]

Although the Indian skin color is very dark brown in all his paintings, in his writings Reck described the Yuchis as olive toned. This is consistent with the experiences of earlier Europeans who first described Indians as tawny

FIGURE 8.3. *The Georgia Indians in the Natural Habitat.* Reck reported that women never had face tattoos but commonly had them down their arms. Note the body positioning is similar to European statues and to De Bry's 1490 engravings of John White's Roanoke drawings. (The Royal Danish Library, Copenhagen, NKS 565 4°: Von Reck's drawings, 20 recto.)

and represents a way of Europeans seeing similarities rather than differences. It was after colonizers placed greater emphasis on racial categories, and after war and disagreements, that Indians became darker skinned or "red."[22]

Despite his many interactions with the Muskogee and Yuchi people, Reck's drawings reveal that he mostly held to ideas about Native Americans that he had learned in Europe. Although he wanted to have good relations with these people and drew and described them sympathetically, he is too steeped in his own culture to escape the German ideas. Visually this is most evident in one of his paintings where the figures are presented in a fashion akin to Theodor De Bry's famous 1590 engravings that were made to accompany Thomas Hariott's report on Virginia (see figure 8.3).[23] Reck titles this drawing *Georgia Indians in Their Natural Habitat,* but it is the least natural of all his paintings. They are posed in a European fashion, similar to De Bry's *Native American in Body Paint,* and there is very little nature or habitat in the background.

In another similarity to the De Bry printing, Reck reported that the Indians were brightly painted, just like the "old Germans" who were described by Tacitus in the Roman era.[24] In 1590 De Bry included pictures of the heavily painted and tattooed "Ancient Picts" at the end of Hariott's report on Virginia, seeming to indicate a common path from uncivilized to civilized for Britons as for Americans. Reck's report followed the same idea that the Yuchi and Muskogee he had met represented some version of people who had not yet "advanced" as much as Europeans, but for whom it was possible to with time.

In the early days, Boltzius's hopes ran high that he would convert all local Native Americans to Christianity. If they needed more evidence that the Indians could be converted, both Reck and Boltzius were excited to hear rumors that, a few hundred miles north of Ebenezer, there was a group of fair-skinned "Welsh Indians."[25] It was believed their ancestors had come from Cornwall, and although Boltzius revealed his true sentiments when he described them as "completely degenerated into Indians," the rumor was that this group still spoke Welsh.[26] This was important news because it signified that the differences they saw in Indians in their dress, manners, and way of life were merely cultural artifacts. Because of this it was assumed it would be easy to convert them to Christianity.

As the Salzburgers began to build Ebenezer they were visited by their nearest neighbors, the Yuchi. These visitors brought food and drink to the Germans and periodically brought a freshly killed deer.[27] This was especially welcomed in Ebenezer because they had little fresh meat in the early period. The Yuchis returned in May 1734 with household goods to trade, but the Salzburgers had very little to trade with them, although Boltzius does not record this fact. In this early period Boltzius was always pleased to have the Yuchi come because they brought supplies and because he still hoped to learn their language and convert them. In the diaries we hear of fewer attempts by any Native American people to bring trade goods, as they likely chose to go a few miles down the river to Savannah where they could get the European goods they desired.

The idea that the local people would welcome Christianity came crashing down quickly for Boltzius. The process actually began almost as soon as he arrived in Georgia. The Salzburgers landed at Savannah on March 12; on March 27 Boltzius witnessed two events in the city that presented conflicting views of Indians. In the first an Indian interceded to stop an Englishman from being whipped in punishment for a crime. After watching fifty lashes, the Indian shouted to the assembled crowd that the penalty of a hundred lashes "is not Christian" and volunteered his own body in exchange.[28] The second incident is recorded in the next sentence in the diaries: an Indian man had been drunk and "cut both ears and all the hair off his . . . wife" because she had been too friendly with an Englishman.[29] Boltzius had personally witnessed the lashing incident and Indian compassion and only heard a rumor about the woman with her ears cut off, yet it was the second story of drunkenness and cruelty that made a mark. He continued to comment on it later and mentioned it to Tomochichi. The chief told him that the whole incident was not correct behavior, but its effect on Boltzius seems to have been permanent.

Despite seeing Indians rarely around their village, Boltzius and the Salzburgers came to view them as nuisances. There were very few positive references to the local Yuchi or Muskogee in the pastor's diaries after just a few years in Georgia. Boltzius wrote that Indians raided their gardens, killed their chickens, and stole their cows. Further, he felt it was particularly dangerous when Yuchis or other Muskogees came to town, as the community tried to remain on good terms, but clearly viewed the Indians as generally drunken and violent. As negative opinions were nurtured, it was easier for Boltzius to see all Indians as the same. It is rare that Boltzius mentions a local person by name, even though we know that one came to live with them for a few weeks while his leg recovered from a wound because Reck drew a picture of him.[30] The Germans picked up anti-Indian sentiment from the other Europeans in the Lowcountry. It was not just the local Yuchi who were difficult; the Salzburgers learned from European traders who passed through Ebenezer that the Muskogees, Chickasaws, and Cherokees who resided inland to the north and west lived the "same lifestyle as the local" Yuchis and were similarly drunken, reinforcing stereotypes.[31] Boltzius recorded in his diary that all Indians had venereal disease, something he could have only surmised through rumor. In 1747 Boltzius wrote that he would like to devote himself full-time to missionary work among the Indians, but they were too warlike and always fighting among themselves to even try to convert them to Christianity.[32] By 1751 Boltzius had completely abandoned any hope for "civilizing" his neighbors when he remarked that someone, probably from the colonial government, should make "serious efforts to convert the Indians."[33]

What had gone wrong? Boltzius blamed the English and the French for corrupting the Indians. He believed the French brought in as much liquor as they could sell, and it was they who spread sexual diseases. Further, the English traders who came out of Charleston and Savannah were irreligious and had taught the Indians only to curse. Part of the problem was that the

Germans came with notions that the Indians were in a natural state, possibly descended from Europeans, and would be easily converted to the faith. They failed to account for the long history of Indian and Euro-American relations. The relative poverty of the Salzburgers in the earliest years meant that they had little to offer the Yuchi, Yamacraw, and Muskogee other than the gospel; they had no extra guns, metal pots, tools, or alcohol to exchange for the deer meat and skins the Americans brought to them.

Also of note is that Boltzius, and possibly the Salzburgers at Ebenezer, seem to have been unaware of the broader issues facing the Yuchi, Muskogee, Cherokee, and Chickasaw as a result of the European invasion of America. The diaries record no understanding that neighboring Yamacraw and Yuchi were remnants of tribes that had been shattered by contact or that they had long experience negotiating with British, French, and Spanish people who wanted their lands. Further, Boltzius seemed not to understand Oglethorpe and the Trustees' desperate need for Indian alliances in British contests with Spain.

Whether they knew it or not, the location of their settlement at the south side of Ebenezer Creek put Salzburgers at the center of disputes between the Yuchi, Yamacraw, Muskogee, and the British over land. It was not just that the Musgrove tract separated the Salzburgers from Savannah, but Ebenezer Creek formed the agreed-upon boundary between the Colony of Georgia and Yuchi land to the north. The Yuchi were a separate people, but the turmoil of European colonization caused them to align with the larger Muskogee Confederation by the time Georgia was established. In the 1730s the Yuchi maintained two settlements, the largest called Yuchi Town by the English and located about thirty miles upriver from Ebenezer. A second large town was another hundred ten miles upriver at a place called Silver Bluff.[34] Because the towns were so far from Ebenezer, the Salzburgers felt that the Yuchis were not using their lands just north of the creek and the soil on that side seemed more fertile and desirable than that on the south side.

From the beginning of the new (moved) settlement along Ebenezer Creek in 1736, Boltzius campaigned to have the Trustees grant them some of this Yuchi land. In June 1736 the Trustees responded firmly that "those lands belong to the Indians, [and] the Trustees have no power to grant them."[35] Some unnamed Salzburger did not wait for approval, and in May 1736 the Yuchis complained to Oglethorpe that a settler has planted four acres and grazed cattle on their land.[36] Because he was in the colony at the time, Oglethorpe personally intervened, kicking out the Salzburger invaders.

This early incident did not deter Boltzius in his campaign to have the

Trustees grant Yuchi land. Finally, in 1741 the Trustees instructed their president, William Stephens, to arrange to purchase the "beautiful" north-of-creek Yuchi land for fifty Salzburgers to settle.[37] Because the Trustees were in London receiving reports that the Yuchi did not use that land, it was easy for them to order settlement there. On the ground in Georgia, Oglethorpe heard of this plan, was angry, and intervened to stop it, reminding the Trustees that the Yuchis were good allies against the Spanish.[38] Oglethorpe also sent a scolding letter to Boltzius in Ebenezer, noting that "the Indians were Natives and Owners of all America" before the British arrived, which is a remarkable sentiment from a man actively colonizing the continent.[39] Further, he excused an incident where some Yuchi apparently took some Salzburger peaches and corn, noting it was part of the traditional hospitality and social system.[40] Boltzius responded to Oglethorpe with due deferential language but added in his letter that "even if the Salzburgers were not to settle there, it would be good if we were given it for pasture."[41] He was not giving up.

The 1730s and 1740s were difficult times for the Yuchi, with continued disputes with their primary adversary, the Cherokee, who lived further north and west. In early 1742 William Stephens, the Trustees' secretary on the ground in Savannah, received word that the Cherokee, the Muskogee, and their Yuchi allies were at war.[42] At issue was their desire for land, access to trade with the British colonies, and age-old animosities. War erupted again in 1749, shortly after the Yuchi relocated their town from the Savannah River to the Chattahoochee. They had moved to live closer to their Muskogee allies, who are also known in history as the Lower Creek (as a distinct group from the Upper Creek, whose towns were along the Coosa and Alabama rivers).[43]

In addition to war with the Cherokee, the Yuchi were pressured into moving by the colonizing Georgians. In 1745 the President's Council, headed by William Stephens, informed the Trustees that the Yuchis "said to claim those lands are of late very much impaired in Number and Strength . . . [with] very few of them remaining" on the land that Boltzius wanted for the Salzburgers.[44] The Council recommended that colonizers now be granted all of the Yuchi lands from Ebenezer all the way past Augusta. In January 1747 the Council gave settler Isaac Barksdale four hundred acres of Yuchi land north of Augusta and another hundred acres to William Barefutt at the site of Yuchi Town.[45] The Council had the support of the Trustees in these actions. Yuchi Town was renamed Mount Pleasant, and British settler Thomas Wiggins built a trading store there.[46]

The Salzburgers also began expanding north of Ebenezer Creek, with the President's Council's blessing. In October 1750 Augsburg philanthro-

pist Christian von Münch wrote that he planned to send more Germans to
Georgia and asked for land grants.[47] A few months later Boltzius sent the
Council a list of nine longtime Salzburger settlers who asked for hundred-
acre grants for the land north of Ebenezer Creek.[48] They intended to exchange their original plots south of the Creek for the better land in the
north. A 1751 transport of Swabian Germans arrived and created the Bethany settlement on the former Yuchi lands.

In Ebenezer in 1752 Boltzius wrote that they "hear and see nothing" of the
Indians, as they had been pushed further inland, seemingly unaware of the
causes for the Yuchi migrations.[49] He still had hope for their souls, he wrote,
but they were too far away and too corrupted by the ungodly English settlers for him to make any effort. In his musing, Boltzius seemed unaware of
the role the colonizing Salzburgers had played in pushing the Yuchi out of
the area. Rather, he saw the failure to convert them as a moral failing on the
part of the Yuchi, their Muskogee allies, and some of the English settlers.

## The "Unchristian Christians"

"We live in a great external peace, set apart from the tumult of the world."[50]
Boltzius was pleased to report that, in 1740, the Salzburgers had created a
harmonious society, remote enough that they were mostly unbothered by
any problems outside of Ebenezer, including the Malcontents' disagreements
developing in Savannah. This is not completely true, as we have already seen
that the Malcontents tried to have the Salzburgers participate in their peti-
tions and found few supporters in Ebenezer. That was not the beginning of
differences between the German and the English Georgians. Almost from
the start of the settlement Boltzius labeled the English people of Savannah
coarse, sinful, and irreligious. He called them degenerate, cruel, and drunken.
Just a few years after arriving he referred to all non-Salzburgers as the "unchristian Christians," meaning that, although they were from Christian England, they were not a Christlike people.[51]

The differences in language, dress, and religion were difficult to overcome
for the English and Germans in Georgia; the greatest tensions were over
the growing divide concerning the Trustees' policies. As noted earlier Boltzius carefully aligned his community with the aims of the Trustees, seeking
to implement their plans and begging for charitable donations for the worthy poor. The Malcontents were a group of British settlers unhappy with the
colony's policies, particularly the ban on slavery and the original system of
tail-male land tenure. It was only a matter of time before the Malcontents

argued that Boltzius and the Germans at Ebenezer were lying about conditions in Georgia, a stance that helped drive a wedge between the Salzburgers and the English in Savannah.

From their earliest arrivals in Georgia, Boltzius had urged his people to keep separated from these non-Lutheran English. Later, the dispute over Trustee policy, and especially over the slavery ban, was the biggest issue that divided the people. In the early years Salzburgers needed money to buy food, and the local projects did not always provide enough work. Consequently, some chose to work for English settlers. Such employment was never long term, usually just a job for a few days or weeks. But Boltzius saw this as a lack of faith that God would provide for their needs. Further, he worried about their souls while they worked for these foreigners, telling Francke that "they plainly suffer harm to their Christianity" by working for the English.[52]

Although Ebenezer was remote, there were some Anglo settlers very nearby. There were the men hired by the Trustees to manage the cowpen at the Old Ebenezer site, and according to Boltzius these Englishmen frequently created problems for the Germans. There were also some Trustee indentured servants assigned to the cowpen who were German-speaking Swiss, but they were apparently of the Reformed faith, not Lutheran, so Boltzius did not fully approve of them. In 1744 two of the Swiss cowpen workers rode into Ebenezer drunk, "disturbing the peace, prophanely Cursing and Swearing, and uttering foul Speeches and reproachfull language against" Boltzius.[53] One of them was said to have seduced (or possibly raped—the language is unclear) a Salzburger girl.[54] For Boltzius, this was more evidence that outsiders were a danger to his flock.

Of course not all Englishmen were bad people. Because Boltzius respected hierarchy and authority, the Salzburgers made alliances easily with many of the colony's leaders and some of the South Carolina plantation elite. Hugh and Jonathan Bryan, for example, were devout Christians and plantation owners from South Carolina who were active supporters of the Salzburgers; as mentioned earlier, they were particularly helpful in providing cattle and provisions. Thomas Causton was the Trustees' first appointed magistrate in Savannah and was responsible for keeping the storehouse. He was a friend to the Salzburgers, probably because he recognized the extra care given to the group by Oglethorpe and the Trustees, his employers. As seen in the dispute over provisions and authority with Vat and Reck, Causton usually sided with Boltzius and usually with the Salzburgers against the English Malcontents.

When William Stephens arrived in Georgia in 1737 he also became a friend of the Salzburgers. Stephens was appointed the Trustees' secretary, later named the president of the colony, and the Salzburgers were immediately deferential to him and his office. Stephens was impressed by the order and success of the Ebenezer settlement, when the reports out of Savannah were of disharmony and difficulty. Their demeanor, accomplishments, and efforts to implement the Trustees' plans may have inclined him to favor the Salzburgers, as most of his reports to the Trustees emphasized successes. Stephens was very loyal to the Trustees and tended to fill his reports with mostly good rather than bad news.[55] Stephens helped the Salzburgers get the Trustees to fund a water-powered gristmill, and it was Stephens who had the unruly Swiss cowpen workers arrested.

Another "good" Englishman was Anglican evangelist George Whitefield, who first visited Ebenezer in 1738 and quickly became an ally of the Salzburgers.[56] Whitefield had been sent to Georgia by the Trustees to meet Anglican religious needs. By the early 1740s Whitefield had left Georgia and rapidly became possibly the most famous traveling evangelist in the British Atlantic world. He used his preaching to help raise money for the Salzburgers. Impressed by their piety, communal unity, and hard work, Whitefield admired the way that "the strong help the weak: and all seem hearty for the Common Good" in their community.[57] Whitefield's donations helped the Salzburgers complete their first church building, named the Jerusalem Church, in 1741.[58] Further, he resolved to send them "Cotton, Spinning Wheels, and a Loom" so the group could begin to make their own clothes and not be dependent upon charitable shipments from Europe.[59] Whitefield wrote to Francke that he was "very happy in the Friendship" of Gronau and Boltzius and that they took "sweet council together, & converse[d] as Christian Friends."[60] For his part Boltzius valued Whitefield's zeal and focus on "the essentials" of religion, although privately the pastor worried about some of Whitefield's doctrine, especially that of Calvinist predestination.[61] Despite this, in general the men got along, and the two held "sweet council" together every two weeks when Boltzius traveled to Savannah to perform church services for the Lutheran servants living there.

Whitefield had been impressed by the orphanage at Ebenezer and determined to build another one in Georgia for British children. The Salzburger orphanage was the first such institution in America; the second belonged to Whitefield, who copied the idea and established his own in Bethesda, south of Savannah. Whitefield brought James Habersham to Georgia to run the Bethesda property, and he too became a friend to the Salzburgers. Later, when Habersham left the orphanage and became an influential merchant and political appointee in the colony, he remained true to his friendship with the Salzburgers. He seemed to favor them when determining wages for working in silk and always reported on them favorably to the London Board of Trade and Plantations.[62]

Boltzius accepted the help of Whitefield and was pleased to work with him in part because the Pietists had a tradition of ecumenical friendships across Protestant religious boundaries. This was true in London, where Ziegenhagen functioned well with his Anglican counterparts. And it was the guiding principle that allowed Urlsperger and Francke to be corresponding members of the SPCK. As long as they behaved in a proper Christian manner, Boltzius was able to work with them. Whitefield, Habersham, the SPCK, and the Trustees were, of course, Anglican. Yet they were instruments of God in helping the Salzburgers and therefore clearly motivated by Christian charity. For these reasons, Boltzius admired and respected them.

Within Ebenezer, and away from the educated elite, Boltzius was less tolerant of non-Lutheran Protestants. He worried about religious divisions that could arise if he was not watchful. Europe had suffered for two hundred years from wars and divisions over which religion was the true faith. Germany was still fractured, with many small sects developing, and the mainline Protestants in Europe were also split between Calvinist and Lutheran churches. For this reason Boltzius was vigilant in looking for potential problems among his own flock. For example, in 1738 he refused to marry Ernst Thilo, the Lutheran doctor sent by Halle, to the widow Anna Dorothea Helfenstein, who practiced the Reformed faith.[63] It was not just that she was a Calvinist, but she had been somewhat troublesome in the community, and Boltzius believed that she felt superior to the Salzburgers. Worse still, her home in Heidelberg had been a gathering spot for a radical religious sect, the Inspirationists. The Community of True Inspiration had their origins in Pietism but focused much more on the idea of individual "inspiration" as the most important way to know God. (In the nineteenth century a group of Inspirationists migrated to Iowa and founded the Amana colonies.) Frau Helfenstein "admitted" her home had been used by the group but denied participating in their beliefs, something Boltzius did not believe, meaning he also thought she was a liar and therefore breaking one of the Ten Commandments.[64] Boltzius and Gronau not only worried about the soul of this woman but also specifically mentioned the fear of creating a "rift in the community, like in Germany" if he allowed non-Lutheran ideas to linger in Ebenezer.[65] In this case, happily, Boltzius's fears were unfounded as the couple did marry and remained important members of the Salzburger community. Thilo stayed in good standing; he had musical training and a strong voice, and it was he who helped Boltzius teach polyphonic singing to the Salzburgers. There were religious divisions in Savannah between the Reformed and Lutheran Germans that the Trustees had sent as indentured servants to relieve the labor shortage. Even though he or Gronau gave biweekly services to the Savannah congregation, Boltzius was worried by the "great antipathy" and "hostility" between the two branches of the faith. He felt that the discord and division were due to the Savannahians' character; they were, to Boltzius, "wicked, Sabbath breaking, and disorderly."[66]

All ecumenical notions departed for the Halle community whenever they encountered the Moravians, a group known as the Herrnhuters in Germany because they had assembled in Herrnhut, Saxony. The Moravians, a Pietist group supported by Count Nicholas Ludwig Zinzendorf in Europe, came to Georgia in 1735. There was a complex history between the two groups, as the head Moravian pastor in America, Bishop August Gottlieb Spangenberg, had trained at Halle.[67] During his time there he was drawn to Herrnhuter ideas. Because of this "apostasy" he was not ordained in Halle, and Johann Martin Boltzius took the position at the orphanage that had originally been intended for Spangenberg. The Halle Lutherans considered Moravian theology dangerous to the soul. To be sure, the Herrnhuters established practices that were very distinct from those of other Protestant sects, including an emphasis on the side wound of Christ as the doorway to salvation. To represent this teaching, Moravian worshipers sometimes entered their church services through a doorway made to look like an open, bleeding wound. Aaron Fogleman argues that the group taught that there were both female and male characteristics in the figure of Jesus, a doctrine that was considered dangerous because it struck at the core nature of the God at the center of Christianity.[68]

The combination of differing theology and a history of personal animosity meant that Boltzius felt he had to blunt the force of the Moravians in Georgia. Since the Trustees had agreed to the Moravians settling in Savannah, Boltzius kept his dispute out of his letters to England and usually out of the official diaries. But the letters to Ziegenhagen and to Germany reveal that he watched the Herrnhuters' activities and tracked where they lived and with whom they spoke.[69] He was an important source of information in the Halle network, providing details about the Moravians' activities and working as an agent to diminish their proselytizing effectiveness in America.

Boltzius first heard the Moravians were coming to Georgia in a letter from Francke. The news was "a reason for weeping and tears."[70] The great concern was that Spangenberg would gain new converts from among the

Salzburgers. This fear was enhanced when Boltzius learned that in Savannah, where the Moravians lived communally, they were able to "draw minds" to the faith, despite what he described as "their sneaky character."[71] Notwithstanding Boltzius's efforts to keep Spangenberg away from Ebenezer, the two met when the Moravian came for a visit in May 1735. They were old acquaintances but not friends, and Boltzius bluntly told Spangenberg that "I had been more distressed than gladdened over his and his peoples' arrival because of their nature and peculiar ways."[72] He was particularly bothered by Spangenberg, who Boltzius believed was "probably . . . trying to stir up animosity" among the Salzburgers by visiting Ebenezer.[73] At the heart of the Halle Pietists' complaint was that the Moravians claimed to still be members of the Lutheran faith. To Boltzius, and the Halle clergy, the group held dangerous doctrine, and by continuing to associate with Lutherans they were actually creating divisions within the church. For Francke, Boltzius, and the Halle Pietists, the Moravians' doctrine imperiled the souls of their followers; but the dissention the sect created within the Lutheran church endangered the souls of everyone.

In addition to his anxiety for his Lutheran flock, Boltzius was concerned for the impressionable new Anglican minister in Savannah, who seemed too intrigued by the Moravians. The new minister was John Wesley, who was sent with his brother Charles by the Trustees. They arrived in February 1736, and John was to stay in Savannah and serve as Anglican priest in town while Charles originally came as Oglethorpe's secretary and was later appointed to be a missionary to the Indians. The Wesleys had traveled to Georgia on the same ship as the Moravians, and John was impressed by their faith and piety on the journey, even when the seas became rough and stormy. In Savannah, in addition to performing his duties as an Anglican priest, Wesley attended what Boltzius termed the Moravians' "spiritual exercises" and was "much captivated by them."[74] Boltzius judged Wesley an earnest and zealous Christian who was being misled. He met with Wesley and tried to dissuade him from Moravian theology and practices.[75] In June 1737 Boltzius and John Wesley walked some distance together through the woods to Thomas Causton's plantation. Along the way these two ministers discussed religion. By the end it appeared that Wesley was cooling to Spangenberg's ideas when he stated that he "could not divine any truly felt and expressed honesty in them."[76] However, Boltzius's triumph was short lived. After Wesley left Georgia in a hurry under a cloud of scandal, he visited the Moravians at Herrnhut. The influence of this group is now acknowledged to have been instrumental in Wesley later establishing the Methodist Church.[77]

Boltzius's Moravian problem in Georgia resolved itself when the group decamped from the colony beginning in the late 1730s. By 1742 they had settled in Pennsylvania's Lehigh Valley, where they are remembered for establishing the towns of Bethlehem and Nazareth and for their devoted focus on their mission to the Indians. Halle Lutherans continued to battle with them though, and Boltzius sympathized with Heinrich Melchior Mühlenberg, who had been sent by Halle to organize Pennsylvania Lutherans in the 1740s. There, he struggled for souls against the Moravian message.

In determining who were good neighbors from among the Euro-American settlers, Boltzius let social standing and religious doctrine be his guide. He respected authority and cultivated good relations among the colonial elite of South Carolina and Georgia for the Ebenezer settlement. Lutherans and Anglican preachers were also considered friends of the community, as long as they were not trying to convert the Salzburgers away from Boltzius's Halle Pietism.

## The Fight over Slavery

It was in the slavery debate that the Salzburgers clashed with English colonizers and also demonstrated the most vigor in civic engagement and wielded the greatest influence on metropole Trustee policies in Georgia. Recall that the Trustees had banned slavery so that "the People being oblig'd to labor themselves for their Support will be . . . more active and useful."[78] Oglethorpe maintained that banning slavery would forestall large tracts of land being owned by one individual, an occurrence that "experience had shown" was not only bad for defense (as people were too spread out to muster) but wasteful because it meant fewer families could settle in an area.[79] In the struggles of the Trustees against the Malcontents, the Salzburgers sided with the Trustees on the intertwined issue of slavery and land ownership because they supported authority, because they were too poor to acquire large plantations and enslaved people, and because of the moral implications of not working for one's own support.[80]

The Salzburgers took on the slavery debate with zeal, with Boltzius sending a steady stream of letters to England and the whole community signing a petition to the Trustees in March 1739 in support of the ban.[81] The issue for the pastors seems not to have been primarily rooted in Christian compassion for the enslaved people and the physical and emotional violence to which they were subjected. Rather, just like the Trustees, the Salzburgers' primary concern was the moral impact of slavery on the enslavers, who, it was felt, could easily become lazy and overly concerned with luxury. Boltzius believed that individual souls in his care, and among the larger colonial society, would be debased by slavery.

Naturally, living in the Lowcountry, the Salzburgers had interactions with slavery and enslaved people. Before they even arrived at Savannah the migrants had seen slavery in action in Charleston. In 1734 Boltzius recorded his impressions of Charleston, noting that there were more African people than Europeans in the city. By then South Carolina was already a majority-enslaved colony. He displayed some sympathy for the Africans, noting that they were worked very hard and were "never urged to become Christians," a dig at the moral character of the enslavers.[82] But he was also critical of the enslaved, who he declared "live like animals" and break the commandment against adultery.[83]

As noted earlier, upon arriving in Georgia the Salzburgers had been lent fourteen enslaved Africans to aid with the first few weeks of settlement. This seems to have hardened Boltzius against the character of the enslaved who he began to see as both lazy and violent.[84] Several times in his diary Boltzius noted that the enslaved workers had to be guarded day and night. After some escapees were recaptured, Boltzius matter-of-factly reported that they received their "regular punishment" of being "badly beaten" and denied food.[85] The loaned enslaved men were forced to help build buildings, fences, and a road for the Salzburgers, but Boltzius hardly mentioned the benefit they derived from the labor. Rather, he saw dealing with these workers as a trial sent by God in order to help the Salzburgers turn to their faith.[86]

The early diary entries of Philip von Reck in 1734 included a little more sympathy for the enslaved people in South Carolina. He noted that a group of Africans he met complained about their owners, and he believed "they have good cause to."[87] Reck wrote that the enslaved were worked relentlessly, given little food, and whipped nearly to death. Boltzius and Reck had both witnessed this extreme violence in Charleston and found it shocking, although they reported slightly different opinions of the enslaved and the enslavers. It should be remembered, too, that it is very likely that they were careful not to be too critical in their written diaries. Although Georgia did not allow slavery, the British Empire certainly profited from the practice. And as a matter of expediency, the Salzburgers needed to be in the good graces of the South Carolina elite, all of whom were enslavers, including their Christian benefactors Hugh and Jonathan Bryan.

From these early encounters Boltzius and Reck rapidly adopted the colonizer's attitudes toward enslaved Africans and came to fear them. In some ways the Germans seemed to adopt the same racial views that Anglo Americans did, but they also recognized the horrific violence that always accompanied slavery. Boltzius saw that the enslaved were badly beaten when they tried to run away, and Reck wrote that the enslaved were treated "very badly." It was because of this cruelty, he noted, that they were all "nursing a secret hatred and waiting for an opportune moment to revolt."[88]

South Carolina's plantation slavery system, like all slave systems in the British Atlantic, had violence at its very core. South Carolina's economy had been mindfully imported from Barbados plantations, where the system was described by Richard Ligon in the 1640s as "the most brutal labor regime" in the Atlantic.[89] In the eighteenth century Georgia Trustee Egmont's Virginia correspondent William Byrd II kept a secret diary in which he nonchalantly reported that he raped his female slaves and had enslaved people on his plantation beaten, burned, and whipped.[90] One enslaved boy kept wetting the bed, so Byrd forced him to drink the urine after he was whipped.

The fear of revolt and runaways was heightened in the Lowcountry during the run-up to the War of Jenkins' Ear in the late 1730s, when Oglethorpe reported that Spanish agents were roaming throughout South Carolina informing enslaved people that they would be freed if they could make it to Florida.[91] Oglethorpe wrote to the Trustees that early in 1739 a small group of men responded to the promises of the Spanish and fled their enslavers, passing through Ebenezer, although Boltzius never recorded that particular incident in the diaries.[92] The great fear among European settlers of a full-scale slave revolt was realized on Sunday, September 9, 1739, south of Charleston along the Stono River. The Stono Rebellion was the largest slave uprising in colonial British North America. In all more than twenty-five Euro-Americans were killed in the revolt, and over fifty African Americans lost their lives in the reprisals.[93] This event sparked fear in Georgia as Oglethorpe and the colony's officials worked to establish patrols near the site of Yuchi Town, where he believed it was easiest for the freedom-seeking people to cross the Savannah River. It seems the Salzburgers were undisturbed by this revolt, as they did not learn about it until September 22, when Oglethorpe bought the town six muskets and some powder for defense.[94] During that visit Oglethorpe told the pastor that houses had been burned and people killed. Although the Stono Rebellion had little practical effect on Ebenezer, it cemented in Boltzius's mind the notion that enslaved people were dangerous.

After five years of experience with neighboring slavery, Boltzius held the opinion that the enslaved Africans were innately "wicked," a nature that was compounded by "unchristian and barbaric treatment" from their enslavers.[95] That is, he believed the practice of slavery in South Carolina damaged both the enslaved and the enslaver. In agreement with the Trustees, Boltzius and Lemke taught the Salzburgers that relying upon the work of another for one's own bread led to moral laziness and debauchery. Their own experience in Georgia, where they were able to build a community and support themselves even in the awful Lowcountry heat, was evidence enough for the Salzburgers and the Trustees to prove that the Malcontents were "idle," immoral people who used the Georgia climate as an excuse to engage in human trafficking of Africans.[96] When the official law banning the importation of African slaves arrived in Georgia in late 1739, Oglethorpe was pleased to report that "the remainder of the idle" people were leaving the colony and "industrious" people were coming to settle there.[97] The Salzburgers' antislavery stance was *the* key support for the Trustees, at a time when they were under attack by the Malcontents in America and by some businessmen in London who deemed the ban impractical at best and damaging to the colony at worst.

Despite this early unified stance against slavery, by the late 1740s Lemke and Boltzius began to report to Halle that some Ebenezer residents did desire to own African people. Boltzius blamed the outsiders—the Malcontents—who, he reported in early 1747, were "slandering" him in Savannah over the Salzburger support of the Trustees' ban.[98] However, slavery had already crept into the community by that time. The Salzburger mills took in grains from throughout the Lowcountry, including from South Carolina, particularly from people who had settled near Purrysburg. Those farmers brought their enslaved people with them to the mills, and Boltzius made clear that the Salzburgers had "never hindered" this practice.[99]

Other inroads came from Purrysburg because some of those settlers regularly associated with the Lutheran community at Ebenezer, including Theobald Kiefer and his son, also named Theobald. The elder Kiefer lived in South Carolina and had purchased three enslaved people, each of whom met a miserable end: one died, one drowned himself, and the third ran away, incurring grave bodily injuries before being captured and sold for a low price.[100] Boltzius took these losses as a sign and in his diary compared Kiefer's experience enslaving people to the New Testament scripture in 1 Timothy, where the Apostle Paul condemns those who "will be rich" who "fall into temptation," which will "drown men in destruction and perdition."[101] Boltzius hoped Kiefer's story would "serve as a warning" to the Salzburgers to avoid enslaving people.[102] It did not. To recoup the losses, the son Kiefer, who lived in Ebenezer, loaned his father money to purchase a man and a woman. This couple produced a child, and in March 1747 Kiefer Jr. asked Boltzius to baptize the African American baby born into bondage in Kiefer's household. Boltzius agreed, with the stipulation that the Kiefers adopt this child and raise him as a Christian.[103] At the baptism Boltzius felt obligated to explain to the congregation why he agreed to the ceremony, stating that he was led by the biblical injunction to spread Christianity to all of the world. He also modified the ritual, including a charge to the witnesses (the Kiefers) to give proper Christian instruction since his "heathen parents are incapable of doing so."[104] This event appears to be the first baptism of an enslaved person in Ebenezer. The lecture at the baptism also underscores that Boltzius, Lemke, and the Salzburgers held the same racial prejudices as their neighbors ("heathen parents") and that their opposition to slavery was rooted in support for the Trustees and the concern over the moral harm that came to the enslaver.

As Boltzius had long feared, the introduction of enslaved Africans to Georgia by the Trustees in 1751 changed the social dynamics in the colony. Wealthy enslavers with large plantations began to dominate the colony economically, politically, and socially, in the same way that enslaving plantation owners did in South Carolina. Most worrisome was that some of the Salzburgers enslaved people. However, it was not until after Boltzius's death in 1765, and just before the American Revolution, that the group experienced severe fractures that tore them apart. By then, Ebenezer was not just a "Salzburger" town but the center of a large German-speaking community.

In the daily lives of the Salzburgers, it is likely the disputes with the disrespectful English, the Moravians, the Malcontents, and the enslaved had little impact. The Ebenezer settlers traveled to Savannah to shop, to sell, and to participate in civil duties such as to sit on a grand jury. But most of the Salzburgers' time was spent in their Ebenezer settlements. It seems that staying put was mostly by choice, as they had opportunities to move. In fact, in the early years of difficulty periodically someone, such as Bichler, would mention Pennsylvania as an option, but in practice very few left Georgia or left the communion of the church. Importantly, Boltzius's efforts to maintain good relations with people in authority were crucial for the success of their settlement. Good reports from William Stephens, George Whitefield, and James Habersham convinced the Trustees and the SPCK that the little community of Salzburgers were the right sort of colonists who deserved continued support.

The greatest concern to Boltzius was that the group remain a strong community who helped one another and remained dedicated to the Lutheran faith. In that he, and the Salzburgers, largely succeeded for nearly two decades. They worked, studied, and worshiped together and continued to participate in the transatlantic Pietist community through books, newspapers, and letters. The combined strength enabled them to survive during the difficult early years and was sustained as they incorporated new transports of Germans.

# EPILOGUE

O n January 1, 1751, it became legal to own slaves in Georgia. This event
is often viewed as the turning point in the fate of the colony: the moment when it left behind the shackles of an unworkable utopian plan for the
opportunity to develop large plantations with the labor of enslaved people.

When Parliament, at the request of the Trustees, allowed slavery in
Georgia, several South Carolinians, including some former Georgia settlers,
and some new adventurers flooded into the colony. The Trustees had also
changed the land laws in 1749, so it was easier to receive grants for large
tracts of up to five hundred acres. A year later the Trustees surrendered their
charter and the Georgia Lowcountry became similar to South Carolina in
economic, labor, and social systems. These changes in land and labor policy brought dramatic changes to Georgia's economy and landscape. Georgia
became a large producer and exporter of the same crops that grew in South
Carolina, namely rice and indigo. In the nineteenth century Georgia was
the original cotton belt. For the Salzburgers, most of whom did not embrace
large-scale plantation slavery, the loss of economic power and connections to
the colony's administrators meant a loss of social capital and influence. Their
importance as a community in the colony declined.

Many Salzburgers did acquire enslaved people, but only a handful ever
participated in the large-scale plantation-style economy that developed
in Georgia. Instead, they continued to focus on family-run farms, usually
with fewer than five African Americans.[1] This was partially because they
were simply too poor to compete with the new English-speaking arrivals.

Ebenezer and the other communities had been economically successful in that they produced a sufficiency for the people, but the Germans had never been wealthy enough as individuals to make expensive purchases such as in enslaved Africans. The key to their success had been the combination of individual subsistence farms and communal economic projects, which was a model that did not fit in the new Georgia.

In addition, the German communities around Ebenezer eschewed large plantations with tens and hundreds of enslaved workers partly because Boltzius still preached against the practice. Boltzius had been against slavery from the beginning, and not just because the Trustees had outlawed the practice. In March 1734, on their journey to Georgia, the first transport stopped at Charleston, where they encountered enslaved African Americans for the first time. Boltzius was not impressed with Charleston and made a list of nine points about the city. Two of the nine were essentially riffs on the same theme: there were a lot of enslaved Africans in Carolina and none of them were Christian.[2] In his dealings with enslaved people Boltzius did pity the African Americans, who were kept in continual poverty and made to work, but he was equally concerned by what he saw in the South Carolina enslavers, believing that they were lazy and cruel, inclined to be drunken and impious.

Pastor Boltzius eventually reconciled himself to slavery, choosing to trust that all things were in the control of God after the Trustees changed policies.[3] He taught that all enslavers had a duty to teach Christianity to the people they owned as property and also had an obligation to be sure they were baptized, as he had done for Kiefer's enslaved boy in 1747.[4] Since Pietist Protestants come to know God through the Word in the Bible, Boltzius urged his parishioners to teach their slaves to read.

The record of baptisms in the Jerusalem Church record books shows that the Salzburgers slowly embraced slavery, and each year from 1757 to 1766 one to two enslaved children were baptized by Boltzius. Theobald Kiefer Jr. had enslaved children baptized about once per year during this time, and he likely had one of the largest holdings of slaves among the Ebenezer settlements. Kiefer was a devout Lutheran, the son of a Purrysburger who had joined the Salzburgers for church services. At the behest of his father, the son was educated at Ebenezer. The father was probably an enslaver when the Salzburgers arrived, as that is implied in the records as the reason why he waited to move to the Georgia side of the Savannah River.

There is also a surprising entry in the church books recording that "Mr. Boltzius's negress Mary gave birth to a girl, March 21, 1758, who was baptized the same day and named Christine."[5] When he died his probate file noted he had enslaved one woman, a housemaid whom he left to his "successor in the ministry."[6] It is unclear if this housemaid was Mary, the mother of Christine, baptized in 1758, as she is not given a name in Boltzius's will. If so, the daughter Christine would have been eight when Boltzius died and should have appeared in his will, as he was strongly against separating families. It is possible the child died. He may have sold Christine. As is often the case when tracking the lives of the enslaved, the records are silent.

A few of the Swabians who had settled with the Salzburgers in the 1750s transports came with their own financial resources; they also had arrived later in the development of the colony, so they were not dependent upon the Trustees and the Protestant philanthropists as much as the earlier groups. As a result, some of the Swabian transport migrants were able to develop larger plantations. John William Gerard de Brahm, who came in the transport funded by Christian Von Münch, amassed large land holdings and purchased numerous enslaved Africans. He and another Swabian, Caspar Wertsch, were the wealthiest Germans in the Ebenezer region.

The pastor's way of accepting slavery in Georgia was to place rules and limits around the practice that would not allow an enslaver to fall into the same habits as the Carolinians. When the Trustees began to entertain accepting slavery, they consulted with Boltzius and other Georgians to help define the rules. The goal was still to avoid an economy like South Carolina's, where plantation owners lived in luxury off the work of other people. Boltzius believed the new law, when it was finalized, was the best they could do while still allowing slavery. The 1750 law limited the number of people a person could own to four enslaved men for every Euro-American man aged sixteen to sixty-five on the plantation. Enslavers who kept more than this four-to-one ratio would be fined each month that they held too many men.[7] Enslaved men could be used only for agriculture, as the skilled craftsmen in the colony were worried about labor competition. Importantly, a white slave owner could be tried for murder if he killed one of his enslaved Africans. Still supporting sericulture as the best export for Georgia, the 1750 law required that owners teach enslaved women how to reel silk from the cocoons.[8] It was the mildest slave code in British America.[9] After the end of Trustee rule in 1752, the Royal Colony of Georgia abandoned these strict rules and adopted South Carolina's practices. Wealth was concentrated with the large landowners, and by 1770 over half of the enslaved people in colonial Georgia were owned by just sixty people.

Arguably the date that had a greater impact on the German settlements around Ebenezer was November 19, 1765, when Johann Martin Boltzius died. He had kept the community unified, under shared faith and culture, despite the Germans' expansion north and south along the Savannah River and the growing disparity in wealth. He had also carefully nurtured the Protestant philanthropists in England and Europe to keep material and moral aid flowing into Georgia. After he died, the small rifts and differences that will always exist in a community began to create larger fissures in the group. Perhaps the most damaging was the split between pastors Christian Rabenhorst and Boltzius's replacement, Christian Friedrich Triebner.

When Rabenhorst was sent to Georgia in 1751 to be the third preacher he was supported by a glebe farm purchased by the Pietists in Germany. Recall that Boltzius, Gronau, and Lemke were all paid salaries by the SPCK and had been somewhat unconcerned about exploiting their lands, so much so that Lemke ignored his plantation and let three poor settlers use the land. Unlike these first three men, Rabenhorst settled near the town of Abercorn, in the mill district, and usually preached at the Zion church, with occasional trips to Savannah. Importantly, Rabenhorst did not receive an SPCK salary, and because he depended upon the income from the property he devoted more energy to developing his plantation, including purchasing some enslaved people and hiring a white overseer. The dependence on slavery and attention to worldly affairs bothered Boltzius at first, but they managed to reconcile, and the two grew to appreciate each other and work well together. Rabenhorst lived near the Abercorn mill district, which had been communal property, with the deed belonging to Boltzius as the pastor of the church. Boltzius passed this ownership to Lemke, who deeded it to Rabenhorst in the 1750s. Rabenhorst leased the mills, and they generated some profit.

Christian Triebner, who was sent to replace Boltzius by the now nearly forty-year partnership of the SPCK and the Halle Pietists, arrived in Ebenezer in 1769. Shortly thereafter he accused Rabenhorst of misappropriating funds from the mill and gaining too much economically from his plantation. The dispute became heated, and the community openly split. Rabenhorst had been in Georgia eighteen years longer than Triebner, but Triebner married Gronau's daughter, interlocking him to the Ebenezer community. Triebner's relatives, including his brother-in-law, the wealthy Caspar Wertsch, and their associates became one faction, while supporters of Rabenhorst formed another. At the Francke Foundations in Halle they were so disturbed by the split in the church caused by the feuding pastors that in

1774 they sent Lutheran reverend Heinrich Mühlenberg from Pennsylvania to mediate, but he had little success.[10] Mühlenberg found Triebner intractable and had greater sympathy for Rabenhorst. In London Ziegenhagen ordered Triebner to be held accountable for his accusations and slander. The point became moot in 1775, when Rabenhorst died and the Americans began the Revolution.

One of the prides of the modern-day Georgia Salzburger Society (a descendants' organization) is John Adam Treutlen. In 1777 Treutlen was elected the first state governor of Georgia, serving less than a year. He had come to the colony in 1744 as a boy, been educated by Boltzius at the school in Ebenezer, and as an adult found prosperity with a plantation and enslaved workers.[11] He had an extraordinary childhood. Like many so-called Salzburgers who came to Georgia later in the 1740s and 1750s, he was a religious exile not from Salzburg but rather from Württemberg. His parents had paid their own way to migrate to Pennsylvania, but the ship was captured by Spanish pirates and they were held in Bilbao.[12] His father died in Spain, and, now penniless, Treutlen and his mother came to Georgia as Trustees' indentured servants. Boltzius urged the Trustees to let the boy come to Ebenezer, and they relented.

Treutlen was a leader in the faction that supported Rabenhorst in his dispute with Triebner. Although the records are incomplete, it appears that the majority of people who supported Rabenhorst sided with the Americans in the war, while those who supported Triebner tended to side with the British. The community was split, and the Triebner-Rabenhorst controversy might have led to greater tensions between the Germans if Ebenezer had not been occupied by the British in 1779 as part of their Southern Campaign.[13] The town of Ebenezer had always been on an important crossroads, situated on the main road to Augusta to the north and near a good crossing of the Savannah River on the way to Charleston. When the Revolutionary War began the Americans turned Ebenezer into a munitions depot and built large earthen fortifications around the town.[14] These earthworks ignored property lines, gardens, and fences. When the British swept in they controlled the town from January 1779 until early January 1781 and were said to use the Salzburgers' Jerusalem Church as a horse stable.

The war severely affected the Salzburgers' pastors. As Triebner was the replacement for Boltzius, his salary was paid by the SPCK, which is why he had stopped in London to meet with them on his way to Georgia.[15] Although he did not keep detailed diaries as Boltzius did, he did send the Society regular updates that were published in their annual reports to members. His letters remind us that the American Revolution was a civil war, fought between neighbors who knew each other well. Understandably, no reports from Triebner were sent at the outbreak of war when the Americans were in Ebenezer, but they picked up again in 1779 after the British Army took Georgia. He informed the SPCK that while the Americans controlled Ebenezer, he and other members of the congregation had lived under a "Tyrranical Government and particular Oppressions."[16] He had refused to take an oath of allegiance to the Patriot cause and was briefly taken prisoner as a result. In 1779 Triebner's account to the SPCK said he had just fifty-four members attending Ebenezer's Jerusalem Church.[17] This drop in attendance may have been because of the divisions in the community, or it may have been a practical outcome of the difficulty of traveling to Ebenezer during war. Surely, someone who was in the Rabenhorst faction, and therefore siding with Governor Treutlen, would not risk travel to have worship services and Holy Communion from the Tory Triebner.

In 1782, after the Americans had won in the South, Triebner and twenty-eight men from Ebenezer left with the British troops.[18] Perhaps one indicator of the economic and social shifts in Georgia after the Trustee period is that Triebner noted that he left behind an estate of nine hundred acres, a large plantation when one considers he was also paid a salary by the SPCK. We do not have records for the twenty-eight men who left with him, who probably also traveled with their families, but we do know Triebner escaped by first going to St. Augustine, Florida, then to the Bahamas, where he was employed by the SPCK to do mission work among the enslaved people there. Triebner, a Halle-trained Lutheran pastor, never returned to German lands. After the Bahamas, he moved to England, where he continued to work for the SPCK. His Ebenezer troubles were not over, though, as Rabenhorst's friends accused Triebner of taking some of the former's estate when he fled America. Making clear that they no longer felt obliged to support people living in the new United States, the SPCK recommended that the Georgians ask the British government for redress.

"Salzburger" governor John Treutlen was also a victim of the civil war for independence. When the British arrived in Savannah he fled across the river to his son's plantation in South Carolina. It was there in early 1782, after the British had surrendered at Yorktown but while personal animosities still raged in the South, that Treutlen was dragged from his bed and murdered.[19]

The American Revolution took another victim: the town of Ebenezer. After being occupied by American, then British, then American armies for years, much of the town was deserted and destroyed. Triebner reported that when under the control of the British the great number of British and Hessian troops in the area around Ebenezer had destroyed nearly all of the fields nearby.[20] When the British troops retreated they, or other men wandering in the countryside, plundered all the surrounding farms of the "Necessaries of Life."[21] Right after the war Ebenezer was briefly made county seat of Effingham County, but that honor was moved to nearby Springfield a year later. By the nineteenth century it was a "dead town," with no inhabitants, although the Jerusalem Church remained.[22]

After Boltzius died the community lost their strong social unity in the battle between Triebner and Rabenhorst. After American independence they lost the charitable support of the SPCK. However, the philanthropic Pietist German network continued to keep ties between continental Europe and America. At the request of the Jerusalem Church congregation, in 1786 the Lutherans sent a replacement Halle-trained pastor to Ebenezer, Johann Ernst Bergmann. He was supported with the income generated by Rabenhorst's old plantation.[23] Although the scale of support diminished, the Francke Foundations continued to send prized Halle medicines and kept a correspondence between themselves and Georgia, just as they continued to partner with the SPCK on other Protestant missions. Bergmann preached in German, which has been cited as the reason some second- and third-generation Salzburgers joined the Methodists and Baptist during the Second Great Awakening in the early nineteenth century.[24] The last letter from Georgia in the Francke Foundations archive is from 1828; it discusses a shipment of medicine and books.[25]

The story of the Salzburgers and German settlements in Georgia complicates our understanding of the Trustee period. They and their leaders, particularly Johann Martin Boltzius, accepted the Trustees' ideas that the Georgia forest could save them. Unlike some of the English-speaking settlers, the community worked to put the Trustees' plans into action. In the end Georgia did provide shelter and physical relief from the persecution they had experienced in Salzburg and Europe. They did build a self-sustaining town, with settlement expanding up and down the Savannah River. And the colony was also a place where many Salzburgers found a greater devotion and commitment to God by worshiping together in their tight-knit community. They surely worked hard, but any successes they had would not have been possible without the continued support of the SPCK and the Halle Pietist network. Their support was part of an effort to spread Protestant Christianity and to blunt the expansion of Catholic empires. In that, they largely succeeded.

The community of Germans never regained the same unity they had during the Trustee period. But many of them and their descendants continued to see the Jerusalem Church as the center of their community. It was briefly occupied by troops again in the 1860s, as William Tecumseh Sherman's army marched to the sea during the Civil War. The church, originally built in the 1730s using donations from the philanthropic network, then rebuilt in 1769, still stands. The town is gone, but the Salzburgers' connections through their faith and shared culture endure.

# NOTES

## Abbreviations

| | |
|---|---|
| Add | Additional Manuscripts |
| AFS | Archiv der Franckeschen Stiftungen, Halle |
| BL | The British Library |
| CR | Candler et al., *Colonial Records of the State of Georgia* |
| *Diary* | Perceval, *Manuscripts of the Earl of Egmont* |
| DR | Urlsperger, *Detailed Reports* |
| GHS | Georgia Historical Society |
| KJV | King James Version |
| *Letterbooks* | Newman, *Henry Newman's Salzburger Letterbooks* |
| *Letters* | Boltzius, *Letters of Johann Martin Boltzius* |
| *Oxford DNB* | *Oxford Dictionary of National Biography* |
| SPCK | Society for Promoting Christian Knowledge |
| SPCK Archives, CUL | SPCK Archives, Cambridge University Library, Department of Manuscripts and University Archives, Cambridge, UK |
| TNA | The National Archives, London, England |

## Foreword

1. Frederick Jackson Turner, *The Rise of the New West, 1819–1829* (New York: Harper & Brothers Publishers, 1906), 57.

## Introduction

1. DR 1:59.
2. DR 1:56.
3. DR 1:59.
4. Whitefield, *Continuation*, 1.

5. U.S. Census Bureau, "Chapter Z: Colonial and Pre-Federal Statistics," pt. 2.

6. TNA CO 5/688, 23 June 1752, p. 195.

7. For example, Miller, "Failure of the Colony." Miller writes of the Trustees' "straight-jacket system," and that "the Colonists chose slavery . . . as necessary preliminaries toward prosperity, and rightly so."

8. Jackson and Spalding, *Forty Years of Diversity*; Coleman, *Colonial Georgia*; Spalding and Jackson, *Oglethorpe in Perspective*; Pressly, *On the Rim*.

9. McIlvenna, *Short Life of Free Georgia*.

10. McIlvenna, *Short Life of Free Georgia*, 3.

11. Piker, "Empire, the Emperor"; Juricek, *Colonial Georgia and the Creeks*; Sweet, *Negotiating for Georgia*; Anderson, *Ethnic Cleansing and the Indian*.

12. For a more detailed discussion of Georgia's role in the life of John Wesley and Methodism, see Hammond, *John Wesley in America*; Hammond and Jones, *George Whitefield*.

13. George Fenwick Jones, *Salzburger Saga*. The authoritative book on the Salzburger expulsion in Europe is Walker, *Salzburg Transaction*.

14. Melton, *Religion, Community, and Slavery*.

15. Betty Wood, *Slavery in Colonial Georgia*.

16. Burnard, *Planters, Merchants, and Slaves*; Hoffer, *Cry Liberty*; Lannen, "Liberty and Slavery"; Jennison, *Cultivating Race*; McCandless, *Slavery, Disease and Suffering*.

17. Engel, *Religion and Profit*.

18. For more information on the makeup of the transports to Ebenezer, see George Fenwick Jones, *Salzburger Saga*.

19. Wokeck, *Trade in Strangers*, 58.

20. Pyrges, *Das Kolonialprojekt EbenEzer*; Pyrges, "Religion in the Atlantic World," in Strom, Lehmann, and Melton, *Pietism in Germany*, 51–70.

21. Parrish, *American Curiosity*; Games, *Web of Empire*.

22. Grabbe, *Halle Pietism*.

23. Kupperman, *Pocahontas and the English Boys*, xi.

## Chapter 1. Exile

1. SPCK, *Further Account of the Sufferings*, 27.

2. SPCK, *Further Account of the Sufferings*, 27.

3. Walker, *Salzburg Transaction*; Melton, *Religion, Community, and Slavery*; Huber and Kastinger Riley, "'Gottes Brünnlein'"; George Fenwick Jones, *Salzburger Saga*; George Fenwick Jones, *Georgia Dutch*. The Reverend P. A. Strobel, who led the Georgia Salzburgers' Jerusalem Lutheran church in the nineteenth century, wrote what is possibly the first full history of the group. As he had no access to German or many British records, his work is based primarily on popular histories and descendants' family stories. Strobel, *Salzburgers and Their Descendants*.

4. Melton, *Religion, Community, and Slavery*, 20–21.

5. Melton, *Religion, Community, and Slavery*, 34–44.

6. Melton, *Religion, Community, and Slavery*, 49.

7. SPCK, *Further Account of the Sufferings*, 41.

8. SPCK, *Further Account of the Sufferings*, 42.

9. SPCK, *Further Account of the Sufferings*, 43.

10. SPCK, *Further Account of the Sufferings*, 37.

11. George Fenwick Jones, *Salzburger Saga*, 6.

12. SPCK, *Further Account of the Sufferings*, 61.

13. Walker, *Salzburg Transaction*, 197–199.

14. Marsch, *Die Salzburger Emigration in Bildern*. A set of two-sided commemorative medals is held in the Salzburg Museum in Salzburg, Austria.

15. SPCK, *Further Account of the Sufferings*, 1, 4.

16. Loewe and Firth, "Martin Luther's 'A Mighty Fortress,'" 132.

17. SPCK, *Further Account of the Sufferings*, 1.

18. SPCK, *Further Account of the Sufferings*, 7, 9.

19. SPCK, *Further Account of the Sufferings*, 7.

20. 22 February 1732, SPCK Minute books, MS A1/14, 135–6, SPCK Archives, CUL.

21. *Letterbooks*, 15.

22. *Letterbooks*, 223.

23. *Diary*, 1:287.

24. Journal of the Trustees, 1732–1737, 12 October 1732, TNA CO 5/686, 20–22.

25. Journal of the Trustees, 20–22.

26. Journal of the Trustees, 20–22.

27. Journal of the Trustees, 20–22.

28. Georgia Trustee Common Council Minutes 1732–36, 24 May 1733, TNA CO 5/689, 59.

29. *Letterbooks*, 276.

30. *Letterbooks*, 333.

31. Melton, *Religion, Community, and Slavery*, 202.

32. Journal of the Trustees, 1732–1737, 26 September 1733, TNA CO 5/686, 137.

33. *Letterbooks*, 322, 326.

34. Journal of the Trustees, 1732–1737, 26 September 1733, TNA CO 5/686, 137.

35. DR 1:39, 59. The first transport included forty-one Salzburger exiles, and their pastor, catechist, and an apothecary. Commissioner Reck, who was not staying in Georgia, made the total that landed forty-five.

36. Melton, *Religion, Community, and Slavery*, 123.

37. DR 1:27.

38. Reck and Boltzius, *Extract of the Journals*, 6; DR 1:67.

39. 1 Samuel 7:12 (KJV). The Salzburgers used the Luther Bible; however, this book uses the King James Version of the Bible for all English translations of scriptural references, except in cases when the Luther Bible differs substantially from the English text. The Luther Bible reads, "Bis hierher hat uns der HERR geholfen." A footnote in the Luther Bible notes the literal Hebrew translation as "Stein der Hilfe" (Stone of Help).

40. DR 1:64.

41. DR 1:69.

42. DR 1:73.

## Chapter 2. The Georgia Trustees

1. James Oglethorpe to George Berkeley, May 1731, in Rand, *Berkeley and Percival*, 277.

2. James Oglethorpe to George Berkeley, May 1731, in Rand, *Berkeley and Percival*, 274.

3. The MPs who were original Trustees include John Perceval, the first Earl of Egmont; James Oglethorpe; Francis Eyles; Rogers Holland; James [Hamilton], Viscount Limerick; Robert More; Thomas Tower; John Page; and John White.

4. Leonard W. Cowie, "Bray, Thomas," *Oxford DNB* (2012).

5. Baine, *Creating Georgia*, 37 and 72.

6. Avalon Project, "Charter of Georgia, 1732," https://avalon.law.yale.edu/18th_century/ga01.asp.

7. Auman, "Give Their Service for Nothing," 101–119.

8. *Diary*, 1:223.

9. *Diary*, 1:267.

10. Spalding, "James Edward Oglethorpe's Quest," 61–63.

11. Harrington, *Oceana and Other Works*, 102.

12. Harrington, *Oceana and Other Works*, 61.

13. Bearcroft and Trustees, *Sermon Preached*.

14. Martyn and Trustees, *Reasons for Establishing*, 29.

15. Martyn and Trustees, *Reasons for Establishing*, 19.

16. Sedgwick, "James Oglethorpe"; Cruickshanks, "John LaRoche."

17. DR 1:69.

18. Hoffer, *Cry Liberty*, 54.

19. TNA CO 5 365/016.

20. Martyn and Trustees, *Account Shewing the Progress*, 9.

21. Martyn and Trustees, *Account Shewing the Progress*, 10.

22. Rothschild, "Horrible Tragedy."

23. Montgomery, *Discourse Concerning the Design'd Establishment*.

24. Montgomery, *Discourse Concerning the Design'd Establishment*, 12–13.

25. Meroney, "London Entrepôt Merchants," 231.

26. *Diary*, 1:220.

27. Jacob M. Price, "Heathcote, Sir Gilbert, First Baronet (1652–1733)," *Oxford DNB*.

28. Oglethorpe, *New and Accurate Account*.

29. Oglethorpe, *New and Accurate Account*, 43.

30. Georgia Trustees, *Select Tracts Relating to Colonies*.

31. 30 June 1732, Urban, *Gentlemen's Magazine*, 825.

32. 20 July 1732, Urban, *Gentlemen's Magazine*, 874.

33. March 1733, Urban, *Gentlemen's Magazine*, 156.

34. *Diary*, 1:282.

35. Meroney, "London Entrepôt Merchants," 236. In the minutes for the Trustees in 1732, nearly every meeting mentions issuing commissions to collect donations. For some examples, see TNA CO 5/686/12, 16, 20, 41, 59, 66, 84, 87, 91.

36. Meroney, "London Entrepôt Merchants," 237.

37. Urban, *Gentlemen's Magazine . . . 1732*, 975.

38. Meroney, "London Entrepôt Merchants," 327.

39. Dunn, "Trustees of Georgia," 533.

40. Dunn, "Trustees of Georgia," 551.

41. Miller, "Failure of the Colony," 1.

42. Crane, "Philanthropists and the Genesis," 64.

43. CR 4:frontmatter.

44. Martyn, *Some Account of the Designs*, 3.

45. Martyn, *Some Account of the Designs*, 4.

46. CR 4:19.

47. Abstract of the General Account of All Monies & Effects from South Carolina, 11 April 1734, Georgia Trustee Manuscripts, 1732–1734, GHS MS 278, item 2.

48. Brigham, "Mark Catesby and the Patronage," 146; Catesby and Hibbert, *Natural History of Carolina*.

49. Moore and Robinson, *Voyage to Georgia*, 32.

50. Moore and Robinson, *Voyage to Georgia*, 30.

51. 7 August 1732 and 5 June 1733, Journal of the Trustees 1732–1737, TNA CO 5/686/10, 102; 10 November 1736, Minutes of the Council of Trustees, 1736–41, TNA CO 5/690/36.

52. Board of Trade and Plantations, Correspondence, TNA CO 5/686/104, 167, and 264.

53. Kupperman, "Puzzle of the American Climate," 1267.

54. Martyn, *Some Account of the Designs*, 31.

55. Martyn, *Some Account of the Designs*, 34.

56. Otterness, *Becoming German*.

57. March 1732, Urban, *Gentlemen's Magazine*, 681.

58. March 1732, Urban, *Gentlemen's Magazine*, 681.

59. Melton, *Religion, Community, and Slavery*, chaps. 1 and 2.

60. 12 October 1732, Journal of the Trustees for Establishing the Colony, 1732–1737, TNA CO 5/686/20.

61. Bearcroft and Trustees, *Sermon Preached*, 12.

62. Bearcroft and Trustees, *Sermon Preached*, 12.

63. 20 August 1735, Egmont, *Journal of the Earl*, 103.

64. Paul Schuster Taylor, *Georgia Plan*, 152.

65. Paul Schuster Taylor, *Georgia Plan*, 56.

66. Dunn, "Trustees of Georgia," 553.

67. Paul Schuster Taylor, *Georgia Plan*, 52.

68. The Malcontents' pamphlets have been collected and published in Reese, *Clamorous Malcontents*.

69. Paul Schuster Taylor, *Georgia Plan*, 173.

70. Paul Schuster Taylor, *Georgia Plan*, 173.

71. Dunn, "Trustees of Georgia," 553.

72. CR 1:620.

73. Dunn, "Trustees of Georgia," 563.

74. Tailfer, Anderson, and Douglas, *True and Historical Narrative*.

75. Martyn and Trustees, *Account Shewing the Progress*.

76. 23 June 1752, CR 5:578.

77. McIlvenna, *Short Life of Free Georgia*, 3.

## Chapter 3. Protestant Philanthropists

1. Samuel Urlsperger to Sir John Philipps, 24 August 1732, *Letterbooks*, 255. Philipps was an influential member of the SPCK.

2. *Letterbooks*, 225.

3. Renate Wilson, *Pious Traders in Medicine*.

4. Gawthrop, *Pietism and the Making*, see especially chap. 9.

5. Matthias, "August Hermann Francke," 104.

6. Ryrie, *Protestants*, 158–163; Stein, "Philipp Jakob Spener (1635–1705)," in Lindberg, *Pietist Theologians*, 84–100.

7. Benjamin Marschke, "Pietism and Politics in Prussia and Beyond," in Shantz, *Introduction to German Pietism*, 472–527.

8. Marschke, "Absolutely Pietist."

9. W. A. Speck, "George, Prince of Denmark and Duke of Cumberland (1653–1708)," *Oxford DNB*.

10. The SPCK still exists today and is best known for publishing a variety of Christian tracts and books. See https://spckpublishing.co.uk.

11. Society for Promoting Christian Knowledge, *Letter from a Residing Member*, 31.

12. Society for Promoting Christian Knowledge, *Letter from a Residing Member*, 33.

13. Nishikawa, "SPCK in Defence," 730–748.

14. Nishikawa, "SPCK in Defence," 736.

15. Nishikawa, "SPCK in Defence."

16. Andrews, "Tranquebar," 3–34.

17. Norman J. Threinen, "Friedrich Ziegenhagen," in Grabbe, *Halle Pietism*, 113–135.

18. SPCK, *Further Account of the Sufferings*.

19. SPCK, *Further Account of the Sufferings*, 3.

20. Threinen, "Friedrich Ziegenhagen," 124.

21. SPCK, *Further Account of the Sufferings*.

22. 28 May 1733, Special Committee for the Salzburgers, SPCK Minute books, MS A1/15, 82, SPCK Archives, CUL.

23. 28 October 1732, SPCK Minute books, MS A1/15, 7, SPCK Archives, CUL.

24. 28 October 1732, SPCK Minute books, MS A1/15, 7, SPCK Archives, CUL.

25. 2 August 1732, Journal of the Trustees for Establishing the Colony, 1732–1737, TNA CO 5/686/5.

26. The SPCK request to Urlsperger is recorded in Henry Newman to Urlsperger, 7 September 1733, *Letterbooks*, 53. Urlsperger's questions on behalf of the Salzburgers are in a letter from Urlsperger to Henry Newman, 27 November 1732, Henry Newman Salzburger letter books (reproductions), MS 93, box 2, folder 4, item 13, Hargrett Rare Book and Manuscript Library, University of Georgia, Athens.

27. *Letterbooks*, 10.

28. CR 1:186.

29. *Diary*, 1:231.

30. Boltzius, "Reliable Answer," 223–261.

31. 31 July 1734, Journal of the Trustees for Establishing the Colony, 1732–1737, TNA CO 5/686/201.

32. 3 December 1734, Journal of the Trustees for Establishing the Colony, 1732–1737, TNA CO 5/686/299.

33. 2 February 1737, Journal of the Trustees for Establishing the Colony, 1732–1737, TNA CO 5/686/350.

34. Newman to Urlsperger, 13 June 1732, *Letterbooks*, 17.

35. Münch to Mr. Mayer, 7 August 1732, *Letterbooks*, 234; Münch to Mayer at London, 24 July 1732, *Letterbooks*, 231.

36. Henry Newman to Vat, 18 September 1733, *Letterbooks*, 57.

37. 29 May 1733, SPCK Minute books, MS A1/15, 86, SPCK Archives, CUL.

38. Henry Newman to Münch, 20 September 1734, *Letterbooks*, 119.

39. Newman to Urlsperger, 20 August 1734, *Letterbooks*, 114.

40. Vat to Newman, 19 October 1734, *Letterbooks*, 490.

41. 24 October 1734, SPCK Minute books, MS A1/16, 12, SPCK Archives, CUL.

42. 29 October 1734, SPCK Minute books, MS A1/14, 12, SPCK Archives, CUL.

43. 5 November 1734, SPCK Minute books, MS A1/16, 16, SPCK Archives, CUL.

44. 29 October 1734, SPCK Minute books, MS A1/16, 15, SPCK Archives, CUL.

45. 21 August 1734, Journal of the Trustees for Establishing the Colony, TNA CO 5/686/207.

46. 15 October 1734, SPCK Minute books, MS A1/16, 9, SPCK Archives, CUL.

47. 15 October 1734, SPCK Minute books, MS A1/16, 10, SPCK Archives, CUL.

48. 21 October 1734, SPCK Letter Account Books and Manuscripts 1732–39, MS 1396, GHS.

49. Simonds to Newman, 23 November 1734, *Letterbooks*, 502.

50. 27 September 1734, SPCK Minute books, MS A1/15, 232, SPCK Archives, CUL.

51. "Currency Converter: 1270–2017," National Archives, https://www.national archives.gov.uk/currency-converter/.

52. Dunn, "Trustees of Georgia," 551.

53. 29 May 1733, SPCK Minute books, MS A1/15, 88, SPCK Archives, CUL.

54. 24 November 1733, SPCK Minute books, MS A1/15, 134, SPCK Archives, CUL.

55. Cowie, *Henry Newman*, 241.

56. 24 November 1733, SPCK Minute books, MS A1/15, 134, SPCK Archives, CUL.

57. DR 15:119.

58. SPCK, *Account of the Society* (1740), 8–9.

59. George Fenwick Jones, *Salzburger Saga*, 115.

60. 18 May 1735, SPCK Minute books, MS A1/16, 72, SPCK Archives, CUL.

61. Invoices and lists of books and medicine for the Ebenezer community, AFS, Missionsarchiv, AFSt/M 5E:4.

62. Vat to Newman, 30 May 1735, Correspondence, original—Board of Trade, TNA CO 5/637/77.

63. 8 October 1736, Correspondence, original—Board of Trade, TNA CO 5/639/12.

64. Francke to Boltzius, 8 September 1745, AFS, Missionsarchiv, AFSt/M 5A 11:32.

65. Renate Wilson, *Pious Traders in Medicine*.

66. 20 December 1738, Minutes of the Council of Trustees, TNA CO 5/690/183.

67. 12 July 1742, Journal of the Trustees for Establishing the Colony, TNA CO 5/687/207.

68. Francke to Boltzius, 24 July 1745, AFS, Missionsarchiv, AFSt/M 5A II:30.

69. Francke to Boltzius, 12 July 1748, AFS, Missionsarchiv, AFSt/M 5A II:81.

70. Münchhausen to Francke, 29 March 1753, AFS, Missionsarchiv, AFSt/M 5E 2:172; Receipt by Johann Wilhelm Breithuth to Münchhausen and Georg Ludwig Waitz, 18 December 1752, AFS, Missionsarchiv, AFSt/M 5E 2:151.

## Chapter 4. The Good Forest

1. DR 1:104–105.

2. DR 2:114–117. The diaries have several examples of Salzburgers who became lost in the woods, although few of them died. In February 1736, for example, Herr Landfelder spent an anxious night in the cold forest before he was found and rescued the next day. DR 3:47.

3. She married Thomas Geschwandel in summer 1736. DR 3:14.

4. Reck, *Von Reck's Voyage*, 26.

5. Boltzius, "Reliable Answer," 468–519.

6. Boltzius, "Reliable Answer," 233.

7. John 1:23 (KJV); Matthew 4 (KJV).

8. Boltzius uses Wüste throughout his official diary, which was printed in Germany and translated for print in England. The English version uses "wilderness," while the German versions use the word *Wüste*. The German-language version was collected and printed in several volumes as *Der ausführlichen Nachrichten Von der Königlich-Groß-Britannischen Colonie Saltzburgischer Emigranten in America . . .* ; the volumes are available in the Salzburger Collection, Crumley Archives, Columbia, S.C.

9. DR 1:106.

10. DR 1:107.

11. Reck and Jones, "Von Reck's Second Report," 322.

12. Reck and Jones, "Von Reck's Second Report," 322.

13. DR 1:106.

14. DR 1:107.

15. Silver, *New Face on the Countryside*, 25.

16. Blackburn, "Conquests for Barbarism," 14. The Oder River swamplands were drained in the eighteenth century by the Prussian government in an effort to reclaim the land and stamp out the unsavory element of the "wasteful" wilderness.

17. *Der ausführlichen Nachrichten . . .*, 7th Continuation, 362, Salzburger Collection, book 67, Crumley Archives. Boltzius wrote, "Wer hätte vor einigen Jahren densten sollen, daß der herr auch grosse Dinge in dieser Wüsten thun würde?"

18. Boltzius to Eva Rosina Boltzius (his mother), 6 May 1734, in *Letters*, 1:74.

19. DR 1:71.

20. Boltzius, "Reliable Answer," 228.

21. Martyn and Trustees, *Account Shewing the Progress*, 6.

22. Martyn and Trustees, *Reasons for Establishing*, 23–25.

23. Watts, *Sermon Preached before the Trustees*, 1. Because these were English sermons, they used the King James Version of the Bible. The Salzburgers, of course, used the Luther Bible. For these verses, the meanings between the two are the same.

24. Bearcroft and Trustees, *Sermon Preached*.

25. Bearcroft and Trustees, *Sermon Preached*, 3.

26. Worster, *Nature's Economy*, 28.

27. Wallmann, "Johann Arndt," 22.

28. Splitter, *Pastors, People, Politics*, 40.

29. Arndt, *True Christianity*, 790.

30. Wallmann, "Johann Arndt," 23.

31. Arndt, *True Christianity*, 791.

32. DR 3:256.

33. Denne, *Duty of Doing All Things*, 5.

34. Denne, *Duty of Doing All Things*, 6.

35. Brigham, "Mark Catesby and the Patronage," 146.

36. Brigham, "Mark Catesby and the Patronage," 141.

37. James Oglethorpe to Hans Sloane, 19 September 1733, BL, Sloane MS 4053, folder 53.

38. Reck, "A Short Report on Georgia and the Indians There," DR 1:137–38.

39. DR 1:141.

40. DR 1:141.

41. Reck and Boltzius, *Extract of the Journals*.

42. Reck, "Short Report on Georgia," DR 1:137.

43. DR 1:137.

44. DR 1:141.

45. Stewart, *"What Nature Suffers to Groe."*

46. The drawings have been attributed to Reck, but there is some scholarly debate about who made them. Kristian Hvidt, who published a book of the drawings along with an introductory commentary, believed Reck drew most of them. See Reck, *Von Reck's Voyage*, 7. George Fenwick Jones argued that the artist may have been one of Reck's servants, Christian Müller. See George Fenwick Jones, *Salzburger Saga*, 32.

47. De Brahm, *Map of South Carolina*.

48. Stewart, "William Gerard De Brahm's 1757 Map," 531.

49. DR 3:99.

50. Stewart, "Whether Wast, Deodant, or Stray," 6, 10.

51. DR 3:99.

52. Silver, *New Face on the Countryside*, 107.

53. DR 3:29.

54. Ethridge, *From Chicaza to Chicakasaw*, 111.

55. Juricek, *Colonial Georgia and the Creeks*, 88.

56. Juricek, *Colonial Georgia and the Creeks*, 88.

57. Johann Martin Boltzius to Eva Rosina Boltzius, 6 May 1734, *Letters*, 1:74.

58. Warde, "Fear of Wood Shortage"; Appuhn, *Forest on the Sea*.

59. Cronon, *Changes in the Land*, 120; Alan Taylor, "Wasty Ways," 13.

60. Reck, *Von Reck's Voyage*, 72. Reck drew a flying squirrel and noted, "If you want

to catch it you must cut down the branch on which it is sitting and then the tree itself."

61. Melton, "From Alpine Miner," 113.

62. Sonnlechner and Winiwarter, "Recht Und Verwaltung," 71.

63. Johann, "Traditional Forest Management," 57. Also see Johann, *Wald Und Mensch.*

64. Wilfing et al., "Environmental Histories," 51. The importance, and even the actuality, of outmigration has been challenged by Jon Mathieu, who noted an overall population increase from 1500 to 1900. Cates, "'The Seasoning,'" 146–158.

65. Wilfing et al., "Environmental Histories," 52.

66. Reck and Boltzius, *Extract of the Journals,* 20.

67. Whitebourne, *Discourse and Discovery of New-Found-Land,* 57; Kupperman, "Puzzle of the American Climate."

68. Allan, "Hales, Stephen."

69. DR 3:99.

70. DR 3:99.

71. Whitefield, *Continuation,* 1.

72. William Stephens, *Journal of the Proceedings,* 1:226.

73. DR 3:33.

74. Johann, *Wald Und Mensch,* 34.

75. DR 6:45.

76. DR 1:69; George Fenwick Jones, *Salzburger Saga,* 15.

77. DR 1:79, 91. Boltzius reported that one of the slaves burned a beehive near a Salzburger hut in May 1734.

78. DR 1:77.

79. DR 1:104.

80. Reck, *Von Reck's Voyage,* 106.

81. These words are marked on Reck's drawings. Most of the drawings of plants or animals include a notation of the Muskogee name, the Yuchi name, and the English or German.

82. DR 2:29.

83. Reck, *Von Reck's Voyage,* 37.

84. Renate Wilson, *Pious Traders in Medicine,* 3.

85. 27 February 1818 letter from Johann Ernst Bergmann to Johann Friedrich Bergold, AFSt/M 5 B 4: 49.

86. DR 2:59.

87. DR 2:59.

88. Renate Wilson, *Pious Traders in Medicine,* 185.

89. DR 3:23.

90. Parrish, *American Curiosity.*

91. Boltzius, "Reliable Answer," 468–519.

92. Boltzius, "Nachrichten Und Anmerkungen."

93. Ewan, "Silk Culture in the Colonies," 137.

94. Joseph Ewan counted and analyzed the breakdown and categorization scheme. See Ewan, "Silk Culture in the Colonies," 138.

## Chapter 5. Subjects

1. DR 1:36.

2. DR 1:36. As a people exiled from their native state, the Salzburgers were free and apparently willing to swear fealty to the British monarch. Boltzius and Gronau were Prussian subjects, and it is not clear if they renounced their rights as Germans in the process of swearing an oath to Britain. The issues of the right of movement and the right to change allegiance had been much debated in Europe. In 1688 Samuel Pufendorf, writing in *The Law of Nature and Nations*, argued that when one moves location and submits to a new government one has forfeited one's "natural" claim to one's home state and sovereign. See McKeown, *Melancholy Order*, 24. In any case, for the Salzburgers and their Halle-trained pastors, the point is somewhat moot as they did not return to Europe.

3. *Letterbooks*, 36.

4. Journal of the Trustees, 24 May 1733, TNA CO 5/686/22.

5. William Blackstone, *Blackstone's Commentaries on the Laws of England*, 4 volumes (Oxford: Clarendon, 1765–1769), 1:362.

6. Ruprecht Steiner to Michel Steiner, November 1738, AFSt/M 5A 7: 50b. "Wir haben hier in Ebenezer viel freiheiten."

7. AFSt/M 5A 7: 49b. "Wir genießen hier alle christliche Freiheit in Religions."

8. DR 3:89.

9. Boltzius, "Reliable Answer," 225.

10. AFSt/M 5A 7:49b.

11. DR 5:280.

12. DR 5:172.

13. DR 5:275.

14. Roeber, *Palatines, Liberty, and Property*, 3.

15. Roeber, *Palatines, Liberty, and Property*, 2, 64.

16. Reck and Boltzius, *Extract of the Journals*, 22.

17. DR 3:12.

18. TNA CO 5/711/12.

19. Boltzius, "Reliable Answer," 252.

20. Johann Martin Boltzius to Eva Rosina Boltzius (his mother), 6 May 1734, *Letters*, 1:401.

21. Boltzius to Gotthilf August Francke, 23 July 1741, *Letters*, 1:333.

22. Boltzius, "Secret Diary," 88. Boltzius started this private diary on 7 February 1736 and did not begin dating his entries until 17 February. This entry occurred sometime between those two dates.

23. DR 3:11.

24. Withuhn, "Salzburgers and Slavery," 175.

25. George Fenwick Jones, *Salzburger Saga*, 53.

26. DR 2:9.

27. Samuel Quincy to Henry Newman, 15 January 1734/1735, *Letterbooks*, 530.

28. Jean Vat to Henry Newman, 10 February 1734, *Letterbooks*, 540.

29. Boltzius and Gronau to Henry Newman, 2 April 1735, *Letterbooks*, 585.

30. Jean Vat to Henry Newman, 30 May 1735, *Letterbooks*, 578.

31. Samuel Quincy to Henry Newman, 15 January 1734/1735, *Letterbooks*, 528.

32. Boltzius, "Secret Diary," 83.

33. George Fenwick Jones, *Salzburger Saga*, 29.

34. *Diary*, 2:437.

35. Henry Newman to Reck, 20 August 1734, *Letterbooks*, 115.

36. Samuel Urlsperger to Henry Newman, 27 March 1735, *Letterbooks*, 543.

37. SPCK [Henry Newman] to James Oglethorpe, 4 June 1736, *Letterbooks*, 192.

38. DR 2:9.

39. DR 2:29.

40. Jean Vat to Henry Newman, 19 April 1735, *Letterbooks*, 539.

41. Parrish, *American Curiosity*, 229.

42. Parrish, *American Curiosity*, 229. Here Parrish is quoting Mark Catesby, the naturalist who traveled in the Lowcountry in the early 1700s.

43. DR 3:19.

44. Jean Vat to Henry Newman, 30 May 1735, *Letterbooks*, 581.

45. Henry Newman to Jean Vat, 18 December 1733, *Letterbooks*, 84.

46. DR 2:41.

47. DR 2:41.

48. Henry Newman to Samuel Urlsperger, 2 January 1735/1736, *Letterbooks*, 184.

49. Henry Newman to Johann Boltzius, 3 June 1736, *Letterbooks*, 190.

50. Boltzius, "Secret Diary," 87.

51. The Georgia Trustees communicated to Oglethorpe that "we cannot proceed in the new settlement intended on the Allatamah." 31 March 1736, *Diary*, 2:252.

52. Boltzius, "Secret Diary," 101.

53. DR 2:181.

54. DR 3:49.

55. DR 3:19.

56. DR 2:156.

57. DR 2:157.

58. Boltzius, "Secret Diary," 89.

59. Boltzius, "Secret Diary," 88.

60. Boltzius, "Secret Diary," 88. See also page 105, in which Boltzius complains that he has not yet heard from Mr. Oglethorpe "how far Mr. Reck's authority extends over the Salzburgers."

61. Egmont, *Journal of the Earl*, 137.

62. DR 3:159–160.

63. DR 3:52.

64. DR 3:53.

65. Boltzius, "Secret Diary," 102.

66. Boltzius, "Secret Diary," 102.

67. Boltzius, "Secret Diary," 105.

68. DR 3:97.

69. DR 3:77.

70. DR 3:61.

## Chapter 6. Community

1. CR 30:103. See also McIlvenna, "Workers, 1733–1736," chap. 2 in *Short Life of Free Georgia*, 23–39.

2. Melton, *Religion, Community, and Slavery*, 193.

3. DR 3:115.

4. Thomas D. Wilson, *Oglethorpe Plan*; John W. Reps, "C2 + L2 = S2? Another Look at the Origins of Savannah's Town Plan," in Jackson and Spalding, *Forty Years of Diversity*, 101–151.

5. *Letters*, 1:191.

6. Shantz, *Introduction to German Pietism*, 120. Chapter 5 presents an overview of the goals and methods at the founding of the Francke Foundations.

7. DR 8:16.

8. DR 5:12.

9. Invoices and lists of books and medicine for the Ebenezer Community, AFS, Missionsarchiv, AFSt/M 5 E:4, items 9–11.

10. Klosterberg, "ABC—Büchlein Und Bilderbibel," 13.

11. Klosterberg, "ABC—Büchlein Und Bilderbibel," 35.

12. Klosterberg, "ABC—Büchlein Und Bilderbibel," 34.

13. Brown, "Devotional Life in Hymns," 211.

14. George Fenwick Jones, *Salzburger Saga*, 55.

15. Julian, *Dictionary of Hymnology*, 396.

16. The Crumley Archives' Salzburger Collection is believed to have come from Ebenezer and surrounding communities. It holds copies of Freylinghausen's hymnal. Freylinghausen, *Geistreiches Gesang-Buch*.

17. DR 2:44.

18. DR 7:12. In the back of volume 7, Jones has compiled a list the forty-five hymns sung in 1740. There may be more that were not recorded by Boltzius. See pages 302–305.

19. *Letters*, 1:105.

20. *Letters*, 1:105.

21. Gotthilf Francke to Ebenezer Community, 2 April 1743, AFSt/M 5A 10:39.

22. Thomas Stephens, *Hard Case*, 3.

23. Thomas Stephens, *Brief Account of the Causes*, 37.

24. DR 8:45.

25. DR 6:161, 163.

26. DR 8:157–158.

27. George Fenwick Jones, *Salzburger Saga*, 68.

28. DR 10:73.

29. George Fenwick Jones, *Salzburger Saga*, 86.

30. George Fenwick Jones, *Georgia Dutch*, 103–104.

31. James Van Horn Melton also noted that Boltzius's rule was "mild" and that the vast majority of Salzburgers chose to stay. Melton, "The Pastor and the Schoolmaster," in Strom, Lehmann, and Melton, *Pietism in Germany*, 226.

32. George Fenwick Jones, *Salzburger Saga*, 69.

33. DR 7:156–158.
34. DR 7:136–137.
35. DR 7:248.
36. "Appendix 1: Texte der ersten Kirchenordnung Ebenezers," in Winde, "Die Frühgeschichte Der Lutherischen Kirche," 210–215.
37. DR 16:177.
38. *Letters*, 1:363. Whitefield contributed £52 toward building a church. *Letters*, 1:320.
39. *Letters*, 1:363.
40. DR 5:318.
41. DR 5:318.
42. DR 5:318.
43. *Letters*, 1:263.
44. *Letters*, 1:363.
45. *Letters*, 1:206.
46. DR 7:171–172.
47. Splitter, *Pastors, People, Politics*, 8.
48. Splitter, *Pastors, People, Politics*, 8.
49. Mühlenberg, *Die Korrespondenz*, 1:42–43.
50. Greene, *Pursuits of Happiness*, 50.
51. Crane, *Southern Frontier*, 1.
52. DR 1:78.
53. DR 1:79.
54. For more about efforts to replicate Halle's programs, see Renate Wilson, "Halle and Ebenezer."
55. Migliazzo, *To Make This Land Our Own*.
56. Migliazzo, *To Make This Land Our Own*, 182–205.
57. DR 9:78.
58. George Fenwick Jones, "Two 'Salzburger' Letters," 55.
59. DR 6:157–159, 192.
60. For example, see *Letters*, 1:221, 275.
61. Alexander Pyrges, "The Ebenezer Communication Network," in Strom, Lehmann, and Melton, *Pietism in Germany*, 199–224.
62. Communal letter from Rastenburg to Ebenezer, 27 January 1742, AFSt/M 5D 12:3.
63. *Letters*, 1:307, 348.
64. Tailfer, Anderson, and Douglas, *True and Historical Narrative*, 161.
65. Melton, "Pastor and the Schoolmaster," 230–231.

## Chapter 7. A Moral Economy

1. Crowley, *This Sheba, Self*.
2. Matson, "Markets and Morality," 477.
3. Crowley, *This Sheba, Self*, 16.
4. See Egmont Papers 1730, BL: Add 46981, which is a set of papers for Egmont from William Taylor, his manager and steward in Ireland.

5. Oglethorpe, *New and Accurate Account*, vii.

6. Genesis 3:19 (KJV).

7. For example, see Psalms 128:2 and 109:11 (KJV).

8. *Letters*, 1:435.

9. Engel, *Religion and Profit*, 39.

10. Roeber, *Palatines, Liberty, and Property*.

11. DR 18:214.

12. Renate Wilson, "Halle and Ebenezer."

13. McCusker and Menard, *Economy of British America*, 180.

14. DR 1:79, 81.

15. Oglethorpe to the Trustees, 4 July 1739, CR 22/2:170.

16. Martyn, *Some Account of the Designs*, 2.

17. Wander, *Deutsches Sprichtwörter-Lexikon*, 1664–1692, 1100–1108.

18. In German, the sayings are "Die alte Kuh gar bald vergisst, dass sie ein Kalb gewesen ist" and "Die Kuh denkt nicht an den Winter, wenn sie in Klee weidet."

19. Mathieu, *History of the Alps*, 51.

20. Mathieu, "From Ecotypes to Sociotypes," 56.

21. Dow, *German Folklore*, 40.

22. For example, see John Frick [Feick], grantor, Deeds, vol. 16, p. 158, Berks County, Pennsylvania, Recorder of Deeds, Reading, Pa. For five pounds, Feick granted water rights for two specific uses: to build a mill race and to water a spot of his neighbor's land for a meadow.

23. Gehrke, "Ante-Bellum Agriculture of the Germans," 147.

24. Glasse, *Art of Cookery*, 2.

25. Hogarth, *O the Roast Beef of Old England*.

26. *Records of the Virginia Company*, 3:12.

27. Anderson, "King Philip's Herds," 602.

28. MacNeil, "Early American Communities," 104.

29. Resolution from the South Carolina General Assembly, 26 January 1732/1733, CR 20:7.

30. DR 3:202.

31. Extract of an English letter, forwarded by Ziegenhagen, from Mr. Von Reck, 1736, received 14 January 1737, AFS, Missionsarchiv, AFSt/M 5A 3:34.

32. George Fenwick Jones, *Salzburger Saga*, 212.

33. Stewart, "Whether Wast, Deodant, or Stray," 5.

34. Stewart, "Whether Wast, Deodant, or Stray," 23.

35. Stewart, "Whether Wast, Deodant, or Stray," 22.

36. Martyn to Boltzius, 31 May 1748, TNA CO 5/668/289.

37. "Inventory and Appraisement of the Estate of the Revd John Martin Boltzius, 1766," Probate Inventories, MS 4000, GHS, roll 22, 214.

38. Stewart, "Whether Wast, Deodant, or Stray," 11.

39. Stewart, "Whether Wast, Deodant, or Stray," 15n25.

40. George Fenwick Jones, *Georgia Dutch*, 212.

41. "Inventory and Appraisement," 214.

42. CR 29:200.

43. 24 December 1735, Journal of the Trustees for Establishing the Colony, TNA CO 5/686/304.

44. DR 2:97.

45. George Fenwick Jones, *Georgia Dutch*, 211.

46. Gallay, *Formation of a Planter Elite*, 21.

47. *Account of the Progress of the Colony*, TNA CO 5/711/24 verso.

48. *Letters*, 1:240.

49. SPCK, *Account of the Society* (1741), 55.

50. In German, the wisdom said, "Eine gute Kuh sucht man in Stall."

51. Anderson, "King Philip's Herds," 604.

52. Stewart, "Whether Wast, Deodant, or Stray," 6.

53. Martyn to Boltzius, 18 July 1750, TNA 5/669/43.

54. Boltzius to Verelst, 13 April 1738, received 13 December 1738, Trustee Correspondence 1737–1741, TNA CO 5/650/79.

55. Boltzius to Vernon, 28 June 1737, Board of Trade Correspondence 1736–1737, TNA CO 5/639/376.

56. *Letters*, 1:168.

57. *Letters*, 1:185.

58. Ziegenhagen to Honorable Gentleman [Benjamin Martyn], 22 February 1736/1737, TNA CO 5/639/35.

59. DR 9:100.

60. DR 9:201.

61. DR 9:225.

62. Boltzius and Gronau to Francke, August 1743, Received 4 February 1744, AFS, Missionsarchiv, AFSt/M 5A 11:3.

63. James Oglethorpe to the Trustees, 18 May 1736, TNA CO 5/638/282.

64. DR 8:388.

65. DR 15:58.

66. DR 15:58.

67. DR 18:112.

68. [SPCK] to Verelst, 9 October 1735, in *S.P.C.K. Early 18th Century Archives*, pt. C, reel 23, 51.

69. DR 7:169.

70. 18 June 1736, Egmont, *Journal of the Earl*, 170.

71. *Letters*, 1:363.

72. CR 4:162.

73. William Stephens, *Journal of the Proceedings*, 2:113.

74. Verelst to Stephens, 29 March 1740, TNA CO 5/667/318.

75. DR 7:179.

76. DR 7:178–181.

77. Verelst to Boltzius, 27 April 1741, TNA CO 5/658/23.

78. DR 7:263.

79. Jones, "Salzburger Mills," 109.

80. DR 18:112.

81. DR 18:112.

82. DR 18:133.

83. George Fenwick Jones, *Georgia Dutch*, 217.

84. DR 11/12:15.

85. Boltzius to Francke, 16 December 1745, AFS, Missionsarchiv, AFSt/M 5A 11:48.

86. Boltzius to Francke, 25 February 1746, AFS, Missionsarchiv, AFSt/M 5A 11:37. Boltzius did not explicitly say he wanted money from Augsburg or Christian von Münch. But he did say that instead of sending linen, he wanted them to send cash. Sending linen was a project financed by Münch, and the implication was to ask him for money. The idea behind the linen donations was that the Salzburgers could sell any that they did not need, thereby clothing themselves and making a little income.

87. CR 1:489.

88. DR 11/12:71.

89. *Letters*, 2:437.

90. CR 1:488.

91. Martyn to Stephens, 18 July 1746, TNA CO 5/668/226.

92. DR 18:228–231. Boltzius wrote a detailed description of the Kurtz affair in his official diary, but the original writing has not been found.

93. Martyn to President [Stephens] and Assistants at Savannah, 11 March 1749, TNA CO 5/668/325.

94. Johann Martin Boltzius to Georgia Trustees, 1 May 1751, TNA CO 5/643/205–206 verso.

95. DR 15:8. The money came from a donation from London court chaplain Samuel Theodor Albinus, who assisted Ziegenhagen beginning in the 1750s.

96. DR 15:4–8.

97. DR 17:23.

98. DR 17:145.

99. Bonner, *History of Georgia Agriculture*, 24.

100. Edmund Sears Morgan, *Gentle Puritan*, 147.

101. Harriot, *Briefe and True Report*, B1 (reverse).

102. Marsh, *Unravelled Dreams*, 131.

103. Marsh, *Unravelled Dreams*, 275.

104. Martyn, *Impartial Enquiry into the State*, 14.

105. Oglethorpe, *New and Accurate Account*, 55.

106. Bearcroft and Trustees, *Sermon Preached*, 13–14.

107. Oglethorpe, *New and Accurate Account*, 58.

108. Boreman, *Compendious Account*, 7.

109. Boreman, *Compendious Account*, 7.

110. Locke, *Observations upon the Growth*.

111. Marsh, "Silk Hopes," 820.

112. Marsh, "Silk Hopes," 834.

113. Martyn, *Impartial Enquiry into the State*, 31.

114. Martyn, *Impartial Enquiry into the State*, 32.

115. Egmont to Mr. Byrd in Virginia, 28 December 1730, Egmont Letters 1727–1730, BL: Add 47032, 261.

116. Martyn, *Impartial Enquiry into the State*, 14.

117. *South Carolina Gazette* (Charleston, S.C.), 14–21 July 1776.

118. "Facts and Observations," 69.

119. Written in 1732 in response to the Trustees, Lambe's letter was published in 1741 in the appendix of Martyn, *Impartial Enquiry into the State*, 74.

120. Brigham, "Mark Catesby and the Patronage," 46.

121. Catesby and Hibbert, *Natural History of Carolina*, 98. The University of North Carolina has digitized Catesby's work. The image of the snake and mulberry can be seen here: http://dc.lib.unc.edu/cdm/ref/collection/dmisc/id/1911.

122. John Perceval to William Byrd II, 28 December 1730, in Byrd, *Correspondence*, 440; William Bryd to Hans Sloane, 31 May 1737, in Byrd, *Correspondence*, 511.

123. Purry's "Description abrégée de l'état present de la Caroline Meridionale" was translated as "A Description of the Province of South Carolina," published as a pamphlet and serialized in the August, September, and October issues of the *Gentlemen's Magazine*. Urban, *Gentlemen's Magazine*, 894–897, 969–970. The full pamphlet has been reprinted as Purry, "Proposals by Mr. Peter Purry."

124. Migliazzo, *To Make This Land Our Own*, 34.

125. Oglethorpe, *New and Accurate Account*, iii.

126. Martyn and Trustees, *Account Shewing the Progress*, 8.

127. Marsh, *Unravelled Dreams*, 272.

128. Coulter and Saye, *List of the Early Settlers of Georgia*, 8.

129. 14 February 1732/1733, Journal of the Trustees for Establishing the Colony, TNA CO 5/686/68; Marsh, *Unravelled Dreams*, 280.

130. DR 3:86.

131. Safley, *Charity and Economy*, 63; the official Aystetten castle website, http://www.schloss-aystetten.de/html/body_geschichte.html.

132. Gertraut Kroehr Boltzius was a Salzburger. Gertraut's sister, Catherina, married Gronau. Both couples probably married in 1735, although no official record survives.

133. Boreman, *Compendious Account*, 14.

134. Boreman, *Compendious Account*, 14.

135. Locke, *Observations upon the Growth*, 67.

136. Boreman, *Compendious Account*, 71.

137. DR 6:76.

138. DR 8:172.

139. DR 8:172.

140. DR 8:509.

141. Migliazzo, *To Make This Land Our Own*, 234; Marsh, *Unravelled Dreams*, 260.

142. DR 8:173.

143. DR 8:189.

144. Journal of the Trustees, 1745–1752, 29 December 1746, TNA CO 5/688/27.

145. *Letters*, 1:394, 1:419, and 1:3.

146. DR 11:10–11.

147. *Letters*, 2:529.

148. Habersham, 13 April 1751, "Diary, 1750–1752," Habersham Family Papers, MS 1787, GHS.

149. "Inventory and Appraisement," 214.

150. DR 17:153.

151. DR 15: 55.

152. George Fenwick Jones, *Georgia Dutch*, 222.

153. DR 18:25.

154. Habersham, 29 April 1751, "Diary, 1750–1751," GHS.

155. Habersham, 29 April 1751, "Diary, 1750–1751," GHS.

156. DR 11:46.

157. DR 11:46.

158. DR 8:172.

159. DR 8:319.

160. Renate Wilson, "Halle and Ebenezer," 285.

161. *Letters*, 2:466.

162. The Lamar Institute found the archaeological remains of the filature. Elliott and Folse Elliott, *Seasons in the Sun*.

163. Renate Wilson, "Halle and Ebenezer," 290.

164. *Letters*, 2:478.

165. Boltzius to Gotthilf August Francke, 21 August 1749, AFS, Missionsarchiv, AF-St/M 5в 1:25.

166. *Letters*, 2:529.

167. 16 November 1749, Journal of Trustees, 1745–1752, TNA CO 5/688/114.

168. 22 February 1748/1749, Journal of Trustees, 1745–1752, TNA CO 5/688/92.

169. Habersham, 18 April 1751, "Diary, 1750–1751," GHS.

170. Habersham, 18 April 1751, "Diary, 1750–1751," GHS; also see 25 May 1751, "Diary, 1750–1751," GHS.

171. Habersham, 26 and 27 April 1751, "Diary, 1750–1751," GHS.

172. John Reynolds to the Lords Commissioners, 12 May 1756, TNA CO 5/645/95.

173. *Letters*, 2:693.

174. Marsh, *Unravelled Dreams*, 375.

175. James Habersham to Earl of Hillsborough, 12 August 1772, *Letterbooks*, Habersham Family Papers, MS 1787, GHS.

176. Boltzius to Trustees, 22 September 1744, Original Correspondence, 1741–1746, TNA CO 5/641/175, stamped pages 439–441.

177. Boltzius to Gotthilf August Francke, 13 May 1762, AFS, Missionsarchiv, Stab/F 32/10, 29; translation from *Letters*, 2:719.

178. DR 15:66.

## Chapter 8. Neighbors

1. DR 1:61.

2. Martyn, *Some Account of the Designs*, 3.

3. DR 1:60.

4. DR 1:166.

5. DR 1:70.

6. Juricek, *Colonial Georgia and the Creeks*, 3, 56.

7. *Letters*, 1:212.

8. Kelton, "Great Southeastern Smallpox Epidemic," 37.

9. Gallay, *Indian Slave Trade*, 297.

10. Gallay, *Indian Slave Trade*, 299.

11. Ethridge, *From Chicaza to Chickasaw*, 149–192.

12. Juricek, *Colonial Georgia and the Creeks*, 39.

13. Juricek, *Colonial Georgia and the Creeks*, 12.

14. Juricek, *Colonial Georgia and the Creeks*, 12.

15. William Verelst, *Audience Given by the Trustees of Georgia to a Delegation of Creek Indians*, 1734–1735, oil on canvas, Winterthur Museum.

16. Reck and Jones, "Von Reck's Second Report," 327.

17. Juricek, *Colonial Georgia and the Creeks*, 32.

18. Kupperman, *Indians and English*, 63.

19. Reck, *Von Reck's Voyage*, 114.

20. *Tomochichi and His Nephew*, De Renne Family Collection of Portraits and Engravings, MS 3704, Hargrett Rare Book and Manuscript Library, University of Georgia, Athens.

21. Reck, *Von Reck's Voyage*, 126.

22. Kupperman, *Indians and English*, 58; Shoemaker, *Strange Likeness*.

23. Harriot, *Briefe and True Report*, 61.

24. "From the Commissioner Baron Von Reck a Short Report on Georgia and the Indians There," DR 1:142.

25. DR 1:121.

26. DR 1:121.

27. DR 1:80.

28. DR 1:67.

29. DR 1:67.

30. Reck, *Von Reck's Voyage*, 106–107.

31. DR 5:175.

32. Boltzius to Reck, 13 July 1747, AFSt/M 5A 11:71.

33. DR 15:245.

34. Juricek, *Colonial Georgia and the Creeks*, 88.

35. Martyn to Boltzius, 10 June 1735, CR 29:151–152.

36. Oglethorpe to Trustees, 10 May 1736, TNA CO 5/654/58.

37. DR 8:417.

38. CR 6:147.

39. DR 8:436–437.

40. DR 8:437.

41. DR 8:444.

42. CR 4 (suppl.): 86.

43. Juricek, *Colonial Georgia and the Creeks*, 88.

44. CR 6:147.

45. CR 6: 171–172.

46. Juricek, *Colonial Georgia and the Creeks*, 88.

47. CR 6:339.

48. CR 6:349.

49. DR 15:245.

50. *Letters*, 1:289.

51. *Letters*, 1:214.

52. *Letters*, 1:195.

53. William Stephens, *Journal of William Stephens*, 1:147; DR 18:138.

54. DR 18:138.

55. Sweet, *William Stephens*.

56. DR 5:135.

57. Whitefield, *Continuation*, 1.

58. Melton, *Religion, Community, and Slavery*, 169.

59. Whitefield, *Continuation*, 1.

60. George Fenwick Jones, "Two 'Salzburger' Letters," 52.

61. DR 5:136DR, 8:12.

62. Habersham's role in building the Savannah merchant community is discussed in Pressly, *On the Rim*. Also see Lambert, *James Habersham*.

63. *Letters*, 1:248.

64. DR 5:158.

65. *Letters*, 1:248.

66. *Letters*, 1:371.

67. Atwood, "Hallensians Are Pietists"; Fogleman, "Shadow Boxing in Georgia," 629–659.

68. Fogleman, *Jesus Is Female*; Craig D. Atwood, "Deep in the Side of Jesus," in Gillespie and Beachy, *Pious Pursuits*, 50–64.

69. *Letters*, 1:223.

70. *Letters*, 1:108.

71. *Letters*, 1:108.

72. *Letters*, 1:127.

73. DR 3:88.

74. *Letters*, 1:171.

75. *Letters*, 1:223.

76. DR 4:92.

77. Hammond, *John Wesley in America*, 79–107.

78. Oglethorpe, *New and Accurate Account*, 30.

79. Oglethorpe, *New and Accurate Account*, 29.

80. For an in-depth analysis of the Salzburgers and the slavery debates, see Melton, *Religion, Community, and Slavery*. Also see Betty Wood, *Slavery in Colonial Georgia*.

81. DR 6:45.

82. DR 1:57.

83. DR 1:57.

84. DR 1:73.

85. DR 1:77.

86. DR 1:95.

87. DR 1:117.

88. DR 1:198n20.

89. Burnard, *Planters, Merchants, and Slaves*, 32.

90. Byrd, *Secret Diary*.
91. CR 22 (part 2): 232–234.
92. CR 22 (part 2): 232.
93. Hoffer, *Cry Liberty*.
94. DR 6:220.
95. DR 6:42.
96. CR 22:120.
97. Oglethorpe to Trustees, 20 October 1739, TNA CO 5/640/405.
98. DR 11:12.
99. DR 11:7.
100. DR 11:32.
101. 1 Timothy 6:9 (KJV).
102. DR 11:32.
103. DR 11:33.
104. DR 11:33.

## Epilogue

1. Melton, *Religion, Community, and Slavery*, 262.
2. DR 1:57.
3. Koch, "Slavery, Mission, and the Perils," 369–393.
4. Betty Wood, *Slavery in Colonial Georgia*. Chapter 4 studies the Salzburgers and slavery. James V. H. Melton, "The Pastor and the Schoolmaster," in Strom, Lehmann, and Melton, *Pietism in Germany*, 229–250.
5. Entries for 1758, Ebenezer Church, *Ebenezer Record Book*, 8.
6. "Inventory and Appraisement of the Estate of the Revd John Martin Boltzius, 1766," Probate Inventories, MS 4000, GHS, roll 22, 214.
7. CR 1:57.
8. CR 1:60.
9. Davis, *Fledgling Province*, 126.
10. Mühlenberg, *Notebook of a Colonial Clergyman*, 147–150.
11. Edna Q. Morgan, *John Adam Treutlen*; George Fenwick Jones, "John Adam Treutlen's Origin and Rise to Prominence," in Jackson and Spalding, *Forty Years of Diversity*, 217–228.
12. George Fenwick Jones, "John Adam Treutlen's Origin," 217.
13. In prosecuting the war, both the Americans and the British used maps of Georgia and South Carolina prepared by Gerard de Brahm, who had been sent by Münch on the second Swabian transport and subsequently been named the colony's chief surveyor. His were the best, most detailed maps of the region.
14. Elliott, *Ebenezer Revolutionary War Headquarters*. Elliott's report includes maps showing the earthworks thrown up to fortify the town.
15. "Some Account of the Saltzburghers Settled at Ebenezer," in SPCK, *Protestant Missions*, 89.
16. "The Mission among the Saltzburghers Settled at Ebenezer," 4 March 1779, in SPCK, *Protestant Missions*.

17. "Mission among the Saltzburghers," 4 March 1779.

18. "Mission among the Saltzburghers," 28 October 1782.

19. George Fenwick Jones, *Salzburger Saga*, 129.

20. "Mission among the Saltzburghers Settled at Ebenezer in Georgia, 1781," in SPCK, *Protestant Missions*, 88.

21. "Mission among the Saltzburghers Settled at Ebenezer in Georgia, 1781," 88.

22. Charles Colcock Jones, *Dead Towns of Georgia*, 11–44.

23. In a 1787 letter to Halle, Bergmann blamed the collapse of Ebenezer on the feud between the Triebner and Rabenhorst factions, more than on the war. See Bergmann to Fabricius, 27 August 1787, AFSt/M 5B 3:30.

24. George Fenwick Jones, *Georgia Dutch*, 195.

25. Müller-Bahlke and Gröschl, *Salzburg, Halle, Nordamerika*, 841.

# BIBLIOGRAPHY

## Archives and Manuscripts Collections
### BRITISH LIBRARY, LONDON, ENGLAND

Bedford to Sloane, 1736, BL Sloane 4055
De Brahm to Knox, 1778, BL Add 24322
Denne Accounts, BL Add 11825 and BL Add 11826
Digby to Newcastle, 1743, BL Add 32700
Egmont Commonplace Book, BL Add 47146
Egmont Letters 1727–1730, 1731, BL Add 47032 and BL Add 47033
Egmont Newsletters, 1730, 1732, and 1733 BL Add 27981, BL Add 47084, BL Add 47085
Egmont Obligation of Religion, 2 vols., BL Add 47204 and BL Add 47205
Egmont Original Correspondence 1730, BL Add 46981
Egmont Religious Writings, BL Add 47207–47209
Egmont (2nd Earl), Journal BL Add 47073
Eyles Petition and Grant in New York, 1731, BL Add 35908 and BL Add 36129
Hales to Birch, 1752, BL Add 4309
Laroche to Hopkins, 1732, BL Add 64929
Newcastle Papers, BL Add 32725
Oglethorpe to Sloane, 1733, BL Sloane 4053
Oglethorpe's "Tour Into the Indian Nations, 1740–42," BL Stowe 792
Oglethorpe to T. Robinson, 1748, BL Add 23827
Shaftesbury to Newcastle, 1749, BL Add 32718
Shaftesbury to T. Birch, 1738–1755, BL Add 4318
Urlsperger to Thompson, 1735, BL Add 23795
Vernon to Buckworth, 1743, BL Add 40776

### CAMBRIDGE UNIVERSITY LIBRARY, CAMBRIDGE, ENGLAND

SPCK Minute Books, SPCK.MS A1/14, MS A1/15, and MS A1/16

## CRUMLEY ARCHIVES,
### COLUMBIA, SOUTH CAROLINA

Salzburger Collection


## FRANCKE FOUNDATIONS ARCHIVE,
### HALLE, GERMANY

Missions Archive, America Division


## GEORGIA HISTORICAL SOCIETY,
### SAVANNAH, GEORGIA

Benjamin Martyn Papers, 1741, MS 545
Charles and Elizabeth Waring Papers, MS 1018
Gentleman's Magazine and Thomas Lediard Articles on Georgia History, 1732–1734, MS 1038
George Fenwick Jones Papers, MS 1924
Georgia Trustees Manuscripts, 1800s, MS 278
Habersham Family Papers, MS 1787
James Edward Oglethorpe and Count Nicolaus Ludwig von Zinzendorf Letters, 1734–1735, MS 1618
James Edward Oglethorpe Papers, MS 595
James Habersham Papers, MS 337
Jones Family Papers, MS 440
Probate Inventories, MS 4000
Savannah Grand Jury Paper, MB 690
Society for Promoting Christian Knowledge Letter Books, Account Books and Manuscripts, Microfilm, MS 1396
Thaddeus Martin Harris Papers, MS 1565
Waring Map Papers, MS 1018


## HARGRETT RARE BOOKS AND MANUSCRIPTS
### LIBRARY, UNIVERSITY OF GEORGIA,
### ATHENS, GEORGIA

Keith M. Read Collection, MS 921
Noble Jones Family Papers, 1754–1838, MS 1127
Sir John Perceval Papers, MS 746
Thomas Stephens Notebooks, 1736–1742, MS 46


## LAMBETH PALACE ARCHIVES,
### LONDON, ENGLAND

Fulham Papers
Secker Papers, MS 1123
SPG Minutes, MS 1124

## THE NATIONAL ARCHIVES, LONDON, ENGLAND

Board of Trade and Secretaries of State: America and West Indies, Original Correspondence, Georgia, CO 5/654 to CO 5/663
Index to Original Correspondence, Georgia, CO 326/19
Journal of the Trustees for Establishing the Colony, CO 5/686, CO 5/687, CO 5/688
Observations on the Right of Great Britain to North America, CO 5/283
Petition of Benjamin Martyn for Money Granted "for the Further Settling and Improving the Colony . . . ," T 1/335/50
Secretaries of State: State Papers Domestic, George II, Letters and Papers, SP 36/21


## Published Primary Sources


*An Account of the Suffering of the Persecuted Protestants in the Archibshoprick of Saltzburg.* London: J. Downing, 1732.
*An Act for Encouraging the Growth of Raw Silk in His Majesty's Colonies or Plantations in America.* London: Thomas Baskett, 1750.
Adair, James. "The History of the American Indians; Particularly Those Nations Adjoining to the Missisippi [*sic*], East and West Florida, Georgia, South and North Carolina, and Virginia: Containing an Account of Their Origin, Language, Manners, . . . With a New Map of the Country Referred to in the History. By James Adair." London: Edward and Charles Dilly, 1775.
"The Archbishop of Saltzburgh's Decree for Expelling His Protestant Subjects." *Historical Register* 17:30–39. London: S. Nevill, 1732.
Archdale, John. *A New Description of That Fertile and Pleasant Province of Carolina: With a Brief Account of Its Discovery, Settling, and the Government Thereof to This Time. With Several Remarkable Passages of Divine Providence during My Time.* London: J. Wyat, 1707.
Arndt, Johann. *Of True Christianity Four Books Wherein Is Contained the Whole Oeconomy of God towards Man; and the Whole Duty of Man towards God. Written Originally in High-Dutch, by the Most Reverend John Arndt, . . . Published in English in the Year Mdccxii: Now Revised, and Rendered More Agreeable to the Original.* 2nd ed. London: Joseph Downing, 1720.
———. *True Christianity: A Treatise on Sincere Repentance, True Faith, the Holy Walk of the True Christian, Etc.* Translated by Rev. Anthony William Boehm. New American ed. Edited by Charles F Schaeffer. Philadelphia: Smith, English, 1868.
Arndt, Johann, Gotthilf August Francke, Research Publications Inc., and Yale University Library. *Johann Arndts . . . Vier Bücher Vom Wahren Christenthum Das Ist, Von Heilsamer Busse, Hertzlicher Reue Und Über Die Sünde.* Microform. Halle: Im Wäysenhause, 1755.
Baine, Rodney M., ed. *Creating Georgia: Minutes of the Bray Associates 1730–1732 & Supplementary Documents.* Athens: University of Georgia Press, 1995.
Bartram, William. *Travels through North & South Carolina, Georgia, East & West Flor-*

*ida, the Cherokee Country, the Extensive Territories of the Muscogulges, or Creek Confederacy, and the Country of the Chactaws; Containing an Account of the Soil and Natural Productions of Those Regions, Together with Observations on the Manners of the Indians.* Electronic ed. Philadelphia: James & Johnson, 1791.

Bateman, Edmund, and Trustees for Establishing the Colony of Georgia in America. *A Sermon Preached before the Honourable Trustees for Establishing the Colony of Georgia, in America, and the Associates of the Late Rev. Dr. Bray at Their Anniversary Meeting, March 19, 1740–1, at the Parish-Church of St. Bride, Alias St. Bridget, in Fleet-Street, London.* London: J. and H. Pemberton, 1741.

Bearcroft, Philip, and Trustees for Establishing the Colony of Georgia in America. *A Sermon Preached before the Honorable Trustees for Establishing the Colony of Georgia in America, and the Associates of the Late Reverend Dr. Bray at Their Anniversary Meeting March 16, 1737–8: In the Parish-Church of St. Bridget, Alias St. Bride, in Fleet-Street London.* London: Printed by J. Willis, 1738.

"Bericht Über Die Geografischen Und Klimatischen Verhältnisse, Die Flora Und Fauna Sowie Die Rechtlichen Bedingungen Der Aufnahme Von Emigranten in Georgia." Frankfurt (Main), 1733.

Berkeley, George, John Perceval, and Benjamin Rand. *Berkeley and Percival.* Cambridge: Cambridge University Press, 1914.

Berriman, William, and Trustees for Establishing the Colony of Georgia in America. *A Sermon Preach'd before the Honourable Trustees for Establishing the Colony of Georgia in America, and the Associates of the Late Rev. Dr. Bray at Their Anniversary Meeting, March 15, 1738–9: In the Parish Church of St. Bridget, Alias St. Bride, in Fleetstreet, London.* London: J. Carter, 1739.

Best, William. *The Merit and Reward of a Good Intention a Sermon Preached before the Honourable Trustees for Establishing the Colony of Georgia in America, and the Associates of the Late Reverend Dr. Bray; at Their Anniversary Meeting, March 18. 1741–2. In the Parish-Church of St. Bride in Fleetstreet. In Which Some Notice Is Taken of a Late Abusive Pamphlet, Intitled, a True and Historical Narrative of the Said Colony. By William Best.* London: W. Innys, 1742.

———. *The Relief of the Persecuted Protestants of Saltzburgh, and the Support of the Colony of Georgia, Recommended in a Sermon Preach'd at St. Laurence-Jewry Church, on Sunday, January 13, 1734.* London: Printed for William Innys and Richard Manby, 1734.

Boehm, Anthony William. *Several Letters Related to the Protestant Danish Mission at Tranquebar in the East Indies.* London: Joseph Downing, 1720.

Boltzius, Johann Martin. *The Letters of Johann Martin Boltzius, Lutheran Pastor in Ebenezer, Georgia: German Pietism in Colonial America, 1733–1765.* 2 vols. Edited by Russell C. Kleckley and Jürgen Gröschl. Lewiston, N.Y.: Edwin Mellen, 2009.

———. "Nachrichten Und Anmerkungen Aus Dem Pflanzenreiche in Georgien, Von Einem Prediger Der Colonie Ebenezer, 1752." *Hamburgishes Magazin* 17, no. 3 (1756): 468–519.

———. "Reliable Answer to Some Submitted Questions Concerning the Land Carolina." Edited by George Fenwick Jones. *William and Mary Quarterly,* Third Series 14, no. 2 (1957): 223–261.

———. "The Secret Diary of Pastor Johann Martin Boltzius." Edited by George Fenwick Jones. *Georgia Historical Quarterly* 53, no. 1 (1969): 78–110.

Boreman, Thomas. *A Compendious Account of the Whole Art of Breeding, Nursing, and the Right Ordering of the Silk-Worm. Illustrated with Figures Engraven on Copper: Whereon Is Curiously Exhibited the Whole Management of This Profitable Insect.* London: Printed for J. Worrall, at the Dove in Bell-Yard, Near Lincolns-Inn; Olive Payne, in Round Court in the Strand; Thomas Boreman, on Ludgate-Hill, 1733.

Brown, Roger Lee, ed. "Thomas Bray of Chirbury." In *The Sayce Papers. Vol 5: Anguish and Achievement,* edited by Roger Lee Brown, 1–3. Welshpool: Gwasg Eglwys y Trallwng, 1999.

Bruce, Lewis, and Trustees for Establishing the Colony of Georgia in America. *The Happiness of Man the Glory of God a Sermon Preached before the Honourable Trustees for Establishing the Colony of Georgia in America, and the Associates of the Late Rev. Dr. Bray: At Their Anniversary Meeting, March 15, 1743, in the Parish Church of St. Margaret, Westminster.* London: Printed by D. Browne, 1744.

Burton, John, and Trustees for Establishing the Colony of Georgia in America. *The Duty and Reward of Propagating Principles of Religion and Virtue Exemplified in the History of Abraham a Sermon Preach'd before the Trustees for Establishing the Colony of Georgia in America: And before the Associates of the Late Rev. Dr. Thomas Bray for Converting the Negroes in the British Plantations, and for Other Good Purposes: At Their Anniversary-Meeting in the Parish Church of St. Mary-Le-Bow: On Thursday March 15, 1732.* London: J. March, 1733.

Byrd, William. *The Correspondence of the Three William Byrds of Westover, Virginia, 1684–1776.* Edited by Marion Tinling. Charlottesville: University Press of Virginia, 1977.

———. *Histories of the Dividing Line Betwixt Virginia and North Carolina.* Edited by William K Boyd. Raleigh: North Carolina Historical Commission, 1929.

———. *The Secret Diary of William Byrd of Westover, 1709–1712.* Edited by Marion Tinling and Louis B. Wright. Richmond, Va.: Dietz Press, 1941.

Candler, Allen Daniel, et al. *The Colonial Records of the State of Georgia.* 32 vols. Athens: University of Georgia Press, 1904–1986.

Catesby, Mark. *The Natural History of Carolina, Florida, and the Bahama Islands; Containing Two Hundred and Twenty Figures of Birds, Beasts, Fishes, Serpents, Insects, and Plants, by Mark Catesby.* London: Benjamin White, 1771.

Catesby, Mark, and Thomas Hibbert. *The Natural History of Carolina, Florida, and the Bahama Islands: Containing the Figures of Birds, Beasts, Fishes, Serpents, Insects, and Plants Particularly the Forest-Trees, Shrubs, and Other Plants, Not Hitherto Described, or Very Incorrectly Figured by Authors. Together with Their Descriptions . . . To Which, Are Added Observations on the Air, Soil, and Waters: With Remarks upon Agriculture, Grain, Pulse, Roots, &C. To the Whole, Is Prefixed a New and Correct Map of the Countries Treated Of.* 2 vols. London, 1731.

*The Clamorous Malcontents; Criticisms & Defenses of the Colony of Georgia, 1741–1743.* Savannah, Ga.: Beehive Press, 1973.

de Brahm, John Gerar William. *Map of South Carolina and a Part of Georgia.* London, 1757. Hargrett Rare Book and Manuscript Library. https://dlg.usg.edu/institutions/guan.

Denne, John. *The Duty of Doing All Things to the Glory of God. A Sermon Preached to the Societies for Reformation of Manners, at the St. Mary-Le-Bow, on Wednesday January the 7th, 1729: An Account of the Designs of the Associates of the Late Dr. Bray*. London: J. Downing, 1730.

Douglass, William. *A Summary, Historical and Political, of the First Planting, Progressive Improvements, and Present State of the British Settlements in North-America. By William Douglass, M.D. Vol. I*. 2 vols. Boston: Rogers and Fowle in Queen-Street, 1749.

Ebenezer Church [Effingham County, Ga.]. *Ebenezer Record Book, Containing Early Records of Jerusalem Evangelical Lutheran Church, Effingham, Ga., More Commonly Known as Ebenezer Church*. Translated by A. G. Voigt, edited by C. A. Linn. Savannah, 1929.

Egmont, John Perceval, Earl of. *Faction Detected, by the Evidence of Facts*. London, 1743.

——. *The Journal of the Earl of Egmont: Abstract of the Trustees Proceedings for Establishing the Colony of Georgia, 1732–1738*. Edited by Robert G. McPherson. Athens: University of Georgia Press, 1962.

Egmont, John Perceval, and Trustees for Establishing the Colony of Georgia in America. *A Journal of the Transactions of the Trustees for Establishing the Colony of Georgia in America*. Edited by Charles Colcock Jones. Savannah, Ga.: Wormsloe, 1986.

"First Parliament of George II: Fifth Session (Part 4 of 4, from 11/2/1732)." In *The History and Proceedings of the House of Commons: Volume 7: 1732–1733*, edited by Richard Chandler, 208–251. London: Chapin, 1742.

Francke, August Hermann. *Pietas Hallensis; or, A Publick Demonstration of the Foor-Steps of a Divine Being Yet in the World. . . .* London: Joseph Downing, 1705.

Francklin, Thomas. *A Sermon Preached before the Honourable Trustees for Establishing the Colony of Georgia in America, and the Associates of the Late Rev. Dr. Bray at Their Anniversary Meeting, March 16, 1749–50. In the Parish Church of St. Margaret, Westminster*. London: R. Francklin, 1750.

Freylinghausen, Johann Anastasius. *Geistreiches Gesang-Buch, auserlesene, so alte als neue, geistliche und liebliche Lieder*. Halle: Francke Foundations, 1733.

Georgia Trustees. *Select Tracts Relating to Colonies*. London: J. Roberts, 1732.

Glasse, Hannah. *The Art of Cookery Made Plain and Easy*. London: Printed for the Author, 1747.

Gordon, Peter. *The Journal of Peter Gordon, 1732–1735*. Edited by E. Merton Coulter. Athens: University of Georgia Press, 1963.

Great Britain, Parliament, House of Commons. *The History and Proceedings of the House of Commons from the Restoration to the Present Time*. Vol. 12. London: Richard Chandler, 1743.

Harrington, James. *The Oceana and Other Works of James Harrington Esq*. London: A. Millar, 1747.

Harriot, Thomas. *A Briefe and True Report of the New Found Land of Virginia of the Commodities and of the Nature and Manners of the Naturall Inhabitants*. London, 1588.

——. *A Briefe and True Report of the New Found Land of Virginia: The 1590 Theodor De Bry Latin Edition*. Charlottesville: Library at the Mariners' Museum by the University of Virginia Press, 2007.

Harvest, George. *Sermon Preached before the Honourable Trustees for Establishing the Colony of Georgia in America, and the Associates of the Late Reverend Dr. Bray at Their Anniversary Meeting, March 16, 1748–9: In the Parish Church of St. Margaret, Westminster.* London: W. Meadows, 1749.

Hays, J. E. *Creek Indian Letters, Talks and Treaties, 1705–1839: In Four Parts / Compiled, Copied and Bound with Authority of John B. Wilson, Secretary of State.* 4 vols. WPA Project P.P. 665-34-3-224. Atlanta: WPA Project, 1939.

Hogarth, William. *O the Roast Beef of Old England ("The Gate of Calais").* London: Tate Britain, Tate Collection, 1748.

Jacobi, John Christian. *Psalmondia Germanica: or, A Specific of Divine Hymns Translated from the High Dutch. . . .* London: J. Young, 1722.

Jones, George Fenwick. "A German Surgeon on the Flora and Fauna of Colonial Georgia: Four Letters of Johann Christoph Bournemann, 1753–1755." *Georgia Historical Quarterly* 76, no. 4 (1992): 891–914.

———. "A Letter by Pastor Johann Martin Boltzius about Bethesda and Marital Irregularities in Savannah." *Georgia Historical Quarterly* 84, no. 2 (2000): 283–294.

———. "Two 'Salzburger' Letters from George Whitefield and Theobald Kiefer II." *Georgia Historical Quarterly* 62, no. 1 (1978): 50–57.

Jones, George F., and Don Savell. "The Fourth Transport of Georgia Salzburgers II: Diary of Mr. Vigera from London to Ebenezer in Georgia in America, London, the 18th Sept. St. V. 1741." *Concordia Historical Institute Quarterly* 56, no. 2 (1983): 52–64.

Journal of the House of Lords Volume 23, 1727–1731. London: HMSO, 1767–1830. British History Online. http://www.british-history.ac.uk/lords-jrnl/vol23/pp337-349.

Kimber, Edward. *A Relation, or Journal, of a Late Expedition to the Gates of St. Augustine, on Florida Conducted by the Hon. General James Oglethorpe, . . . By a Gentleman, Voluntier in the Said Expedition.* London: T. Astley, 1744.

King, James. *A Sermon Preached before the Honourable Trustees for Establishing the Colony of Georgia, in America and the Associates of the Late Rev. Dr. Bray, at Their Anniversary Meeting, March 17, 1742–3.* London: J. Clarke, 1743.

Kleiner, John W., and Helmut T. Lehmann, eds. *The Correspondence of Heinrich Melchior Mühlenberg: 1740–1747.* Vol. 1. Camden, Maine: Picton Press, 1986.

Kramer, Johann Matthias, Benjamin Martyn, and James Edward Oglethorpe. *Neueste Und Richtigste Nachricht Von Der Landschaft Georgia in Dem Engelländischen Amerika: Worinnen Enthalten: 1. Die Original-Berichte, Welche Die Königlichen Commissarien Über Die Beschaffenheit Dieser Landschaft Eingeschicket Haben. 2. Ein Zuverlässiger Bericht Derer Vornehmsten Privilegien, Freyheiten Und Wohlthaten, So Alle Diejenigen Zu Geniessen Haben, Die Sich in Dieser Fruchtbaren Provinz Häusslich Niederlassen; Nebst Einem Unterricht Für Selbige Zu Ihrer Dahinreise.* Göttingen: Verlegts Johann Peter Schmid, 1746.

Lawson, John. *A New Voyage to Carolina.* Edited by Hugh T. Lefler. 1709. Reprint, Chapel Hill: University of North Carolina Press, 1967.

Lee, Daniel. "Roman Law, German Liberties and the Constitution of the Holy Roman Empire." In *Freedom and the Construction of Europe*, edited by Quentin Skinner and Martin van Gelderen, 256–273. New York: Cambridge University Press, 2013.

Lewis, Andrew. "Henry Muhlenberg's Georgia Correspondence." *Georgia Historical Quarterly* 49, no. 4 (1965): 424–454.

Locke, John. *Observations upon the Growth and Culture of Vines and Olives: The Production of Silk: The Preservation of Fruits. Written at the Request of the Earl of Shaftesbury: To Whom It Is Inscribed: By Mr. John Locke. Now First Printed from the Original Manuscript in the Possession of the Present Earl of Shaftesbury.* London: W. Sandby, 1766.

Mantiano, Don Manuel de. "Letters of Don Manuel De Montiano, Siege of St. Augustine." In *Collections of the Georgia Historical Society*, edited by Otis Ashmore and George Baldwin VII, 1–70. Savannah, Ga.: Savannah Morning News, 1909.

Martyn, Benjamin. *An Impartial Enquiry into the State and Utility of the Province of Georgia.* London: W. Meadows, 1741.

———. *Some Account of the Designs of the Trustees for Establishing the Colony of Georgia in America.* London, 1732.

Martyn, Benjamin, and Georgia Trustees for Establishing the Colony of Georgia in America. *Reasons for Establishing the Colony of Georgia, with Regard to the Trade of Great Britain, the Increase of Our People, and the Employment and Support It Will Afford to Great Numbers of Our Own Poor, as Well as Foreign Persecuted Protestants. With Some Account of the Country, and the Design of the Trustees.* London: W. Meadows, 1733.

Martyn, Benjamin, and Trustees for Establishing the Colony of Georgia in America. *An Account Shewing the Progress of the Colony of Georgia in America from Its First Establishment.* London, 1741.

Meager, Leonard. *The English Gardener, or, A Sure Guide to Young Planters and Gardeners in Three Parts.* London: J. Wright and John Hancock, 1683.

Milfort, Louis. *Memoirs; or, A Quick Glance at My Various Travels and My Sojourn in the Creek Nation.* Savannah, Ga.: Beehive Press, 1972.

Montgomery, Robert. *A Discourse Concerning the Design'd Establishment of a New Colony to the South of Carolina, in the Most Delightful Country of the Universe.* London, 1717.

Moore, Francis, and Jacob Robinson. *A Voyage to Georgia. Begun in the Year 1735. Containing an Account of the Settling the Town of Frederica, in the Southern Part of the Province; and a Description of the Soil, Air, Birds, Beasts, Trees, Rivers, Islands, &C. With the Rules and Orders Made by the Honourable the Trustees for That Settlement; Including the Allowance of Provisions, Cloathing, and Other Necessaries to the Families and Servants Which Went Thither. Also a Description of the Town and County of Savannah, in the Northern Part of the Province; the Manner of Dividing and Granting the Lands, and the Improvements There with an Account of the Air, Soil, Rivers, and Islands in That Part.* London: Jacob Robinson in Ludgate-Street, 1744.

Mühlenberg, Heinrich Melchior. *Die Korrespondenz Heinrich Melchior Mühlenbergs, Aus Der Anfangszeit Des Deutschen Luthertums in Nordamerika.* 2 vols. Edited by Kurt Aland. New York: Walter De Gruyter, 1986.

———. *The Notebook of a Colonial Clergyman.* Translated and edited by Theodore G. Tappert and John W. Doberstein. Philadelphia: Mühlenberg Press, 1959.

National Society Colonial Dames of America in the State of Georgia, Atlanta Town Committee, and Georgia Department of Archives and History. *Abstracts of Colo-*

*nial Wills of the State of Georgia, 1733–1777.* Atlanta: Published by the Atlanta Town Committee of the National Society Colonial Dames of America in the State of Georgia for the Dept. of Archives and History in the Office of Secretary of State, State of Georgia, 1962.

Newman, Henry. *Henry Newman's Salzburger Letterbooks.* Edited by George Fenwick Jones. Athens: University of Georgia Press, 1965.

*A New Voyage to Georgia by a Young Gentleman. Giving an Account of His Travels to South Carolina, and Part of North Carolina. To Which Is Added, a Curious Account of the Indians. By an Honourable Person. And a Poem to James Oglethorpe.* 2nd ed. London: J. Wilford, 1737.

Nourse, Timothy. *Campania Faelix or, a Discourse of the Benefits and Improvements of Husbandry: Containing Directions for All Manner of Tillage, Pasturage, and Plantation; . . . To Which Are Added, Two Essays: I. Of a Country-House. II. Of the Fuel of London.* 2nd ed. London: Tho. Bennet, 1706.

Oglethorpe, James Edward. *General Oglethorpe's Georgia: Colonial Letters, 1733–1743.* Edited by Mills Lane. Savannah, Ga.: Beehive Press, 1975.

———. *A New and Accurate Account of the Provinces of South-Carolina and Georgia: With Many Curious and Useful Observations on the Trade, Navigation, and Plantations of Great-Britain, Compared with Her Most Powerful Maritime Neighbours in Antient and Modern Times.* London: J. Worrall, 1733.

———. *Some Account of the Design of the Trustees for Establishing Colonys in America.* Edited by Rodney M. Baine and Phinizy Spalding. Athens: University of Georgia Press, 1990.

Oglethorpe, James Edward, and Rodney M. Baine. *The Publications of James Edward Oglethorpe.* Athens: University of Georgia Press, 1994.

Ostervald, J. F. *The Grounds and Principles of the Christian Religion, Explain'd in a Catechetical Discourse for the Instruction of Young People. Rendered into English by Mr. Hum. Wanley: And Revised by Geo. Stanhope.* 3rd ed. London: J. Downing, 1734.

Panse, Karl. *Geschichte Der Auswanderung Der Evangelischen Salzburger Im Jahr 1732. Ein Beitrag Zur Kirchengeschichte. Nach Den Quellen Bearbeitet.* Leipzig, 1827.

Perceval, John, Earl. *The Controversy in Relation to the Test and Corporation Acts Clearly Disputed, in a Dialogue between a Dissenter and a Member of the Establish'd Church.* London, 1733.

———. *Manuscripts of the Earl of Egmont. Diary of Viscount Percival Afterwards First Earl of Egmont.* 3 vols. London: HMSO, 1920.

———. *The Thoughts of an Impartial Man upon the Present Temper of the Nation; Offer'd to the Consideration of the Freeholders of Great-Britain.* London, 1733.

Petty, William. *Several Essays in Political Arithmetick by Sir William Petty, . . . The Fourth Edition, Corrected. To Which Are Prefix'd, Memoirs of the Author's Life.* London: D. Browne, J. Shuckburgh, and J. Whiston and B. White, 1755.

Purry, Peter. "Proposals by Mr. Peter Purry, of Newfchatel, for Encouragement of Such Swiss Protestants as Should Agree to Accompany Him to Carolina, to Settle a New Colony. And, Also a Description of the Province of South Carolina, Drawn up at Charlestown, in September 1731." In *Historical Collections of South Carolina: Embracing Many Rare and Valuable Pamphlets, and Other Documents, Relating to the History of That State*, edited by B. R. Carroll, 2, 121–140. New York: Harper & Brothers, 1836.

Rand, Benjamin, ed. *Berkeley and Percival: The Correspondence of George Berkeley, afterwards Bishop of Cloyne and Sir John Percival, afterwards Earl of Egmont*. Cambridge: Cambridge University Press, 2014.

Reck, Philipp Georg Friedrich von. *Kurz Gefasste Nachricht Von Dem Etablissement Derer Salzburgischen Emigranten Zu Ebenezer, in Der Provinz Georgien in Nord-America Wie Solche Auf Verlangen*. Hamburg: F.C. Ritter, 1777.

———. *Von Reck's Voyage: Drawings and Journal of Philip Georg Friedrich Von Reck*. Edited by Kristian Hvidt. Savannah, Ga.: Beehive Press, 1980.

Reck, Philipp Georg Friedrich von, and Johann Martin Boltzius. *An Extract of the Journals of Mr. Commissary Von Reck, Who Conducted the First Transport of Saltzburgers to Georgia: And of the Reverend Mr. Bolzius, One of Their Ministers. Giving an Account of Their Voyage to, and Happy Settlement in That Province*. London: M. Downing, 1734.

Reck, Philip Georg Friedrich von, and George Fenwick Jones. "Von Reck's Second Report from Georgia." *William and Mary Quarterly* 22, no. 2 (1965): 319–333.

*The Records of the Virginia Company of London*. Vol. 3. Edited by Susan Myra Kingsbury. Washington, D.C.: Government Printing Office.

Reese, Trevor R., ed. *The Clamorous Malcontents: Criticisms and Defenses of the Colony of Georgia, 1741–1743*. Savannah, Ga.: Beehive Press, 1973.

———, ed. *The Most Delightful Country of the Universe: Promotional Literature of the Colony of Georgia, 1717–1734*. Savannah, Ga.: Beehive Press, 1972.

———. *Our First Visit in America: Early Reports from the Colony of Georgia, 1732–1740*. Savannah, Ga.: Beehive Press, 1974.

Ridley, Glocester, and Trustees for Establishing the Colony of Georgia in America. *A Sermon Preached before the Honourable Trustees for Establishing the Colony of Georgia in America, and the Associates of the Late Reverend Dr. Bray at Their Anniversary Meeting, March 20, 1745–6, in the Parish Church of St. Margaret, Westminster*. London: J. Clarke, 1746.

Rohrbach, Lewis Bunker, Hermann Gollub, Herbert Nolde, Samuel Urlsperger, and George Fenwick Jones. *The Salzburger Expulsion Lists*. Rockport, Maine: Picton Press, 1999.

Rundle, Thomas. *A Sermon Preached at St. George's Church Hanover Square, on Sunday February 17, 1733/4 to Recommend the Charity for Establishing the New Colony of Georgia. By T. Rundle*. London: T. Woodward and J. Brindley, 1734.

Sibbald, George. *Notes and Observations on the Pine Lands of Georgia: Shewing the Advantages They Possess, Particularly in the Culture of Cotton: Addressed to Persons Emigrating, and Those Disposed to Encourage Migration to This State: Together with a Plan of Emigration, for Their Immediate Settlement: To Which Is Added a Geographical Sketch of the State of Georgia, with a Comparative View of the Population of 1791, and 1801, and the Exports of the Years 1791 & 1800*. Augusta, Ga.: 1801.

Smith, Samuel. *A Sermon Preach'd before the Trustees for Establishing the Colony of Georgia in America and before the Associates of the Late Rev. Dr. Thomas Bray, ... At Their First Yearly-Meeting, in the Parish Church of St. Augustin, on Tuesday February 23,*

*1730/31. By Samuel Smith, . . . To Which Is Annexed Some Account of the Designs Both of the Trustees and Associates.* London: J. March and Messieurs Mount and Page, 1733.

Smith, Samuel, Thomas Bray, Benjamin Martyn, Trustees for Establishing the Colony of Georgia in America. *A Sermon Preach'd before the Trustees for Establishing the Colony of Georgia in America, and before the Associates of the Late Rev. Dr. Thomas Bray, for Converting the Negroes on the British Plantations, and for Other Good Purposes. At Their First Yearly-Meeting, in the Parish Church of S. Augustin, on Tuesday February 23, 1730–31.* London: J. March and Messieurs Mount and Page, 1733.

Society for Promoting Christian Knowledge. *An Account of the Origin and Designs of the Society for Promoting Christian Knowledge.* London: Joseph Downing, 1733.

———. *An Account of the Society for Promoting Christian Knowledge.* London: M. Downing, 1740.

———. *An Account of the Society for Promoting Christian Knowledge.* London: M. Downing, 1741.

———. *An Account of the Society for Promoting Christian Knowledge.* London: M. Downing, 1743.

———. *An Account of the Society for Promoting Christian Knowledge.* London: M. Downing, 1744.

———. *An Account of the Society for Promoting Christian Knowledge.* London: J. Oliver, 1746.

———. *A Further Account of the Sufferings of the Persecuted Protestants in the Archbishoprick of Saltzburg: Taken from Authentick Papers.* London: Jos. Downing, 1733.

———. *A Letter from a Residing Member of the Society for Promoting Christian Knowledge in London, to a Corresponding Member in the Country.* London: J. Downing, 1714.

———. *Protestant Missions to the East Indies from 1732 to 1785.* London, 1785.

———. *S.P.C.K. Early 18th Century Archives.* London: World Microfilms, 1976.

———. *A Translation of a Letter out of High Dutch.* London, 1739.

Stephens, Thomas. *A Brief Account of the Causes That Have Retarded the Progress of the Colony of Georgia, in America: Attested upon Oath: Being a Proper Contrast to a State of the Province of Georgia, Attested upon Oath: And Some Other Misrepresentations on the Same Subject.* London, 1743.

———. *The Castle-Builders; or, The History of William Stephens, of the Isle of Wight, Esq; Lately Deceased. A Political Novel, Never before Published in Any Language.* London, 1759.

———. *The Hard Case of the Distressed People of Georgia.* London, 1742.

Stephens, William. *A Journal of the Proceedings in Georgia Beginning October 20, 1737. By William Stephens, Esq; to Which Is Added, a State of That Province, as Attested upon Oath in the Court of Savannah, November 10, 1740.* 3 vols. London: W. Meadows, 1742.

———. *The Journal of William Stephens.* 2 vols. Edited by E. Merton Coulter. Athens: University of Georgia Press, 1958.

———. *A State of the Province of Georgia, Attested upon Oath in the Court of Savannah, November 10, 1740.* London: W. Meadows, 1742.

Tailfer, Patrick, Hugh Anderson, and David Douglas. *A True and Historical Narrative of the Colony of Georgia in America from the First Settlement Thereof until This Present Period: . . . By Pat. Tailfer, M.D. Hugh Anderson, M.A. Da. Douglas, and Others.* Charles-Town, S.C.: P. Timothy, 1741.

Thoresby, Ralph, and Trustees for Establishing the Colony of Georgia in America. *The Excellency and Advantage of Doing Good Represented in a Sermon Preached before the Honourable Trustees for Establishing the Colony of Georgia in America, and the Associates of the Late Reverend Dr. Bray, on Their Anniversary Meeting, March 17, 1747–8: In the Parish Church of St. Margaret, Westminster: To Which Is Annex'd a Letter of Samuel Loyd, Esq., Concerning the Nature and Goodness of the Georgia Silk.* London: W. Meadows, 1748.

Thorpe, Francis Newton. *The Federal and State Constitutions, Colonial Charters, and Other Organic Laws of the States, Territories, and Colonies Now or Heretofore Forming the United States of America.* Buffalo, N.Y.: W.S. Hein, 1993.

Trustees for Establishing the Colony of Georgia in America. *The General Accompt of All Monies and Effects Received and Expended by the Trustees for Establishing the Colony of Georgia in America . . . From the Ninth Day of June, . . . 1735, to the Ninth Day of June, . . . 1736.* London, 1736.

———. *The General Account of All Monies and Effects Received and Expended by the Trustees for Establishing the Colony of Georgia in America . . . From the Ninth Day of June . . . 1732, . . . To the Ninth Day of June, . . . 1733.* London, 1733.

Urban, Silvanus. *The Gentlemen's Magazine, or Monthly Intelligencer, for the Year 1732.* London: F. Jefferies, 1732.

———. *The Gentlemen's Magazine, or Monthly Intelligencer, for the Year 1733.* London: F. Jefferies, 1733.

Urlsperger, Johann August. *About the Excellence of the Georgian English Colony in Comparison with Other Colonies.* Lanham, Md.: University Press of America, 2008.

Urlsperger, Samuel. *Ausführliche Nachrichten von der Koniglich-Gross-Brittanischen Colonie Saltzburgisher Emigranten in America.* Halle: Verlegung des WäysenHauses, 1735–1752.

———. *Detailed Reports on the Salzburger Emigrants Who Settled in America.* 18 vols. Edited by George Fenwick Jones. Athens: University of Georgia Press, 1968.

Walpole, Horace. *Memoirs of the Reign of King George the Second.* 3 vols. New York: AMS Press, 1970.

Warren, Robert, and Trustees for Establishing the Colony of Georgia in America. *Industry and Diligence in Our Callings Earnestly Recommended in a Sermon Preached before the Honourable Trustees for Establishing the Colony of Georgia, in America, and the Associates of the Late Rev. Dr. Bray: At Their Anniversary Meeting, March 17, 1736–7, at the Parish Church of St. Bride, Alias St. Bridget, in Fleet-Street, London.* London: W. Meadows, 1737.

Watts, George. *A Sermon Preached before the Trustees for Establishing the Colony of Georgia in America; at Their Anniversary Meeting in the Parish-Church of St. Bridget, Alias St. Bride, in Fleetstreet, London: On Thursday, March 18. 1735. Published at the Particular Request of the Trustees.* London: M. Downing, 1736.

Wesley, John. *An Extract of the Revd. Mr. John Wesley's Journal from August 12, 1738 to Nov. 1, 1739.* 2nd ed. Bristol: Felix Farley, 1748.

————. *An Extract of the Rev. Mr. John Wesley's Journal, from His Embarking for Georgia, to His Return to London. No. I and II.* London: G. Whitfield, 1797.

————. *The Journal of John Wesley.* 4 vols. London: J. M. Dent, 1906.

————. *The Letters of the Rev. John Wesley.* Standard ed. Edited by John Telford. London: Epworth Press, 1931.

————. *A Short View of the Difference between the Moravian Brethren, Lately in England; and the Reverend Mr. John and Charles Wesley. Extracted Chiefly from a Late Journal.* London: W. Strahan, 1745.

Whitebourne, Richard. *A Discourse and Discovery of New-Found-Land....* London: Felix Kyngston, 1620.

Whitefield, George. *A Continuation of the Account of the Orphan-House in Georgia, from January 1740/1 to June 1742. To Which Are Also Subjoin'd, Some Extracts from an Account of a Work of a Like Nature, Carried on by the Late Professor Franck . . . By George Whitefield.* Edinburgh: T. Lumisden and J. Robertson, 1742.

————. *A Continuation of the Reverend Mr. Whitefield's Journal from a Few Days after His Return to Georgia to His Arrival at Falmouth on the 11th of March 1741.* London: W. Strahan, 1741.

————. *A Journal of a Voyage from London to Savannah in Georgia. In Three Parts. Part I. From London to Gibraltar. Part II. From Gibraltar to Savannah. Part III. From Savannah to London.* 5th ed. London, 1739.

————. *A Letter to the Reverend Mr. John Wesley in Answer to His Sermon, Entitled, Free-Grace. By George Whitefield.* Philadelphia: Benjamin Franklin, 1741.

Woodward, Josiah. *An Account of the Rise and Progress of the Religious Societies in the City of London, &c. And of Their Endeavours for Reformation of Manners. By Josiah Woodward, D.D.* 6th ed. London: M. Downing, 1744.

## Online Sources

Avalon Project: Documents in Law, History, and Diplomacy. Lillian Goldman Law Library, Yale Law School. https://avalon.law.yale.edu.

Bio-bibliographisches Register zum Archiv der Frankeschen Stiftungen. Francke Foundations. https://digital.francke-halle.de/fsbio.

Historical Maps Database. Digital Library of Georgia, Hargrett Rare Book & Manuscript Library, University of Georgia. https://dlg.usg.edu/collection/guan_hmap.

*New Georgia Encyclopedia.* University of Georgia. http://www.georgiaencyclopedia.org.

*Oxford Dictionary of National Biography.* http://www.oxforddnb.com.

Picturing the New World: The Hand-Colored De Bry Engravings of 1590. University of North Carolina. https://dc.lib.unc.edu/cdm/landingpage/collection/debry.

Virtual Vault. Georgia Archives. https://vault.georgiaarchives.org.

Von Reck's Drawings, NKS 565 4°. Royal Library of Denmark http://www5.kb.dk /permalink/2006/manus/22/eng.

## Secondary Sources

Adam, Thomas, and Ruth V. Gross. *Traveling between Worlds: German-American Encounters.* 1st ed. Walter Prescott Webb Memorial Lectures. College Station: Texas A&M University Press, 2006.

Allan, D. G. C. "Hales, Stephen (1677–1761)." In *Oxford Dictionary of National Biography* (2004).

Allen, W. O. B., and Edmund McClure. *Two Hundred Years: The History of the Society for Promoting Christian Knowledge, 1698–1898.* London: Society for Promoting Christian Knowledge, 1898.

Anderson, Gary Clayton. *Ethnic Cleansing and the Indian: The Crime That Should Haunt America.* Norman: University of Oklahoma Press, 2014.

Anderson, Virginia DeJohn. *Creatures of Empire: How Domestic Animals Transformed Early America.* New York: Oxford University Press, 2004.

———. "King Philip's Herds: Indians, Colonists, and the Problem of Livestock in Early New England." *William and Mary Quarterly,* Third Series 51, no. 4 (1994): 601–624.

Andrew, Donna T. *Philanthropy and Police: London Charity in the Eighteenth Century.* Princeton, N.J.: Princeton University Press, 1989.

Andrews, Edward E. "Tranquebar: Charting the Protestant International in the British Atlantic and Beyond." *William and Mary Quarterly,* Third Series 74, no. 1 (January 2017): 3–34.

Appuhn, Karl. *A Forest on the Sea: Environmental Expertise in Renaissance Venice.* Baltimore: Johns Hopkins University Press, 2009.

Armitage, David, and M. J. Braddick. *The British Atlantic World, 1500–1800.* New York: Palgrave Macmillan, 2002.

Arthur, Linda L. "A New Look at Schooling and Literacy: The Colony of Georgia." *Georgia Historical Quarterly* 84, no. 4 (2000): 563–588.

Atwood, Craig D. "The Hallensians Are Pietists; Aren't You a Hallensian?" *Journal of Moravian History* 12, no. 1 (2012): 47–92.

Auman, Karen. "'Give Their Service for Nothing': Bubbles, Corruption, and Their Effect on the Founding of Georgia." *Eighteenth-Century Studies* 54, no. 1 (Fall 2020): 101–119.

Baine, Rodney M. "James Oglethorpe and the Early Promotional Literature for Georgia." *William and Mary Quarterly,* Third Series 45 (1988): 100–106.

Beiler, Rosalind J. "Dissenting Religious Communication Networks and European Migration, 1660–1710." In *Soundings in Atlantic History,* edited by Bernard Bailyn and Patricia L. Denault, 210–236. Cambridge, Mass.: Harvard University Press, 2009.

Benton, Lauren A. *Law and Colonial Cultures: Legal Regimes in World History, 1400–1900.* Studies in Comparative World History. New York: Cambridge University Press, 2002.

Berg, Johannes van den, and J. P. van Dooren, eds. *Pietismus Und Reveil: Referate Der Internationalen Tagung, Der Pietismus in Den Niederlanden Und Seine Internationalen Beziehungen, Zeist, 18.-22. Juni 1974.* Leiden: Brill, 1978.

Black, Jeremy. *British Politics and Society from Walpole to Pitt, 1742–1789.* New York: St. Martin's, 1990.

———. *George II: Puppet of the Politicians?* Exeter: University of Exeter Press, 2007.

———. *Great Powers and the Quest for Hegemony: The World Order since 1500.* New York: Routledge, 2008.

———. *The Hanoverians: The History of a Dynasty.* London: Hambledon and London, 2004.

Blackburn, David. "'Conquests for Barbarism': Taming Nature in Frederick the Great's Prussia." In *Nature in German History,* edited by Christof Mauch, 10–30. New York: Berghahn Books, 2006.

Bonner, James C. *A History of Georgia Agriculture, 1732–1860.* Athens: University of Georgia Press, 1964.

Braun, G., and Susanne Lachenicht. *Hugenotten Und Deutsche Territorialstaaten: Immigrationspolitik Und Integrationsprozesse = Les Etats Allemands Et Les Huguenots: Politique D'immigration Et Processus D'integration, Pariser Historische Studien.* Munich: Oldenbourg, 2007.

Brecht, Martin, U. Deppermann, and Hartmut Lehmann. *Geschichte Des Pietismus.* 2 vols. Göttingen: Vandenhoeck und Ruprecht, 1995.

Brewer, John. *The Sinews of Power: War, Money, and the English State, 1688–1783.* 1st Am. ed. New York: Knopf, 1989.

Brigham, David R. "Mark Catesby and the Patronage of Natural History in the First Half of the Eighteenth Century." In *Empire's Nature: Mark Catesby's New World Vision,* edited by Amy R. W. Meyers and Margaret Beck Pritchard, 91–145. Chapel Hill: University of North Carolina Press, 1998.

Brown, Christopher Boyd. "Devotional Life in Hymns, Liturgy, Music, and Prayer." In *Lutheran Ecclesiastical Culture, 1550–1675,* edited by Robert Kolb, 205–259. Boston: Brill, 2008.

Brunner, Daniel L. *Halle Pietists in England: Anthony William Boehm and the Society for Promoting Christian Knowledge.* Arbeiten Zur Geschichte Des Pietismus. Göttingen: Vandenhoeck & Ruprecht, 1993.

Bultmann, W. A., and P. W. Bultmann. "The Roots of Anglican Humanitarianism: A Study of the Membership of the SPCK and the SPG, 1699–1720." *Historical Magazine of the Protestant Episcopal Church* 33, no. 1 (1964): 3–48.

Burnard, Trevor. *Planters, Merchants, and Slaves: Plantation Societies in British America, 1650–1820.* Chicago: University of Chicago Press, 2015.

Busch, Gudrun, and Wolfgang Miersemann, eds. *"Geist=Reicher" Gesang: Halle Und Das Pietistische Lied.* Hallesche Forschungen. Tübingen: Max Niemeyer Verlag, 1997.

Bushman, Richard Lyman. "Markets and Composite Farms in Early America." *William and Mary Quarterly,* Third Series 55, no. 3 (1998): 351–374.

Butler, Jay Jordan. "Agrarianism and Capitalism in Early Georgia, 1732–1743." Master's thesis, University of Wyoming, 1949.

Calloway, Colin G., Gerd Gemünden, and Susanne Zantop. *Germans and Indians: Fantasies, Encounters, Projections.* Lincoln: University of Nebraska Press, 2002.

Carson, James Taylor. *Making an Atlantic World: Circles, Paths, and Stories from the Colonial South.* Knoxville: University of Tennessee Press, 2007.

Cates, Gerald L. "'The Seasoning': Disease and Death among the First Colonists of Georgia." *Georgia Historical Quarterly* 64, no. 2 (1980): 146–158.

Chaplin, Joyce E. *An Anxious Pursuit: Agricultural Innovation and Modernity in the Lower South, 1730–1815*. Chapel Hill: University of North Carolina Press, 1993.

Claydon, Tony, and Ian McBride, eds. *Protestantism and National Identity: Britain and Ireland, c.1650–c.1850*. Cambridge: Cambridge University Press, 1998.

Coclanis, Peter A., ed. *The Atlantic Economy during the Seventeenth and Eighteenth Centuries: Organization, Operation, Practice, and Personnel*. The Carolina Lowcountry and the Atlantic World. Columbia: University of South Carolina Press, 2005.

Coleman, Kenneth. *Colonial Georgia: A History*. A History of the American Colonies. New York: Scribner, 1976.

———, ed. *A History of Georgia*. Athens: University of Georgia Press, 1977.

———. "The Southern Frontier: Georgia's Founding and the Expansion of South Carolina." *Georgia Historical Quarterly* 56, no. 2 (1972): 163–174.

Conner, William H., Thomas W. Doyle, and Ken W. Krauss. *Ecology of Tidal Freshwater Forested Wetlands of the Southeastern United States*. Dordrecht: Springer, 2007.

Coulter, E. Merton, and Albert B. Saye. *A List of the Early Settlers of Georgia*. Athens: University of Georgia Press, 1949.

Cowen, David L. "The Trustees' Garden at Savannah." *Pharmacist Quarterly* 60, no. 2 (1983).

Cowie, L. W. *Henry Newman: An American in London, 1708–43*. London: SPCK, 1956.

Crane, Verner W. "The Philanthropists and the Genesis of Georgia." *American Historical Review* 27, no. 1 (1921): 63–69.

———. *Southern Frontier, 1670–1732*. 2nd ed. Tuscaloosa: University of Alabama Press, 2004.

Cronon, William. *Changes in the Land: Indians, Colonists, and the Ecology of New England*. New York: Hill & Wang, 1983.

Crowley, John E. *This Sheba, Self: The Conceptualization of Economic Life in Eighteenth-Century America*. Baltimore: Johns Hopkins University Press, 1974.

Cruickshanks, Eveline. "John LaRoche." In *The History of Parliament*. https://historyofparliamentonline.org.

Dahlberg, Sandra L. "'Doe Not Forget Me': Richard Frethorne, Indentured Servitude, and the English Poor Law of 1601." *Early American Literature* 47, no. 1 (2012): 1–30.

Daniels, Christine, and Michael V. Kennedy, eds. *Negotiated Empires: Centers and Peripheries in the Americas, 1500–1820*. New York: Routledge, 2002.

Davis, Harold E. *The Fledgling Province: Social and Cultural Life in Colonial Georgia, 1733–1776*. Chapel Hill: University of North Carolina Press, 1976.

Davis, Richard Beale. *Intellectual Life in the Colonial South, 1585–1763*. 3 vols. Knoxville: University of Tennessee Press, 1978.

Davison, Lee. *Stilling the Grumbling Hive: The Response to Social and Economic Problems in England, 1689–1750*. New York: St. Martin's, 1992.

Dorwart, Reinhold A. "Cattle Disease (Rinderpest?): Prevention and Cure in Brandenburg, 1665–1732." *Agricultural History* 33, no. 2 (1959): 79–85.

Dow, James R. *German Folklore: A Handbook*. Westport, Conn.: Greenwood, 2006.

Duffy, Eamon. "Correspondence Franternelle: The SPCK, the SPG, and the Churches of Switzerland in the War of Spanish Succession." In *Reform and Reformation: England and the Continent C. 1500–C. 1750*, edited by Derek Baker, 251–280. Oxford: Oxford University Press, 1979.

Dunn, Richard S. "The Trustees of Georgia and the House of Commons, 1732–1752." *William and Mary Quarterly*, Third Series 11, no. 4 (1954): 551–565.

Edelson, S. Max. *Plantation Enterprise in Colonial South Carolina*. Cambridge, Mass.: Harvard University Press, 2006.

Elliott, Daniel T. *Ebenezer, an Alpine Village in the South Georgia Swamp*. Watkinsville, Ga.: LAMAR Institute, 1988.

———. *Ebenezer Revolutionary War Headquarters: A Quest to Locate and Preserve*. Lamar Institute Publication Series. Box Springs, Ga.: LAMAR Institute, 2003.

———. *Ebenezer Town Lots and Their Owners*. Athens, Ga.: LAMAR Institute, 1989.

———. *The Lost City Survey: Archaeological Reconnaissance of Nine Eighteenth Century Settlements in Chatham and Effingham Counties, Georgia*. Watkinsville, Ga.: LAMAR Institute, 1990.

Elliott, Daniel T., and Rita Folse Elliott. *Seasons in the Sun: 1989 & 1990 Excavations at New Ebenezer*. Watkinsville, Ga.: LAMAR Institute, 1991.

Engel, Katherine Carté. *Religion and Profit: Moravians in Early America*. Philadelphia: University of Pennsylvania Press, 2009.

———. "The SPCK and the American Revolution: The Limits of International Protestantism." *Church History* 81, no. 1 (2012): 77–103.

Ethridge, Robbie Franklyn. *Creek Country: The Creek Indians and Their World*. Chapel Hill: University of North Carolina Press, 2003.

———. *From Chicaza to Chickasaw: The European Invasion and the Transformation of the Mississippian World, 1540–1715*. Chapel Hill: University of North Carolina Press, 2013.

Ewan, Joseph. "Silk Culture in the Colonies." *Agricultural History* 43, no. 1 (1969): 129–142.

"Facts and Observations Relative to the Culture of Silk." *Fessenden's Silk Manual and Practical Farmer* 1, no. 5 (1835): 65–70.

Fogleman, Aaron Spencer. *Hopeful Journeys: German Immigration, Settlement, and Political Culture in Colonial America, 1717–1775*. Philadelphia: University of Pennsylvania Press, 1996.

———. *Jesus Is Female: Moravians and the Challenge of Radical Religion in Early America*. Philadelphia: University of Pennsylvania Press, 2007.

———. "Shadow Boxing in Georgia: The Beginnings of the Moravian-Lutheran Conflict in British North America." *Georgia Historical Quarterly* 83, no. 4 (1999): 629–659.

Fries, Adelaide L. *The Moravians in Georgia, 1735–1740*. Raleigh, N.C.: Edwards & Broughton, 1905.

Gallay, Alan. *The Formation of a Planter Elite: Jonathan Bryan and the Southern Colonial Frontier*. Athens: University of Georgia Press, 1989.

———. *The Indian Slave Trade: The Rise of the English Empire in the American South, 1670–1717*. New Haven, Conn.: Yale University Press, 2002.

Games, Alison. *The Web of Empire: English Cosmopolitans in an Age of Expansion, 1560–1660.* New York: Oxford University Press, 2008.

Gawthrop, Richard L. *Pietism and the Making of Eighteenth Century Prussia.* New York: Cambridge University Press, 1993.

Gehrke, William H. "The Ante-Bellum Agriculture of the Germans in North Carolina." *Agricultural History* 9, no. 3 (1935): 143–160.

Gillespie, Michele, and Robert Beachy, eds. *Pious Pursuits: German Moravians in the Atlantic World.* New York: Berghahn Books, 2007.

Grabbe, Hans-Jürgen, ed. *Halle Pietism, Colonial North America, and the Young United States.* Stuttgart: Franz Steiner Verlag, 2008.

Greene, Jack P., ed. *Exclusionary Empire: English Liberty Overseas, 1600–1900.* New York: Cambridge University Press, 2010.

———. *Pursuits of Happiness: The Social Development of Early Modern British Colonies and the Formation of American Culture.* Chapel Hill: University of North Carolina Press, 1988.

Hahn, Steven C. *The Invention of the Creek Nation, 1670–1763.* Indians of the Southeast. Lincoln: University of Nebraska Press, 2004.

Hammond, Geordan. *John Wesley in America: Restoring Primitive Christianity.* Oxford: Oxford University Press, 2014.

Hammond, Geordan, and David Ceri Jones, eds. *George Whitefield: Life, Context, and Legacy.* Oxford: Oxford University Press, 2016.

Hancock, David. *Citizens of the World: London Merchants and the Integration of the British Atlantic Community, 1735–1785.* New York: Cambridge University Press, 1995.

Haver, Charlotte E. *Von Salzburg Nach Amerika: Mobilität Und Kultur Einer Gruppe Religiöser Emigranten Im 18. Jahrhundert.* Paderborn, Germany: Ferdinand Schöningh, 2011.

Herget, Winfried. "Anders Als Der Rest Der Welt: Die Puritaner in Der Amerikanischen Wildnis." In *Colonial Encounters: Essays in Early American History and Culture*, edited by Hans-Jürgen Grabbe, 29–50. Heidelberg: Universitätsverlag Winter, 2003.

Herz, Dietmar, and John David Smith. "'Into Danger but Also Closer to God': The Salzburgers' Voyage to Georgia, 1733–1734." *Georgia Historical Quarterly* 80, no. 1 (1996): 1–26.

Hicks, Anthony. "The Shaftesbury Collection." In *Handel Collections and Their History*, edited by Terrence Best, 87–107. Oxford: Clarendon, 1993.

Hinderaker, Eric, and Peter C. Mancall. *At the Edge of Empire: The Backcountry in British North America.* Baltimore: Johns Hopkins University Press, 2003.

Hoffer, Peter Charles. *Cry Liberty: The Great Stono River Slave Rebellion of 1739.* New York: Oxford University Press, 2012.

Hoyer, Gerhard. "Samuel Urlsperger, Der Bedeutendste Repräsentant Des Hallischen Pietismus in Süddeutschland Und Große Freund Und Förderer Der Salzburger Emigranten." In *August Herman Francke und die Salzburger Emigration 1731/1732: Vortragssammlung*, 17–23. Halle (Saale): Salzburger Verein e.V. Bielefeld, 2001.

Huber, Ulrike, and Helene M. Kastinger Riley. "Die Vertreibung Der Protestantischen Unangesessenen Aus Dem Erzbistum Salzburg Im Winter 1731/32." *Salzburg Archiv* 28, (2002): 129–160.

————. "'Gottes Brünnlein Hat Wassers Die Fülle.' Ein Abriß Der Geschichte Der Nach Ebenezer Im Amerikanischen Georgia Ausgewanderten Salzburger." *Salzburg Archiv* 26 (1999): 111–162.

Hudson, Charles M., Thomas J. Pluckhahn, and Robbie Franklyn Ethridge. *Light on the Path: The Anthropology and History of the Southeastern Indians.* Tuscaloosa: University of Alabama Press, 2006.

Isaacs, Tina. "The Anglican Hierarchy and the Reformation of Manners, 1688–1738." *Journal of Ecclesiastical History* 23 (1982): 391–411.

Jackson, Harvey H., and Phinizy Spalding, eds. *Forty Years of Diversity: Essays on Colonial Georgia.* Athens: University of Georgia Press, 1984.

Jennison, Watson W. *Cultivating Race: The Expansion of Slavery in Georgia, 1750–1860.* Lexington: University Press of Kentucky, 2012.

Johann, Elizabeth. "The Impact of Industry on the Landscape and Environment of Austria Prior to the First World War." *Forest & Conservation History* 34, no. 3 (1990): 122–129.

————. "Landscape Changes in the History of the Austrian Alpine Regions: Ecological Development and the Perception of Human Responsibility." In *Forest Biodiversity: Lessons from History for Conservation*, edited by O. Honnay, K. Verheyen, B. Bossuyt, and M. Hermy, 27–40. Cambridge, Mass.: CABI Publishing, 2004.

————. "Traditional Forest Management under the Influence of Science and Industry: The Story of the Alpine Cultural Landscapes." *Forest Ecology and Management* 249 (2007): 54–62.

————. *Wald Und Mensch: Die Nationalparkregion Hohe Tauern (Kärnten).* Klagenfurt: Verlag des Kärntner Landesarchivs, 2004.

Jones, Charles Colcock, Jr. *The Dead Towns of Georgia.* Collections of the Georgia Historical Society. Savannah, Ga.: Morning News Steam Printing House, 1878. Reprint, 1974.

Jones, George Fenwick. *The Georgia Dutch: From the Rhine and Danube to the Savannah, 1733–1783.* Athens: University of Georgia Press, 1992.

————. *The Germans of Colonial Georgia, 1733–1783.* Rev. ed. Baltimore: Genealogical, 1996.

————. "The Salzburger Mills: Georgia's First Successful Enterprises." *Yearbook of German-American Studies* 23 (1988): 105–115.

————. *The Salzburger Saga: Religious Exiles and Other Germans along the Savannah.* Athens: University of Georgia Press, 1984.

Julian, John. *A Dictionary of Hymnology.* Vol. 1: *Setting Forth the Origin and History of Christian Hymns of All Ages and Nations.* London: John Murray, 1907.

Juricek, John T. *Colonial Georgia and the Creeks: Anglo-Indian Diplomacy on the Southern Frontier, 1733–1763.* Gainesville: University Press of Florida, 2010.

Kelton, Paul. "Great Southeastern Smallpox Epidemic." In *Transformation of the Southeastern Indians, 1540–1760*, edited by Robbie Franklyn Ethridge and Charles M. Hudson, 21–37. Jackson: University Press of Mississippi, 2002.

Kimbrough, S. T. "Charles Wesley in Georgia." *Methodist History* 45, no. 2 (2007): 77–110.

Klose, Nelson. "Sericulture in the United States." *Agricultural History* 37, no. 4 (1963): 225–234.

Klosterberg, Brigitte. "ABC—Büchlein Und Bilderbibel: Kinder- Und Jugendlitertur in Franckens Stiftungen." Halle, Germany: Franckesche Stiftungen, 2000.

Koch, Philippa. "Slavery, Mission, and the Perils of Providence in Eighteenth-Century Christianity: The Writings of Whitefield and the Halle Pietists." *Church History* 84, no. 2 (June 2015): 369–393.

Kupperman, Karen Ordahl, ed. *America in European Consciousness, 1493–1750.* Chapel Hill: University of North Carolina Press for the Institute of Early American History & Culture, Williamsburg, 1995.

———. "Controlling Nature and Colonial Projects in Early America." In *Colonial Encounters: Essays in Early American History and Culture,* edited by Hans-Jürgen Grabbe, 69–88. Heidelberg: Universitätsverlag Winter, 2003.

———. "Fear of Hot Climates in the Anglo-American Colonial Experience." *William and Mary Quarterly,* Third Series 41, no. 2 (1984): 213–240.

———. *Indians and English: Facing Off in Early America.* Ithaca, N.Y.: Cornell University Press, 2000.

———. *Pocahontas and the English Boys: Caught between Cultures in Early Virginia.* New York: New York University Press, 2019.

———. "The Puzzle of the American Climate in the Early Colonial Period." *American Historical Review* 87, no. 5 (1982): 1262–1289.

Küster, Hansjörg. *Geschichte Des Waldes: Von Der Urzeit Bis Zur Gegenwart.* Munich: Verlag C.H. Beck oHG, 1998.

Lachenicht, Susanne. "Huguenot Immigrants and the Formation of National Identities, 1548–1787." *Historical Journal* 50, no. 2 (2007): 1–23.

———, ed. *Religious Refugees in Europe, Asia and North America: 6th–21st Century.* Hamburg: LIT, 2007.

Lambert, Frank. *James Habersham: Loyalty, Politics, and Commerce in Colonial Georgia.* Athens: University of Georgia Press, 2005.

Lannen, Andrew. "Liberty and Slavery in Colonial America: The Case of Georgia, 1732–1770." *The Historian* 79, no. 1 (Spring 2017): 32–55.

Lehmann, Helmut, Hermann Wellenreuther, and Renate Wilson, eds. *In Search of Peace and Prosperity: New German Settlements in Eighteenth-Century Europe and America.* University Park: Pennsylvania State University Press, 2000.

Lindberg, Carter, ed. *The Pietist Theologians.* Malden, Mass.: Blackwell, 2005.

Loewe, Andreas, and Katherine Firth. "Martin Luther's 'A Mighty Fortress.'" *Lutheran Quarterly* 32 (2018): 125–145.

Longenecker, Stephen L. *Piety and Tolerance: Pennsylvania German Religion, 1700–1850.* Metuchen, N.J.: Scarecrow Press, 1994.

———. *Shenandoah Religion: Outsiders and the Mainstream, 1716–1865.* Waco, Tex.: Baylor University Press, 2002.

Lowood, Henry E. "The Calculating Forester: Quantification, Cameral Science and the Emergence of Scientific Forestry Management in Germany." In *The Quantifying Spirit in the 18th Century,* edited by Tore Frängsmyr, J. L. Heilbron, and Robin E. Rider, 315–342. Berkeley: University of California Press, 1990.

MacDonald, David R. *The Transit of the Anglican Mind to the Maryland Colony: Thomas Bray and the Bray Libraries of Christ Church Durham, Nanjemoy, Maryland, 1696–1701.* South Bend, Ind.: Cloverdale Books, 2007.

MacNeil, A. R. "Early American Communities on the Fundy: A Case Study of Annapolis and Amherst Townships, 1767–1827." *Agricultural History* 63, no. 3 (1989): 101–119.

Mancall, Peter C., and Joshua L. Rosenbloom. "Exports and the Economy of the Lower South Region, 1720–1770." *Research in Economic History* 25 (2008): 1–68.

Mancke, Elizabeth. "The Languages of Liberty in British North America, 1607–1776." In *Exclusionary Empire: English Liberty Overseas, 1600–1900*, edited by Jack P. Greene, 25–49. New York: Cambridge University Press, 2010.

Marsch, Angelika. *Die Salzburger Emigration in Bildern.* Weißenhorn: Anton H. Konrad Verlag, 1986.

Marschke, Benjamin. "Absolutely Pietist: Patronage, Factionalism, and State-Building in the Early Eighteenth-Century Prussian Army Chaplaincy." PhD dissertation, University of California, Los Angeles, 2003.

Marsh, Ben. *Georgia's Frontier Women: Female Fortunes in a Southern Colony.* Athens: University of Georgia Press, 2007.

———. "Silk Hopes in Colonial South Carolina." *Journal of Southern History* 78, no. 4 (2012): 807–854.

———. *Unravelled Dreams: Silk and the Atlantic World, 1500–1840.* New York: Cambridge University Press, 2020.

———. "The Very Sinews of a New Colony: Demographic Determinism and the History of Early Georgia Women, 1732–1752." In *Gender, Race and Religion in the Colonization of the Americas*, edited by Nora E. Jaffary. Burlington, Vt.: Ashgate, 2007.

Mathieu, Jon. "From Ecotypes to Sociotypes: Peasant Households and State-Building in the Alps, Sixteenth-Nineteenth Centuries." *History of the Family* 5, no. 1 (2000): 55–74.

———. *History of the Alps 1500–1900: Environment, Development and Society.* Translated by Matthew Vester. Morgantown]: West Virginia University Press, 2009.

Matson, Cathy. "Markets and Morality: Intersections of Economy, Ethnics, and Religion in Early North America." *Early American Studies* 8, no. 3 (2010): 475–481.

Matthias, Markus. "August Hermann Francke (1663–1727)." In *The Pietist Theologians*, edited by Carter Lindberg, 100–114. Malden, Mass.: Blackwell, 2005.

Mauch, Christof, ed. *Nature in German History.* New York: Berghahn Books, 2006.

Mauelshagen, Carl. *Salzburg Lutheran Expulsion and Its Impact.* New York: Vantage, 1962.

McCain, James Ross. *Georgia as a Proprietary Province: The Execution of a Trust.* Spartanburg, S.C.: Reprint Co., 1972.

McCandless, Peter. *Slavery, Disease and Suffering in the Southern Lowcountry.* New York: Cambridge University Press, 2011.

McCusker, John J. "How Much Is That in Real Money? A Historical Price Index for Use as a Deflator of Money Values in the Economy of the United States." *Proceedings of the American Antiquarian Society* 101, no. 2 (1991): 297–373.

McCusker, John J., and Russell R. Menard. *The Economy of British America, 1607–1789.* Chapel Hill: University of North Carolina Press, 1985.

McIlvenna, Noeleen. *The Short Life of Free Georgia: Class and Slavery in the Colonial South.* Chapel Hill: University of North Carolina Press, 2015.

McKeown, Adam M. *Melancholy Order: Asian Migration and the Globalization of Borders*. New York: Columbia University Press, 2008.

Melton, James V. H. "Confessional Power and the Power of Confession: Concealing and Revealing the Faith in Alpine Salzburg, 1730–1734." In *Cultures of Power in Europe during the Long Eighteenth Century*, edited by H. C. Scott and Brendan Simms, 133–157. Cambridge: Cambridge Univ Press, 2007.

———. "From Alpine Miner to Lowcountry Yeoman: Transatlantic Worlds of a Georgia Salzburger, 1693–1761." *Past & Present* 201 (2008): 97–140.

———. *Religion, Community, and Slavery on the Colonial Southern Frontier*. New York: Cambridge University Press, 2015.

Merchant, Carolyn. "Reinventing Eden: Western Culture as a Recovery Narrative." In *Uncommon Ground: Rethinking the Human Place in Nature*, edited by William Cronon, 132–170. New York: Norton, 1996.

Meroney, Geraldine. "The London Entrepôt Merchants and the Georgia Colony." *William and Mary Quarterly*, Third Series 25, no. 2 (1968): 230–244.

Migliazzo, Arlin C. *To Make This Land Our Own: Community, Identity, and Cultural Adaptation in Purrysburg Township, South Carolina, 1732–1865*. Columbia: University of South Carolina Press, 2007.

Miller, Randall M. "The Failure of the Colony of Georgia under the Trustees." *Georgia Historical Quarterly* 53, no. 200 (1969): 1–17.

Montgomery, Horace, ed. *Georgians in Profile: Historical Essays in Honor of Ellis Merton Coulter*. Athens: University of Georgia Press, 1958.

Morgan, Edmund Sears. *The Gentle Puritan: A Life of Ezra Stiles, 1727–1795*. New York: Norton, 1984.

Morgan, Edna Q. *John Adam Treutlen: Georgia's First Constitutional Governor. His Life, Real and Rumored*. Springfield, Ga.: Historic Effingham Society, 1998.

Morgan, Philip D. *Slave Counterpoint: Black Culture in the Eighteenth-Century Chesapeake and Lowcountry*. Chapel Hill: University of North Carolina Press, 1998.

Müller-Bahlke, Thomas J., and Jürgen Gröschl, eds. *Salzburg, Halle, Nordamerika: Ein Zweisprachiges Find- Und Lesebuch Zum Georgia-Archiv Der Franckeschen Stiftungen*. Halle: Verlag der Franckeschen Stiftungen im M. Niemeyer, 1999.

Nishikawa, Sugiko. "The SPCK in Defence of Protestant Minorities in Early Eighteenth-Century Europe." *Journal of Ecclesiastical History* 56, no. 4 (2005): 730–748.

Obst, Helmut. *A.H. Francke Und Die Franckeschen Stiftungen in Halle*. Göttingen: Vandenhoeck & Ruprecht, 2002.

Otterness, Philip. *Becoming German: The 1709 Palatine Migration to New York*. Ithaca, N.Y.: Cornell University Press, 2004.

Owen, Davis. *English Philanthropy: 1660–1960*. Cambridge, Mass.: Harvard University Press, 1964.

Ozment, Steven E. *Ancestors: The Loving Family in Old Europe*. Cambridge, Mass.: Harvard University Press, 2001.

———. *The Reformation in the Cities: The Appeal of Protestantism to Sixteenth-Century Germany and Switzerland*. New Haven, Conn.: Yale University Press, 1975.

Parker, Anthony W. *Scottish Highlanders in Colonial Georgia: The Recruitment, Emigration, and Settlement at Darien, 1735–1748*. Athens: University of Georgia Press, 1997.

Parrish, Susan Scott. *American Curiosity: Cultures of Natural History in the Colonial British Atlantic World*. Chapel Hill: University of North Carolina Press, 2006.

Pichler, Sandra. "Die 'Georgia Salzburger' Zur Kulturellen Un Ethnischen Indentität Von Einwanderern." Universität Salzburg, 1998.

Pietschmann, Horst, ed. *Atlantic History: History of the Atlantic System, 1580–1830*. Veröffentlichung Der Joachim Jungius-Gesellschaft Der Wissenschaften Hamburg. Göttingen: Vandenhoeck & Ruprecht, 2002.

Piker, Joshua. "Colonists and Creeks: Rethinking the Pre-revolutionary Southern Backcountry." *Journal of Southern History* 70, no. 3 (2004): 503–540.

———. "The Empire, the Emperor, and the Empress: The Interesting Case of Mrs. Mary Bosomworth." In *European Empires in the American South*, edited by Joseph P. Ward, 149–168. Jackson: University Press of Mississippi, 2017.

Pressly, Paul M. *On the Rim of the Caribbean: Colonial Georgia and the British Atlantic World*. Athens: University of Georgia Press, 2013.

Pyrges, Alexander. *Das Kolonialprojekt EbenEzer: Formen und Mechanismen protestantischer Expansion in der atlantischen Welt des 18. Jahrhunderts*. Stuttgart: Franz Steiner Verlag, 2015.

———. "German Immigrants at the Ebenezer Settlement in Colonial Georgia, 1734–1850: Integration and Separatism." PhD dissertation, Kansas State University, 2000.

Rebel, Hermann. *Peasant Classes: The Bureaucratization of Property and Family Relations under Early Habsburg Absolutism, 1511–1636*. Princeton, N.J.: Princeton University Press, 1983.

Reese, Trevor R. "Benjamin Martyn, Secretary to the Trustees of Georgia." *Georgia Historical Quarterly* 38, no. 2 (1954): 142–147.

———. *Colonial Georgia*. Athens: University of Georgia Press, 1963.

Riotte, Torsten. "Britain and Hanover." In *A Companion to Eighteenth-Century Europe*, edited by Peter H. Wilson, 354–367. Malden, Mass.: Blackwell, 2008.

Roeber, A. G. "'The Origin of Whatever Is Not English among Us': The Dutch-Speaking and the German-Speaking Peoples of Colonial British America." In *Strangers within the Realm: Cultural Margins of the First British Empire*, edited by Philip D. Morgan and Bernard Bailyn, 220–283. Chapel Hill: University of North Carolina Press, 1991.

———. *Palatines, Liberty, and Property: German Lutherans in Colonial British America*. Baltimore: Johns Hopkins University Press, 1998.

Rogal, Samuel J. *Essays on John Wesley and His Contemporaries: The Texture of Eighteenth-Century English Culture*. Lewiston, N.Y.: Edwin Mellen Press, 2006.

Rogers, George A., and R. Frank Saunders. *Swamp Water and Wiregrass: Historical Sketches of Coastal Georgia*. Macon, Ga.: Mercer University Press, 1984.

Rohrer, S. Scott. *Wandering Souls: Protestant Migrations in America, 1630–1865*. Chapel Hill: University of North Carolina Press, 2010.

Rose, Craig. "The Origins and Ideals of the SPCK, 1699–1716." In *The Church of England, C. 1689–1833: From Toleration to Tractarianism*, edited by Colin Haydon, 172–190. Cambridge: Cambridge University Press, 1993.

Rothschild, Emma. "A Horrible Tragedy in the French Atlantic." *Past & Present* 192 (August 2006): 67–108.

Russell, David Lee. *Oglethorpe and Colonial Georgia: A History, 1733–1783.* Jefferson, N.C.: McFarland, 2006.

Ryrie, Alec. *Protestants: The Faith That Made the Modern World.* New York: Viking, 2017.

Saunt, Claudio. *A New Order of Things: Property, Power, and the Transformation of the Creek Indians, 1733–1816.* New York: Cambridge University Press, 1999.

Schmidt, Martin. "Das Hallische Waisenhaus Und England Im 18 Jahrhundert: Ein Beitrag Zu Den Thema: Pietismus Und Oikumene." *Theologische Zeitschrift* 7 (1951): 38–55.

———. "Epochen Der Pietismusforschungs." In *Pietismus Und Reveil: Referate Der Internationalen Tagung, Der Pietismus in Den Niederlanden Und Seine Internationalen Beziehungen, Zeist, 18.-22. Juni 1974,* edited by Johannes van den Berg and J. P. van Dooren, 22–79. Leiden: Brill, 1978.

Schneider, Hans. *German Radical Pietism.* Lanham, Md.: Scarecrow Press, 2007.

Schnurmann, Claudia, and Hartmut Lehmann, eds. *Atlantic Understandings: Essays on European and American History in Honor of Hermann Wellenreuther.* Atlantic Cultural Studies. Hamburg: Lit, 2006.

Schwarz, Reinhard. *Samuel Urlsperger (1685–1772): Augsburger Pietismus Zwischen Aussenwirkungen Und Binnenwelt.* Berlin: Akademie Verlag, 1996.

Scomp, H. A., and Norman Vincent Turner. *History of the Salzburgers: As Written by Professor H. A. Scomp in 1907.* Macon, Ga.: Norman Vincent Turner, 2002.

Sedgwick, Romney R. "James Oglethorpe." In *The History of Parliament.* https://historyofparliamentonline.org.

Shantz, Douglas H. *An Introduction to German Pietism: Protestant Renewal at the Dawn of Modern Europe.* Baltimore: Johns Hopkins University Press, 2013.

Shoemaker, Nancy. "How Indians Got to Be Red." *American Historical Review* 102, no. 3 (1997): 625–644.

———. *A Strange Likeness: Becoming Red and White in Eighteenth-Century North America.* New York: Oxford University Press, 2006.

Silver, Timothy. *A New Face on the Countryside: Indians, Colonists, and Slaves in South Atlantic Forests, 1500–1800.* New York: Cambridge University Press, 1990.

Smith, Marvin T., Robbie Franklyn Ethridge, and Charles M. Hudson. *The Transformation of the Southeastern Indians, 1540–1760.* Jackson: University Press of Mississippi, 2002.

Sonnlechner, Christoph, and Verena Winiwarter. "Recht Und Verwaltung in Grundherrschaftlichen Waldordnungen Niederösterreichs Und Salzburgs (16.-18. Jahrhundert)." *Naturnutzung und Naturschutz in der europäischen Rechts- und Verwaltungsgeschichte* 11 (1999): 57–85.

Spady, James O'Neil. "Bubbles and Beggars and the Bodies of Laborers: The Georgia Trusteeship's Colonialism Reconsidered." In *Constructing Early Modern Empires: Proprietary Ventures in the Atlantic World, 1500–1750,* edited by L. H. Roper and Bertrand Van Ruymbeke, 213–268. Boston: Brill, 2007.

Spalding, Phinizy. *Oglethorpe in America.* Chicago: University of Chicago Press, 1977.

Spalding, Phinizy, and Harvey H. Jackson. *Oglethorpe in Perspective: Georgia's Founder after Two Hundred Years.* Tuscaloosa: University of Alabama Press, 1989.

Splitter, Wolfgang. "The Fact and Fiction of Cotton Mather's Correspondence with

German Pietist August Hermann Francke." *New England Quarterly* 83, no. 1 (2010): 102–122.

———. "The Germans in Pennsylvania Politics, 1758–1790: A Quantitative Analysis." *Pennsylvania Magazine of History and Biography* 122, no. 1/2 (1998): 39–76.

———. *Pastors, People, Politics: German Lutherans in Pennsylvania, 1740–1790.* Trier: Wissenschaftlicher Verlag Trier, 1998.

Stewart, Mart A. *"What Nature Suffers to Groe": Life, Labor, and Landscape on the Georgia Coast, 1680–1920.* Athens: University of Georgia Press, 1996.

———. "'Whether Wast, Deodant, or Stray': Cattle, Culture and the Environment in Early Georgia." *Agricultural History* 65, no. 3 (1991): 1–28.

———. "William Gerard De Brahm's 1757 Map of South Carolina and Georgia." *Environmental History* 16 (2011): 524–535.

St. George, Robert Blair. *Possible Pasts: Becoming Colonial in Early America.* Ithaca, N.Y.: Cornell University Press, 2000.

Strobel, P. A. *The Salzburgers and Their Descendants Being the History of a Colony of German (Lutheran) Protestants Who Emigrated to Georgia in 1734, and Settled at Ebenezer, Twenty-Five Miles above the City of Savannah.* Baltimore: T. Newton Kurtz, 1855.

Strom, Jonathan, Hartmut Lehmann, and James V. H. Melton, eds. *Pietism in Germany and North America, 1680–1820: Transmissions of Dissent.* Farnham: Ashgate, 2009.

Sweet, Julie Anne. *Negotiating for Georgia: British-Creek Relations in the Trustee Era, 1733–1752.* Athens: University of Georgia Press, 2005.

———. *William Stephens: Georgia's Forgotten Founder.* Baton Rouge: Louisiana State University Press, 2010.

Taylor, Alan. "'Wasty Ways': Stories of American Settlement." *Environmental History* 3, no. 3 (1998): 291–310.

Taylor, Paul Schuster. *Georgia Plan: 1732–1752.* Berkeley: Institute of Business and Economic Research, 1971.

Temple, Sarah Blackwell Gober, and Kenneth Coleman. *Georgia Journeys, Being an Account of the Lives of Georgia's Original Settlers and Many Other Early Settlers from the Founding of the Colony in 1732 until the Institution of Royal Government in 1754.* Athens: University of Georgia Press, 1961.

Thomas, Keith. "James Edward Oglethorpe, 1696–1785." Oglethorpe Tercentenary Commission Lecture, Corpus Christi College, Oxford, 1996.

———. *Man and the Natural World: Changing Attitudes in England, 1500–1800.* New York: Oxford University Press, 1996.

Thompson, Andrew C. *Britain, Hanover and the Protestant Interest, 1688–1756.* Studies in Early Modern Cultural, Political and Social History. Rochester, N.Y.: Boydell Press, 2006.

———. "The Protestant Interest and the History of Humanitarian Intervention, C. 1685–1756." In *Humanitarian Intervention: A History*, edited by Brendan Simms and D. J. B. Trim, 67–89. Cambridge: Cambridge University Press, 2011.

U.S. Census Bureau. *Historical Statistics of the United States, Colonial Times to 1970, Part 2.* Series z1–19. September 1975.

Van Dühlmen, Richard. *Kultur und Alltag in der Frühen Neuzeit, Erster Band: Das Haus und seine Menschen, 16.-18. Jahrhundert.* Munich: Verlag C. H., 1990.

Viazzo, Pier Paolo. *Upland Communities: Environment, Population and Social Structure in the Alps since the Sixteenth Century.* Cambridge: Cambridge University Press, 1989.

Von Stetten, Paul. *Kunst Gewerb—Und Handwerks Geschichte Der Reichs-Stadt Augsburg, 1779–88.* Vol. 1. Augsburg: C. H. Stage, 1779.

Wagner, Gillian. *Thomas Coram, Gent., 1668–1751.* Woodbridge: Boydell Press, 2004.

Walker, Mack. *German Home Towns: Community, State, and General Estate, 1648–1871.* Ithaca, N.Y.: Cornell University Press, 1998.

———. *The Salzburg Transaction: Expulsion and Redemption in Eighteenth-Century Germany.* Ithaca, N.Y.: Cornell University Press, 1992.

Wallmann, Johannes. "Johann Arndt (1555–1621)." In *The Pietist Theologians*, edited by Carter Lindberg, 21–37. Malden, Mass.: Blackwell, 2005.

Wander, Karl Friedrich Wilhelm. *Deutsches Sprichwörter-Lexikon. Ein Hausschatz Für Das Deutsche Volk.* Vol. 2. Leipzig: F.A. Brockhaus, 1870.

Warde, Paul. "The Environmental History of Pre-industrial Agriculture in Europe." In *Nature's End: History and the Environment*, edited by Sverker Sörlin and Paul Warde, 70–92. New York: Palgrave Macmillan, 2009.

———. "Fear of Wood Shortage and the Reality of the Woodland in Europe, C.1450–1850." *History Workshop Journal*, no. 62 (2006): 28–57.

Wenger, Diane E. *A Country Storekeeper in Pennsylvania: Creating Economic Networks in Early America.* State College: Pennsylvania State University Press, 2008.

Wharton, Charles H. *The Natural Environments of Georgia.* Atlanta: Georgia Department of Natural Resources, Environmental Protection Division, Geologic Survey Branch, 1989.

Wilfing, H., V. Winiwarter, C. Sonnlechner, and Project Group Environmental History. "Environmental Histories: The Long-Term Interaction of Society and Nature in Three Austrian Villages." *Die Bodenkultur* 53 (2002): 45–54.

Wilkins, Thomas Hart. "Sir Thomas Jekyll and His Impact on Oglethorpe's Georgia." *Georgia Historical Quarterly* 91, no. 2 (2007): 119–134.

Williams, Raymond. *Culture and Materialism: Selected Essays.* London: Verso, 2005.

———. "Ideas of Nature." In *Problems in Materialism and Culture: Selected Essays*, 67–85. London: NLB, 1980.

Wilson, David K. *The Southern Strategy: Britain's Conquest of South Carolina and Georgia, 1775–1780.* Columbia: University of South Carolina Press, 2005.

Wilson, Renate. "Halle and Ebenezer: Pietism, Agriculture and Commerce in Colonial Georgia." PhD dissertation, University of Maryland, 1988.

———. "Philanthropy in 18th-Century Central Europe: Evangelical Reform and Commerce." *Voluntas* 9, no. 1 (1998): 81–102.

———. *Pious Traders in Medicine: A German Pharmaceutical Network in Eighteenth-Century North America.* University Park: Pennsylvania State University Press, 2000.

Wilson, Thomas D. *The Oglethorpe Plan: Enlightenment Design in Savannah and Beyond.* Charlottesville: University of Virginia Press, 2012.

Winde, Hermann. "Die Frühgeschichte Der Lutherischen Kirche in Georgia: Dargestellt Nach Den Archivalien Der Franckeschen Stiftungen in Halle Und Der Universitätsbibliothek in Tübingen." PhD dissertation, Martin-Luther-Universität Halle-Wittenberg, 1960.

Withuhn, William L. "Salzburgers and Slavery: A Problem of Mentalité." *Georgia Historical Quarterly* 68, no. 2 (1984): 173–192.

Wokeck, Marianne. "The Dynamics of German-Speaking Immigration to British North America." In *Major Problems in American Colonial History*, edited by Karen Ordahl Kupperman, 212–221. Boston: Houghton Mifflin, 2000.

———. *Trade in Strangers: The Beginnings of Mass Migration to North America*. University Park: Pennsylvania State University Press, 1999.

Wood, Allen W. "Rational Theology, Moral Faith and Religion." In *The Cambridge Companion to Kant*, edited by Paul Guyer, 394–416. Cambridge: Cambridge University Press, 1992.

Wood, Betty. *Gender, Race, and Rank in a Revolutionary Age: The Georgia Lowcountry, 1750–1820*. Athens: University of Georgia Press, 2000.

———. *Slavery in Colonial Georgia, 1730–1775*. Athens: University of Georgia Press, 1984.

Worth, John E. *The Struggle for the Georgia Coast: An 18th-Century Spanish Retrospective on Guale and Mocama*. Athens: American Museum of Natural History, University of Georgia Press, 1995.

# INDEX

disease, 76, 77, 92, 116, 150; cattle, 124; dysentery, 103; malaria, 104
distance, as tool, 92–93, 97, 124
Dunn, Richard, 32

East Prussia Salzburgers, 111
Ebenezer, 2, 7; building of, 20, 73; charity in, 84; destruction of, 178; expansion of, 100; naming of, 20, 89; religious services in, 101, 105, 110; relocation of, 69, 72
—buildings in: churches, 106, 162; factories, 143; orphanages, 109, 138; schools, 109
Ebenezer Creek, 91, 158; flooding of, 64, 127
economic infrastructure projects, 115, 142
economy: of Ebenezer, 115, 122, 131; of South Carolina, 115, 133, 167
Egmont, Earl of (John Perceval), 23, 32, 41, 66
English Georgians, 98, 112, 160
environmental determinism, 4
Eveleigh, Samuel, 34

farming, 115; destruction of, 120; fields for, 72; plantation-style, 75, 145
Fielding, Henry, 118
Firmian, Leopold Anton Eleutherius von, 12–14
Fogleman, Aaron, 164
Francke, August Hermann, 44, 47; beliefs of, 44–45, 84; *Pietas Halensis*, 45
Francke, Gotthilf August, 47, 103
Francke Foundation in Halle, 8, 16, 43; establishment of, 44; medicine from, 56, 77, 103, 178; publishing of, 44, 77, 102, 111
Frederick III/I (king), 44–45
Freylinghausen, Johann Anastasius, 103

Gallay, Allan, 150
Gastein Valley, 17, 99, 117
George, Prince of Denmark, 45
George II (king), 25
Georgia charter, 24–25, 29, 41
Georgia forest, 2, 62, 71, 178; clear-cut harvesting of, 71–72, 74; Salzburger disappearances within, 59–60
Georgia plan: benefits for British Empire, 28, 30, 113; ideal society, 27, 39, 41, 63, 113; land inheritance, 18, 25–26, 28, 39, 41, 160; land ownership, 18, 26, 28, 33, 39, 72; promise of disinterest, 24, 29, 31; research for, 33; slavery ban, 25–28, 33, 41, 160
Georgia Salzburgers, death of, 21, 60, 86, 175

Georgia soil, 68–70, 87, 90
Georgia Trustees, 1, 17; divisions within, 41; end of, 2–3, 41; failure of, 3; formation of, 23–24; goals of, 23, 29, 32, 37, 42, 89; members of, 24, 28–29, 34; publications of, 30–32, 64, 116; relationship with Salzburgers, 35, 37; seal of, 31, 41, 132
—funding of: for botany, 34–35, 67; by commercial donors, 31; lack of, 57; from Parliament, 32, 40; by religious donors, 31
Georgia wildlife, 74
Great Southeastern Smallpox Epidemic, 150
Gronau, Israel Christian: background of, 19, 44, 54; death of, 57
Gröschl, Jürgen, 11

Habersham, James, 141, 144, 146, 162
Hales, Robert, 46
Hales, Stephen, 24, 34, 67
hard work, 85, 114, 162, 171
Harrington, James, 26. *See also* Agrarian Law
Harriott, Thomas, 155, 156
Heathcote, Gilbert, 29
Hogarth, William, 118
holidays, 117
homogenous community, 107, 162
Houston, William, 34, 67
hurricanes, 66
Hvidt, Kristian, 154
hymns, 15, 102–103, 126

ideal settlers. *See* worthy poor
indentured servants, 110, 161, 164

Jerusalem Church, 162, 173, 176, 179
Jones, George Fenwick, 5, 10, 140
Jones, Noble, 93

Kalcher, Margaretha, 84, 138
Kalcher, Ruprecht, 84, 138
Kiefer, Theobald, Jr., 110, 169, 173
Kipahalgwa, 152–153
Kleckley, Russell C., 11
Kogler, Georg, 128, 129
Kroehr, Catharina, 136, 139, 140
Kroehr, Gertraut, 136; manager of silk business, 139–144
Kupperman, Karen O., 9
Kurtz, 130

Printed in the United States
by Baker & Taylor Publisher Services